The Dogs Who Grew Me

A TRIBUTE TO THE SIX DOGS WHO TAUGHT ME WHAT REALLY MATTERS IN LIFE

Ann Pregosin

CAPITAL
BOOKS, INC.
Sterling, Virginia

Capital Books, Inc.
P.O. Box 605
Herndon, Virginia 20172-0605

ISBN 1-892123-62-2 (alk. paper)

Library of Congress Cataloging-in-Publication Data

Pregosin, Ann.
    The dogs who grew me : a tribute to the six dogs who taught me what really matters in life / Ann Pregosin.
    p. cm.
    ISBN 1-892123-62-2
    1. Dogs.   2. Dogs—Anecdotes.   3. Human-animal relationships.
    4. Pregosin, Ann.   I. Title.
    SF426.2 .P74   2002
    636.7—dc21   2001047712

Printed in the United States of America on acid-free paper that meets the American National Standards Institute Z39-48 Standard.

First Edition

10 9 8 7 6 5 4 3 2 1

The Dogs Who Grew Me

Also by Ann Pregosin

How Not to Kill Your Houseplants

For David and lovely Lexie,
who embody so much
of what is right and good
in this world.

Contents

Acknowledgments

I would like to thank Kathleen Hughes, publisher of Capital Books, for giving me the opportunity to write this book. I would also like to thank Noemi Taylor for being such a pleasure to work with in every possible way. As always, I thank my agent, Elizabeth Knappman Frost, for her wonderful guidance and support. A nod of great appreciation goes to the works of Stanley Coren, ever an inspiration and source of wonderful dog information. I especially thank my sister Paula for her unfailing enthusiasm as she listened to passages herein and encouraged me to "Keep writing!" I thank my supportive husband David and my lovely daughter Lexie for their patience and understanding throughout. Last, never least, it is the six wonderful dogs who have graced my life and continue to grace it, who propelled this labor of love from start to finish. They're all here in my heart, and now on the pages that follow.

Introduction

While it delves with depth into myriad training and other dog issues, this book is not about what we can do to our dogs to change them, alter them, readjust them. Rather, this book is about what a dog does for us; what, *as is*, he can teach us; how, like few other forces, at all stages of our lives, a dog can shape us, mold us, expand us, improve us as people, if only we had eyes to see.

The Dogs Who Grew Me is a memoir about the six dogs who have shared my life and grew me as a person. Moppet, the sweet little black American cocker spaniel who came from a pet shop on Flatbush Avenue in Brooklyn, whose presence, whose very existence, was the focal point of my childhood in the fifties. Della, my beautiful black Great Dane, whose devotion saw me through college, the start of my own business (to which she and the three dogs after her would accompany me every day), the end of one marriage, and the beginning of the next. Timber, the extraordinary wolf hybrid a little closer to the forest than her all-dog counterparts, whose exceptional beauty, inside and out, graced my thirties. Boo, my iron-willed, highly intelligent rottweiler who guarded me through my early forties until cancer brought this immensely powerful dog in the prime of his life to his knees in one terrible week. Daisy, the chocolate American cocker spaniel I bought for my daughter nine years ago so she, too, would know the immense pleasure of a little dog to share her childhood with. And Tyler, my lovely four-year-old Bernese mountain dog, who is teaching me, like no dog before him, the joy of living.

The emphasis throughout is on the dogs. How typical—as five distinct breeds are represented here—each dog was (or is) of his or her respective breed. Who they were as individuals, and those qualities that made each one so unique. Then, their effect on my life: how they saw me through the turbulent times; how their presence enhanced and, in some cases, induced the happy times; the invaluable lessons they taught me at so many turns; how they grew me as a person. And how grateful I am to have been taught so eloquently by each one of them what really matters in life.

The life lessons here are as seemingly simple (but ultimately profound) as the unfettered joy of a walk down the street, and the appreciation of creature comforts (good food and a warm bed at the end of a hard day), and as noble as perseverance, learning the rules, the foibles of excessive rigidity and self-defeating aggression, developing patience, enduring pain, and welcoming joy. They speak to birth and motherhood: How often I have thought that if I can be half the mother my Great Dane, Della, was to ten puppies, how lucky my one daughter will be. They speak to the gift of good health, the adjustments to be made as youth gives way to age, how death must be accepted as a part of life. And, oh, how essential to really live the life that came before. These are but some of the lessons these six dogs have taught me, all this without ever uttering a single word, their eloquence by example.

Further, each section paints the larger backdrop: the historical or cultural context of the respective decade in which each dog's life (some of them overlapping) occurred. The fifties with cocker spaniels running all over, when life was supposed to be so simple and uncomplicated. The sixties when all hell broke loose and no self-respecting hippie would be caught dead with a pedigree dog. The seventies when everything, pedigree-prejudice included, settled back down. The eighties when the pursuit of the dollar and the pedigree dog came back into vogue. And the nineties, termed The Decade of the Dog, particularly the purebred dog, with sweet-natured breeds like the Labrador and golden retriever leading the pack, and also with notable representation of the highly protective breeds like the rottweiler and pit bull.

Mixed in with the individual lessons each dog taught me are the lessons they all taught me. Like that most fundamental idea that, just like these dogs, love comes in many sizes and shapes. But the differences in style of love, for dogs and humans alike, must never be allowed to obscure the underlying magic: the love itself being offered. Also, if dog breeds are different—indeed, the human race has worked mighty hard to make them different—then maybe, by extension, we can not only accept, but enjoy the differences between people, not to mention individuals therein. As we are not all the same. We are who we are.

This said, bring on the dogs!

All knowledge, the totality of all questions and answers, is contained in the dog.

—Franz Kalfa, *Investigations of a Dog*

1

This Little Girl's Moppet

My life with dogs began some forty years ago in a little pet shop that stood on Flatbush Avenue in Brooklyn. I was with my mother, my skinny six-year-old legs donned in *red* blue jeans (yes, kids in the fifties, or this kid anyway, wore red blue jeans), my torso adorned in a white T-shirt, as I stood there looking down at the little tribe of baby cocker spaniels doing the puppy dance in the front window for me. And one of them—the thought was so wonderful as to be almost unbearable—was going to be mine.

Five more times I would stand on this same pinnacle of joy. In the future, however, it would be preceded by careful research into breeds, contacting breeders, phone calls to determine each other's "suitability" and availability of litters. The car trips to visit the kennels in New Jersey or the wilds of upstate New York. Then, some weeks or months later would come the glorious pick-up day when the longed for puppy (sometimes not your choice to make, but the breeder's) finally appeared. But this time, my first time, my research was very simple: I wanted a cocker spaniel puppy and I had already paid a great psychological price for her.

But first things first, why a cocker spaniel? The fifties were awash with spaniels; they were also liberally splashed with German shepherds. Look at any baby boomer's collection of old black-and-white family photos, and there's a cocker spaniel somewhere in there. Look a little longer, and German shepherds start turning up. (Far more prevalent, of course, was the mixed breed, the mongrel, the mutt. And we would have one of these too; he was my father's dog, Beau, and we'll get to him later.)

1

But I was not a German shepherd kind of kid. I was a cocker spaniel kid. The status that came along with owning a shepherd meant nothing to me. That "police dog" thing held no appeal whatsoever. I wanted what I saw in the backyards and at the end of all those leashes of my early childhood: I wanted sunny. I wanted cheerful. Lively. Small. I wanted sweet. I wanted—and oh, how I needed—*loving*. The dog who would give me all these things beyond my wildest dreams was right there in that pet shop window. Her name was Moppet. Like a life jacket tossed to a floundering person, she didn't exist to save me, but save me in some important ways, she did.

To understand who she was and what she did for me, you must understand who I was then, what the world felt like in the fifties, and the sense of deprivation that had begun to color me troubled.

I wasn't thrown into locked closets, or denied food, the stuff of real deprivation. My deprivation was of a personal nature, a sometime misery framed in an upper-middle-class setting. My father (New York born and raised) was a brilliant doctor, thus bestowing much glory upon his offspring that when, for instance, the three of us had occasion to walk through the waiting room of his office, we would set off the flurry of mummers, "They're the '*doctor's children*.'" When we were pre-teenagers, he would buy us all English racer bikes and send us to private schools. My mother, blond, very pretty, and German and Irish, was the mid-westerner reared on milk and corn who raised not a few eyebrows in her home town of Keokuk, Iowa, when, as a college student, she fell in love with the handsome Italian medical student at the University of St. Louis. And married him. And then came to big bad New York (more fodder for brow-raising) to eventually settle in Bay Ridge, Brooklyn, in a two-story house above my father's office with a backyard on a street populated by other doctor families living in adjoined two-story houses above their offices.

It was here that my parents raised their children, three of them; and where, when I was about four years old, that deprivation, that sometime misery, set in. It wasn't anybody's fault. It stemmed from birth order. It is what is now called "middle-child syndrome," compounded and made worse by the fifties culture that valued boys and devalued girls.

That is, I was sandwiched between my older sister and younger brother, the second, in other words, of two girls—followed by a *boy*—a most unenviable position much emphasized at social events, most especially family gatherings, when, for instance, my sister Paula would walk into the room and be greeted by howls of "Look at you! How tall you've grown! And how pretty!" Then the chorus turned to my brother, with the refrain "What a big boy you are now! And how handsome!" This was accompanied by the affectionate running of somebody's hand over my brother's crew cut and a warm nod of approval for its perfect flatness. But when my turn came to hear the accolades and take a courtesy, it was as though the family revelers had run out of gas. My expectations were met with initial silence. It's not that they lost interest, there was no interest. They'd already seen the original, the first-born daughter with the long braids. They'd paid homage to the son who would carry on the name. So who was—and frankly, who cared about—this *second* daughter? Lest the impression be left that I was totally ignored, my turn for recognition would come later in the heart sinking, "Oh, you must be Paula's sister." Or, "I didn't know Brother (my brother's nickname) had two sisters."

While it could be argued that some of the manners at these gatherings needed a little looking into, these weren't vicious people. They meant no harm. They were average people caught up in their own life dramas.

They were also people very much a product of an era that bears little resemblance to the current culture (fermented in the eighties and nineties) that is so child-centered, so child-correct that it bends over backwards in pretzel fashion to acknowledge and make each and every little person at any gathering, anywhere, feel mighty important. And God forbid you should fail to compliment even the kid gleefully running his nails down a blackboard. Not so in the fifties. This was an adult-oriented culture. The kid doing the nails on the blackboard would have seen it ejected right out the window. The little girl who felt invisible against the glory of her sister and brother just needed to forget this nonsense and go play with her dolly.

The literature of the time backed up these stances. There were not fifty books being published every five minutes on "child rearing" (the term didn't even exist), some ten of them focused on the significance of birth order, nor books that zeroed in on "middle-child syndrome," nor books that would have something to say about bunks beds versus two single beds, or the role eye color would play in later career choices. All this—the good and the trumped up—would come later. This was the era of stay-at-home mothers taking their cues from Dr. Spock, who told the mothers who read his book—in between making grilled cheese sandwiches and ladling out Campbell's soup—how to extricate ear wax from the uncooperative three year old. Beyond earwax, there were bouts of appendicitis to think about. There was measles to deal with. Polio was claiming its last victims. So Dr. Spock didn't give a damn about birth order. He was too busy—and so were our mothers—dealing with the "real" issues of everyday life.

So, nobody gave a hoot about "middle-child" something or other. But it's not as though I moved through life as one of the walking wounded. Far from it. My nickname was "Smiley," and you don't get called Smiley for nothing. Unlike my sister who, as this family story has it, was born and then "cried for a whole year," I was a happy baby; not a peep out of me. Yes, it's true I let out a good holler when I woke up one day to an inch-worm inching its way along the crib railing, but minutes later I was playing contentedly with my toys. I loved the Raggedy Ann wallpaper in the room I shared with my sister. I easily made little friends in kindergarten and first grade. I was so glad we had a cat. But the "Smiley" in me was no match for the increasingly murky middle-child void that kept coming after me, chipping away at me, replacing my optimism with worry, my spontaneity with self-consciousness. And I had no defenses against it, no solution to it. I was old enough to feel the pain, but too young to know how to get out from under it—until, at age six, something and someone intervened

That "something" was a scalp aliment (not ringworm, but some obscure condition for which no name was ever provided) that came on the heels of a debilitating scarlet fever and chicken pox summer. The cure, my parents told me, required I get my shoulder length hair cut. In return for which—here's where the "someone" came in—they promised to get me a dog.

So off I went with my father, for some ungodly reason, to get the deed done. And done it was one summer morning that was otherwise sunny: the barber chair, the barber, my father standing there, as the sniping started and pieces of hair began to fall away and continued to fall. At some point so, also, did the tears. But the tears didn't stop the scissors. They continued to snip . . . up to my ears . . . past my ears, only stopping when the blurred vision looking back at me in the mirror was that of a little girl's stunned face below a jagged crew cut, her heart pounding with shock and humiliation. One thought and one thought alone sustained me:

the puppy who would be the reward for this butchery of my hair. She was faceless and nameless at this point; all I had was the idea of her that kept me from completely unraveling.

Which begs the question, Did my father not prepare me for this desecration of my hair? The answer is he said "short," but what he failed to tell me was how short. This "short" was devastation. It was a short that for years would spin nightmarish dreams of scissors and people suddenly coming up behind me and cutting off my hair. So, yes, it could be said my father failed miserably in informing me the true nature of this therapeutic haircut, no less preparing me for its aftermath. Looking back, I have to chalk it up to the fact that his was a doctor's clinical approach: Cut the hair (virtually) off, end of scalp problem. Also, being male, it could be said he didn't understand, or forgot, or chose to forget, the degree to which even a little six-year-old girl's sense of femaleness is caught up with her hair. (In his defense, let the record show that when, in the years to come, the topic of this infamous hair cut would rear its sensitive head, the look on my father's face suggested at some point he had come to understand what happened this day. Let the record also show my hair did grow in gloriously, this fact thrown in with the footnote that I have worn my hair long ever since.)

So home I went with my new look. If my own eyes, and the wind whipping around my ears, didn't tell me how freakishly chopped off my hair was, the initial shocked looks on my mother's face and Paula and Brother's faces certainly did. My father, wanly backed up by mother, would do his best to pass this butchery off as an "Italian Boy Haircut"— thereby rendering it, what, desirable? Something you would seek out for yourself to make a fashion statement? At six?

For weeks I walked around in the Italian Boy do. People who didn't know me simply assumed the skinny little kid with the jagged crew cut was a boy. Bad enough, since I was a girl. The real problem, of course, came with people who did know me: the kids on my block, the kids at school, who were of a bent that sniffs out a weakness and zooms in to exploit it. No sniffing needed here; my head was a beacon for taunts. Now even before the butchery of my hair, I was a sensitive kid. Now I was a super-sensitive kid. But I was no idiot. There was no point trying to explain to my tormentors, "Don't you know? This is an Italian Boy Hairdo!" because it would have been met with sneers of "Oh, really? Well you look like you stuck your head in a lawn mower!"

I endured the taunts. I endured the wind whipping around my ears. I have a vague memory of briefly resorting to a scarf to cover my shorn dome, but it drew even more attention to the problem. So I cast the scarf aside and took my licks and prayed my hair would grow quickly to release me from this torture, holding tight in my mind to the little dog who would be the reward for all this.

But hair doesn't respond to prayers. Time is a little deaf too. When you need it to speed up, it only slows down. But one day has to follow another, and they did, six long weeks of them until the day finally came that brought me with my mother to that pet shop on Flatbush Avenue. And there I stood—white T-shirt, red blue jeans, butchered hair—looking down at the baby cocker spaniels in the front window. And what a classic puppy cluster they were: six or seven shiny little black bodies (some all black, others with patches or streaks of white on their chests) gaily jumping around on the newspaper; some tripping and flopping all over each other; others gaily chewing on each other's ears, then diving down to get at a leg, which led to more "serious" play-tussles replete with baby growling. And then—every puppy cluster has one—there was the puppy all tuckered out and fast asleep on her side, her belly rising and falling, totally oblivious to the lively pandemonium around her.

All this I took in as I stood there, trying to separate them in my mind and see who each puppy was, when a little miracle happened. One puppy extricated herself from the jumble of play and marched right over to the glass partition, inches away from my rapt gaze, to stand up on her hind legs with her front legs pressed against the glass, and peer up at me with dancing little brown eyes. A littermate hopped over and nipped at her legs to get her to forget this distraction and come back and rejoin in the fun. But she didn't. She stood there, sweet and little, doing the balancing act against the glass on wobbly legs, her eyes shining, her little tail vibrating. A moment later, she let go her front legs (or may be they simply slid off the glass) to land with a tiny thud back down on the newspapers. Hardly deterred, she jumped right back up, looking straight at me with the sweetest expression I ever saw. My heart moved in a way I had never experienced before. In that instant, I knew who she was, and I loved her.

I don't remember if I asked my mother, who was standing directly behind me, for her input in the selection process, but I suspect at some point I did. I do remember finally tearing my eyes off this wonderful little creature, turning around to my mother, and uttering the words as classic as the scene that led up to it: *"This one. I want this one."*

The pet shop owner stepped over, reached into the front window to pick Moppet up, and carried her over to the counter. A moment later, the front door opened. I turned my head for a second and saw a kid accompanied by his mother enter the shop and head straight for the aisles of fish tanks. When I turned back, the pet shop owner was placing Moppet on the counter in front of me and I couldn't believe my eyes. It was all coming true. The hair for the puppy, the pain for the puppy, and here she was. As caught up as I was in this moment, it was a momentous moment for her, too. Only days ago she had parted from her mother, a minute ago she'd been plucked from her littermates. Now, all alone and high up on this hard counter, she stood on wobbly legs, uncertain. I put my hands on her to steady her (and yes, to make sure she didn't fall off) and what my hands felt instantly registered in the heart. It was pure joy.

All thoughts of the injustice of waiting six long weeks for this day evaporated into the air. If I'd remembered the last time I felt overlooked at some gathering, I couldn't remember it now. If I'd known how bad red blue jeans were, I wouldn't have cared about that either. Nothing mattered to me but this warm, soft little puppy already sporting—my fingers ventured to touch them—the gentle little curls in her cocker spaniel ears, the soft little neck under the ears, and—my hands couldn't believe such riches—the tender body covered in the soft black fur. I looked into her eyes. They were still bright, but tinged with worry. The counter was so high, her surroundings so new. But she was willing—I felt her body start to relax—to be comforted by my hands that stroked her as I told her not to worry, that everything was going to be all right.

How many times in life do we want something desperately and then actually get it? My heart could hardly take it in. The miracle of this soft little creature in my gentle clasp exceeded my wildest dreams. But even here, the happiest moment of my childhood, life can still exact its toll. There was one more coin, one more little piece of pain, to pay for this joy. As the kid and his mother who'd been strolling the aisles of fish tanks now approached the counter, that coin dropped a moment later with the words that would echo up through the decades: "Oh, look, mommy," he said, "the little boy's getting a puppy."

I tell this story now with a smile on my face, but at the time this sentence cut off my breath. It sliced through my happiness like a hatchet through a birthday cake. But while his words had staying power—they survived four decades intact—he meant no harm. This boy, endowed with normal vision, simply sang out a perfectly legitimate observation. But that kid could have said the little boy *with two heads* is getting a puppy and it wouldn't have mattered for long. Moppet was already working her magic. Her gifts had begun. She was already my buffer, the golden little nugget nestled in my heart, who made this final payment in pain, the reminder of how I looked, fall away to nothing. And indeed, this is the last incidence I can remember of innocent remarks, or deliberate taunts, engendered by the infamous Italian Boy Haircut.

As my mother prepared to pay for Moppet, she didn't produce a wad of cash from her purse or hand over the magical piece of plastic. This was the fifties. Nobody had wads of cash (not in their bag, anyhow), and credit cards didn't exist. Then again, no wad of cash would be necessary. My Moppet would cost all of twenty-five dollars. (Yes, a far cry from the one thousand to fifteen hundred dollars that buys a purebred dog nowadays.)

Even if my mother had brought a suitcase of money, six-year-old me would not walk out of this pet shop on Flatbush Avenue with a truckload of dog stuff in tow. Borrowing another page from the fifties that parallels the point I'm about to make, I cite the fact that the train set my brother and everybody else's brother got did not consist of the train, a mile of track, a train station, a village, a mountain, a tunnel, a bridge, and a thousand play people to move around all this. The train set of the fifties was two items: the train, and a little circle of track that got set up in the living room. Kids sat watching that train run around the circle till they got bleary eyed.

So it was with dogs. You didn't get the dog and a leash, a collar, a dog bed, a dog coat, a food bowl, a water bowl, a month's supply of special puppy food, and a dog book or two to pull it all together. Hell, no! Like the train, this was the no-frills dog acquisition fifties. The frills hadn't been invented. There were no matching collars and leashes. There were plain leather flat collars with a buckle. There were chain-link leashes that ended in the leather loop for the hand. The "match" was made when you clipped the leash onto the collar.

As for dog coats, Lassie and Rin Tin Tin never wore them, and neither did any other dog I ever saw in my childhood. (Which makes me now wonder how did the little short-haired dogs survive the winters of my youth? Did their owners carry them around under their thick wool coats? Did they wrap the shivering little masses in wads of safety-pinned blankets, and take the whole business out for a walk?) As for that other amenity, the dog bed, there wasn't the plethora of beds and cushions of every imaginable size, material, style, and purpose, with monogramming Fido's initials all but de rigueur. The dog bed industry was in its infancy. All it had managed to come up with was the one-size-fits-all brown wicker basket with the one-color cushion. And you didn't see too many of these in the typical household because, as any baby boomer can attest, the dog bed of the fifties was the floor. Or—and here's where things got fancy—a floor with a rug. And no, the rug did not come monogrammed. But no matter. Fido was mighty grateful for the rug.

So, six-year-old me did not walk out this day with a truckload of dog stuff. I walked out with Moppet and one other item: a collar. The rest—a dog bowl, a *leash*?—would come later. On the other hand, that I received the collar but no leash amazes me even to this day. Is it possible I was just too excited to think about a leash? Or maybe I just plain forgot because I already had what I wanted: the little black American cocker spaniel puppy with the white splash down her throat and chest who I would name Moppet.

This may be the perfect place to pause and take a look at the cocker spaniel and its history, and see its Breed Standard as set forth by the American Kennel Club.

Historically, the spaniel family is a large one with roots of considerable antiquity that date back to England and mention of the "Spanyell" as early as 1368. This "Spanyell" came to be divided into two groups: the land spaniel and the water spaniel. A further division was applied to the land spaniels on the basis of size, separating the "cockers" and the very small "toy" spaniels from spaniels of larger size. Then, cocker and toy spaniels themselves were separated, this division based upon function. The toys, maintained as pets and "lap comforters," eventually became the English toy spaniels; whereas the cockers, hunting dogs, retained their early classification as sporting dogs.

The cocker spaniel is the smallest member of the Sporting Dog Group, his name, the "cocker," "cocking spaniel," and finally "cocker spaniel," deriving from his proficiency at flushing out and retrieving the woodcock, an upland game bird. While the cocker spaniel owes his derivation to England, he was fully developed in the United States, hence he is now called the American cocker spaniel.

In temperament, the same characteristics that made the cocker spaniel so effective and pleasant a sporting dog make him the wonderful companion dog he is today. He has an inherent desire to hunt, and takes to water readily. He's a bright, eager learner. He's energetic but gentle, playful, willing, very eager to please, and very affectionate and loving with his owner.

In appearance, the cocker spaniel has a sturdy, compact body. He weighs between twenty-five and thirty-five pounds. A male stands fifteen inches at the shoulders, whereas a female measures fourteen inches at the shoulder. They come in solid black or black with tan trim. Or ASCOB (Any Solid Color Other Than Black), which includes the buffs (cream to red colored), the browns (chocolate colored), or brown with tan trim. They also come in parti-color (two or more colors, one of which is always white).

Did Moppet's genes create a cocker true to her breed? She was a *fifties* cocker down to her toenails. Yes, it's true, as will be told, she fell a little short in some areas, but she excelled in those other traits that define a cocker spaniel: loving, happy, gentle, playful, willing. Her take on these traits was a dream come true. But she didn't wave the magic wand that would instantly dissolve the middle-child syndrome in me, or reverse the culture at large that put boys on pedestals and girls at their base. You change yourself in this world (indeed, if it comes from outside yourself, it can be taken away). What other people—or other entities—can do is inspire you; they can plant seeds of inspiration. If the soil isn't receptive, the seed dies, the idea is lost, as there was no place for inspiration to take hold. But the soil in me was highly receptive to the seeds Moppet planted. So, yes, there can be defining moments in life, and getting Moppet was one of them.

So home she came, and like a light switch turned on, there was suddenly this wonderfulness in my life.

Her traits were exactly what I needed. My traits were exactly what she needed. For fourteen years we would each give exactly what the other needed. And it started in that pet shop when this wonderful little creature looked past my hair and insecurities, which meant nothing to her, and saw me. And chose me. The pleasant little cocker in her was nice, delightfully nice, to my sister and brother, and she was most agreeable with my mother and father, but it was me she looked to. If I left a room, she got up and ran after me. The *any dog* in her that found the cat most interesting joined forces with the sporting dog in her that had her running around the house after the cat, who quickly figured out (cats are masters at making this determination) that this little dog in hot pursuit wasn't into the hunt, as in "kill." It was all play with Moppet. But if Moppet lost her rapt audience—that would be me—the merry chase was over as she deserted the cat to come along with me.

Small little acts, these, not the stuff you write a play around. Taken out of context, they sound like nothing, but put back into the context of my early childhood, they were everything. They were the antidote to feeling invisible. The antidote to feeling second choice. But they were not, of course, the cure. Real change is a process, not a moment, not even moments as sweet as these that Moppet engendered. But from small beginnings that were not small to me, came the inspiration for large things that are large that would grow in me: *You matter. Be yourself. And be*—she would help me find this—*what matters to you.*

Which brings me to Moppet's most outstanding trait, her greatest gift: she is the dog who taught me how to love, how to recognize it, delight in it (I was a fast learner here), and, just as important, how to love back. It was an extraordinary lesson to learn at any age, much less six.

Now, my parents loved me. But—this is one of those little "but's" that makes the difference between night and day—I didn't *feel* loved, which, when I was six, translated into feeling unlovable, not deserving of love. Enter the little dog who, from the top of her little domed cocker spaniel head to the tip of her little cocker tail, was all about love. Nothing was more important to her. Not food. Not play. Not comfort. Not sleep. And not, as we've already established, chasing the cat. For Moppet— here comes the first miracle—I was synonymous with love. And—here comes the second miracle—so was she for me. And it wasn't a love that needed translating because a dog, any dog, is nothing if not the great communicator of emotions in a language readily understood by humans.

While I wish you good luck in "reading" a cow, you can "read" a horse. That is, their ears prick forward when they're relatively happy and lay flat to the head when they're angry. But you need a "horse whisperer" or some other equestrian expert to tell you what else is going on in that beautiful head. Marine parks would like us to think that the smile on a porpoise's face is because he's having so much fun jumping through the hoops, but what's really happening in his great brain may not be the stuff of a smile at all. I daresay if he could escape, he would take himself back to sea and never look back with a real smile on his face.

But a dog's smile is real. So is the wag of his tail. So are the rest of his emotions. He won't wag his tail if he isn't happy. And he doesn't whine if he isn't upset.

But way beyond this, a dog is a dictionary of communication, with ears that move around, a tail (on dogs so endowed) that rises and falls, with that ridge of fur that rises up on his back when sufficiently provoked, with myriad barks and whines and vocalizations—all of it employed in body language that conveys a host of information about what he's feeling at any given moment. In all these emotions, the dog is incapable of deception. He is the embodiment of sincerity, and in this sincerity, no animal conveys love like a dog. Indeed, a dog can't show love if he doesn't feel it, which makes it very, very real. But some dogs specialize in love. Cockers are among these. And among cockers, there are individual dogs who live by love, and for it. Moppet was one of these.

It was right there, not under her skin, but in her skin, her eyes, her body language, this desire for and pleasure in being touched and picked up, and being comforted when something scared her. Most importantly, it was her desire to be close to the one who gave her these things. This need for affection, for contact, for closeness, for love in its myriad forms connected right down to her soul because it was who she was. As I leapt to the lovely task of giving her what she needed, I discovered that this was also who I was. Little miracle worker that she was, she didn't teach me the word "water" that opened up someone else's world. She taught me Love and it changed my world.

The saying exists—and it's a good one—that you can't love someone else until you love yourself. In my case, it was loving someone else that taught me how to love myself. But it didn't change me overnight. What it all came down to was the life-altering conclusion I reached when I was six that if this unquestionably lovable and loving dog found me lovable, then maybe I was.

Last, I didn't know it at six, but I would eventually figure out that often enough the closer people are to you, the more complicated—and yes, sometimes the more convoluted—is the love that holds you so close. Not so with dogs. And not so with Moppet. Her love was most uncomplicated. It was simple and straightforward. And it wasn't a some-times love. It was an everyday love. A freely given love.

Was hers that wildly touted dog virtue of "unconditional love"? If I had kicked her ten times a day would she have loved me the same? Of course not. It's true dogs are infinitely more resilient of mistreatment and, yes, more forgiving of that mistreatment than we humans are. But just like any other highly intelligent and emotional creature, a dog's love for us is much connected to how we treat him, how kind we are, how patient, consistent, and how loving we are. While the term "unconditional love" as applied to dogs (which has become virtually synonymous with dogs) didn't even exist in the fifties, had I understood it, I would not have wanted it. As love-starved as I felt, any love that was unconditional would have lost its value to me. Real love, love based upon kindness and goodness, was what I needed and wanted from Moppet. And real love is what I got.

Mixed in with these life lessons, and those to come, were lessons galore about the practical aspects of taking care of a dog, and these were as rich and instructive in their way as the life lessons Moppet taught me. While many of them speak to all dogs, some of them are much connected to cocker spaniel traits, or Moppet's particular version of these traits.

I remember well the adorable puppy Moppet was. Along with that adorableness came a creature greatly in need of care. She needed to be kept out of danger. She needed to be fed. She needed to be provided fresh water. She needed to be groomed, and housetrained. She needed to be trained, period. To walk on a leash. To understand basic commands. And to do all this reliably and agreeably so she could be what a cocker spaniel was in the fifties and still is: a good companion dog.

Feeding and watering Moppet was a cinch. Far from drudgery, I discovered what pleasure there was in filling her bowl with dog food and watching her eat. Indeed, to this very day, unless I'm really busy, I don't throw food at my two dogs and race away. I take a moment or two to stand there and watch them start eating, and what I feel is the same pleasure and satisfaction in providing for them that I felt with Moppet. So remembering to feed her was not a problem. Neither was remembering to fill her water bowl. Where I fell short, of course, was in many aspects of the cleaning up after her. The splashed water, the little pieces of food on the kitchen floor. The little tumbleweeds of black fur that rolled across the floor on a summer breeze because I forgot to brush her in the first place and then forgot to chase down the evidence of my forgetfulness with the broom and dustpan.

These aspects of care are not breed specific. They apply to every dog. The next three items speak directly to specific cocker spaniel traits and the special care or attention they require.

The first relates to that physical attribute that more than any other identifies this breed: those long sweet cocker spaniel ears. These are not the no-care smooth-coated flap ears that beagles sport. They are certainly not the no-care, if long haired, upright ears that German shepherds come with. Cocker spaniel ears grow fur, lots of it, on the upper and undersides of the ear. If this fur is not regularly groomed, it first turns into myriad curls, then into clumps of intertwined curls. These clumps join forces with other clumps, making larger clumps. And so it goes. And this is just the outside of the ears. Now comes the inside, the ear canal. In here, the cocker demonstrates another trait that can also be troublesome: the prodigious production of earwax, which if not regularly removed, collects dirt and grime. Not a pretty sight, but not exactly a health issue at first. However, this unaesthetic grimy ear canal can escalate into a health issue because it is the perfect environment for the highly contagious and tenacious ear mite that thrives in this dark, moist, warm environment, especially with the lack of air-circulation those flopped-over furry cocker spaniel ears provide. And here they feed on skin debris, often causing secondary infections that, like ear mites, are not easily gotten rid of. Indeed they can hang on for weeks.

Suffice it to say six-and-seven-and-beyond-year-old me was not up to the task of Moppet's cocker spaniel ears. While the ear mite thing only happened a few times (which required we take her to the vet for treatment), the proficiency and the frequency of my grooming of Moppet's furry ears would not have qualified them for the show ring.

Regularly brushing the rest of the body is also most important. Some cockers come with silky textured fur that's a breeze to maintain. But most grow fur that intertwines into myriad curls, and these are the cockers who need regular grooming to keep those curls in bound—or regular visits to the professional groomer to do it for you. In Moppet's case, the curling fur was restricted to her famous ears.

The next cocker spaniel trait that can be problematic has to do with housetraining, the learning of the essential *we do not pee in the house, we pee outside*. Like many a spaniel, especially a female, this was a concept that simply did not and would not compute in Moppet's brain. Indeed, she peed all over the house, just like the rest of the cockers in the fifties were peeing all over their houses (and, just like our current cocker spaniel, absenting the most carefully timed schedule, more or less lets it fly as the spirit moves her). So yes, housetraining was an issue with Moppet.

But was this a function of her intelligence? Hardly. To cite Stanley Coren's *The Intelligence of Dogs, Canine Consciousness and Capabilities*—in which he ranks the "obedience" or "working intelligence" of seventy-nine dog breeds on a descending scale of one to seventy-nine (with the Border collie in the number one slot as the most intelligent and the Afghan hound at number seventy-nine as the least intelligent), Mr. Coren's ranking of the cocker spaniel in the very respectable number twenty slot says what we have here is a highly intelligent dog infinitely capable of understanding that which is explained to her, followed soon after (this soon defined as five to fifteen repetitions of instruction) by compliance. Mr. Coren—and his myriad data culled from the results of obedience competitions and the hundreds of obedience trail judges who assisted in its interpretation—is so right. Cocker spaniels are bright, eager learners *if* they agree the training idea has merit. If it's meaningful to them. If it makes sense to them. But housetraining— the hold it till you get outside—is a concept that did not make sense to Moppet.

This is not to say she didn't understand the consequences that followed a little indoor water spree. When I came upon the little puddle in the middle of the floor and asked her, "What's *that*? Did you do *that*?" she knew exactly what the "that" referred to. She also understood the tone of "bad dog" and the finger wagging that accompanied it. She was sorry and crestfallen as she watched me clean up this puddle and the thousand more to come. She was equally sorry as she watched my mother clean up her thousand puddles. Even so, she was forever perplexed as to why her little owner and her other humans made such faces and such a fuss over a little water on the floor.

Which begs the question: Is this free-to-pee trait exhibited by some cocker spaniels, particularly females, a bladder issue? Or is it a head issue? I suspect it is both. It's the head that often isn't wired to connect to this specific area of training. And it's also the bladder that seems to quickly reach capacity, then gives out to its urges. This conclusion is much fortified by the fact that the cocker spaniel is hardly diffident about its owner's wishes; this is a breed that is nothing if not eager to please. If it can. In the housetraining arena, Moppet simply couldn't.

Could she have done better in different or more capable hands? With different equipment, or any equipment to aid in the teaching of the lesson? Of course she might have. Moppet was my first dog. I had no prior experience to bring to her training. While my mother backed up my efforts (or picked up the slack where my efforts fell off), I was responsible for Moppet's housetraining. I didn't have the myriad books on dog training available now that delve into housetraining as the core topic any dog needs to learn AFAP, as fast as possible. But even without this guidance, I figured out some of the rudiments on my own, which came down to this: Take her out often. Of course, my often wasn't often enough. Or my timing wasn't precise enough. Or I just wasn't fast enough. It would occur to me that it had been "a while" since she'd been out, so I'd get the leash and call her to the front door, only to discover she'd peed in the hallway on the way to the door. I resorted to sometimes tying her up. It didn't work. She'd walk out as far as the leash would let her and comfortably pee there, then walk herself back to dry land.

What this fiasco of housetraining really needed is that piece of equipment that didn't exist in the fifties: the dog crate, the restraining box that builds on the fundamental fact that dogs are loath to eliminate where they sleep or eat. Its proper use—not as a jail cell, but as a safe and pleasant place to learn to mentally and physically hold the pee until it's time to go outside—might have made for significant headway with the very resistant Moppet. Or certainly have improved the outlook here. But could it have made her even seventy-five percent "sure" in the house? I doubt it. Many are the conversations I have now with owners of female cocker spaniels who, even with all their fancy crates and sixteen dog books for guidance, still keep the rolls of paper towels very handy.

So it could be said the floors and rugs of my early childhood took quite a beating. But (this is easy for me to say, though not so easy for my mother to say) if the price of life with Moppet meant getting out a rowboat to stay above the water level she generated, I would have gladly gotten out that rowboat.

Before we leave the exhaustive topic of water vis-à-vis cocker spaniels, a quick word on another trait exhibited by many female cockers: "submissive urination:" the sudden and uncontrollable wetting that can accompany being very excited or frightened. Moppet spared us the "frightened" kind that some cockers exhibit, for instance, at the awful sight of the veterinarian. But she was wont to occasionally engage in the "excited" kind when I came home after being away at school all day and she was so excited to see me, she couldn't help but pee some of that excitement.

The standard cure for this, which I didn't know at the time: Don't get the water flowing by adding your own wildly happy greeting to the excitement of a cocker who's already whipped herself into a frenzy of happiness. Instead, let your greeting be low key. This doesn't mean ignore her. Just walk in calmly and take a minute or two before you say a nice little hello.

The next trait I'll discuss, consummate paper shredder, is one I have never come across in any dog book or breed description of a cocker spaniel (or in any conversation with fellow spaniel owners), so I must assume it was a Moppet trait, and hers alone. It evidenced itself every single day of her life—given the opportunity. The opportunities were many in a household that, like any other, contained myriad paper products: books, newspapers, mail, magazines, comic books, medical journals, homework. Should any such object—a tissue, a stamp—be left within her reach, or fall within her reach, it became fair game. Thus, when, as they are wont to, a paper napkin slipped off a lap at the dining table and sailed down to the floor, Moppet was on it in a second, manically shredding it into a thousand little pieces. If my mother did something as normal as put down her *Good Housekeeping* magazine to go answer the phone, she came back to a little blizzard of paper rubble with one happy little Moppet in its center.

What purpose all this shredding served only Moppet knew. Was there something intrinsically wrong with an intact magazine? Did a whole sheet of homework somehow offend her? Did it connect with some hard-wired need in her to rout out the birds in the underbrush of a piece of paper by reducing their cover literally to shreds? I don't have the answers to these questions. What I can say is we would never train the paper shredder out of Moppet. So we trained ourselves to put paper objects out of her reach. We must not have been too successful here, or she was too good an opportunist, because my childhood memories are much littered with little pieces of paper courtesy of the little cocker in our midst.

Water events and paper aside, what about the rest of Moppet's training? Here she was the "bright, eager learner" referred to earlier. While the training as offered up by six-and-seven-and-on-up me was not of a highly sophisticated level, Moppet easily learned all the things any dog needs to learn. She came when she was called, which was, as with any dog, very, very important, to her well-being and safety. She did a nice "sit," planting her little bottom down on the floor. She did a reasonable "stay" unless I backed away too far. She walked on a leash very nicely, not exactly at my side, but close enough to call it heeling. She understood that if I was sitting on the sofa and patted the cushion next to me, that meant hop up, and so she did. And if I told her "off," she understood to hop off. All these things she did most reliably and agreeably like the wonderful companion dog she was.

Indeed, Moppet defined that wonderful word: the "companion" in a companion dog. Her presence, her very existence, had fast become the focal point of my childhood, the ground zero of things good, things reliable. Things I could count on. Things I loved. She slept on my bed. Is there anything more wonderful than going to sleep every night with your childhood dog right there with you? I don't think so. She tagged me around the house. If I stopped to pick up a book and sat down in a chair to read it, she sat down next to the chair. If I really got into reading this book, she laid down and went to sleep. I can remember going outside to sit down on the porch steps that led down to our backyard; there would come the brush of soft fur against my side as Moppet sat down next to me, and we'd have a moment there in the air and warm sunshine, together.

The companion dog in Moppet also came out in that sweet trait she had in overflow: an inborn willingness to try something new, or put up with something old not of her choosing. It wasn't because she needed more excitement in her life. It was to please the companion she had in me. Nowhere was this willingness demonstrated more vividly than in our adventures with a prized possession of my childhood: my red wagon.

I can't remember who came first: Moppet or the wagon. But I do remember peeking through the slats of the Venetian blinds in the living room one Christmas, and how my heart leapt at the sight of my father secreting it down the sidewalk, in a vain attempt to get it into the house undetected. I didn't load my wonderful wagon with dolls or toys for passengers. What doll or Jack-in-the-Box could compare with my living, breathing, little Moppet for a passenger? On the other hand, no Jack-in-the-Box needed coaxing to stay put. Moppet did. What little dog in her right mind would choose to stay in this metal box on wheels, lurching and sliding around while her owner gleefully towed her up and down the block? But stay she did. Putting up with my chatter, and all manner of passersby who reached down to pet her as we rolled along. But there came a point when even her willingness to endure this noisy game of rumbling up and down the sidewalk began to run thin, and she did the only thing she could: she hopped out.

A yell or two got her to hop back in, until, two minutes later, she jumped out again and it was clear she was not going to voluntarily get back in that wagon. So I picked her up and put her back in with the admonition to "stay there." But in the time it took me to walk the step or two to pick up the handle so we could get going again, she jumped back out, her clenched body language and the look in her eyes saying, "I'm *really* not enjoying this. It's time to do something else." I hope I praised her for indulging me for so long, as I indulged myself with the thought that there would be more wagon days for us.

And there were. The next time I might have pulled her down the block and turned the corner to gaily rumble past the storefronts on Fifth Avenue. Or in the spirit of real adventure, it might have been a walk all around the block, big doings this, until Moppet's final hop out delivered with that apologetic but firm look in her eyes said the wagon thing was done for this day, too. But no love lost here. Indeed love gained, especially in hindsight, for the little dog who went as far as she could go to please me, and in so doing, made my red wagon days all the sweeter.

She made all my days sweeter. She also made them more vivid, more colorful, more interesting, more everything because of those traits in her that were who she was, that kept pointing me to who I was and what really mattered, or would matter, to me.

Thus it was Moppet who first showed me what would become a lifelong pleasure: the simple and profound glory of a walk down the street with your dog, and what the walk becomes because of the dog. Of course, this event was preceded by much excitement as she jumped around by the front door. In the beginning, I took this to only mean she needed to pee (which, of course, she did). But this act completed, the joy didn't fall off. This was the tiny prelude to what really mattered: the walk, being outside. It was the street trees on our block whose trunks she sniffed; the weeds growing in a tree well where she paused to pick up messages; the squirrel flitting about in a neighbor's front garden who caught her eye; the sparrow flying overhead; the dandelion sprouting up between a crack in the sidewalk; the breeze gently ruffling her fur, as she lifted up her nose to sniff this breeze. It was nature that this little cocker spaniel experienced with such excitement. It was Nature's unexpected little gifts of sight and sound and scent and movement that made her come alive. And her joy in these things made me come alive to them, opening up my fascination with the natural world and its animals and plants, their habitats, and the fragile miracle all this is. Because nature isn't someplace else, or some other time. It's right here and now. It's the glory of a simple little walk down the street if you have a dog to show you the way.

Today I walk a different dog on a different street. The horticulturalist that I am can recite the botanical names of the trees and shrubs we pass. The lifelong reader of zoology in me can tell you the internal workings of a bird or an earthworm we might come across. But what I see and feel inside is what Moppet showed me when I was six.

And then came Beau, my father's dog. His arrival tells like a *Leave It to Beaver* episode with the homespun storyline: He followed my sister home one day from the butcher shop. The longer version (I had to check with Paula to get it) has her standing at the butcher shop counter; she had just handed up the money, and the butcher had handed her down the brown paper bag with the meat in it. Then he did what he always did: he reached over the counter a second time to hand her his usual treat, a slice of baloney wrapped in a little piece of paper. My sister hated baloney, but she didn't want to hurt his feelings. So she thanked him, left the store, and the moment she was out of eyesight, she did what she always did: she put the baloney in the back pocket of her jeans, and started for home.

Unbeknownst to her, a stray dog honed in on that pocket and trailed her all the way home until, walking up the front stoop of our house, she turned around, and saw him. So it was baloney that brought Beau to us. Had my sister liked baloney and eaten this slice, there wouldn't be this tale to tell.

He was a brown, medium-sized mixed breed dog who gave the impression he was much larger, with ears that stood up when he was interested in something, then folded back to their resting position against his head when that interest subsided. He had a long tail that curled upward (unless he did something bad, in which case the curl sagged to a droop until he was forgiven), and a highly expressive face. No doubt he had some German shepherd in him. Then again, in the fifties there wasn't an owner of a brown medium-sized mixed breed who didn't announce with pride how Scruffy had "some shepherd" in him. This aside, what really defined Beau, apart from his ample intelligence, was the distinct air of masculinity he gave off. This masculine mutt was irresistibly drawn to my father (and vice versa) and I can still see the two of them masculine-ing their way down the street together.

I can't remember the exact day Beau arrived. In reconstructing these early dog years, there was just Moppet. Then there was Beau, too. But I can tell you his arrival didn't set off the classic refrain of "Can we keep him?! Can we keep him?!" On the contrary, my mother and father were happy to oblige young Beau looking for someplace to put down roots.

So, first he found the baloney. Then he found us, the fifties family with a mother and a father and three kids and a cat named Kitty. Then, one step farther through the door, he found Moppet. And promptly fell in love with her.

I, much taken with Disney's newly released *Lady and the Tramp*, imagined him the "Tramp" to Moppet's "Lady," a conception I would impart to any adult, stopping strangers on the street (this was an era when it was okay to talk to strangers) to tell them how the little black cocker spaniel before their very eyes was named Lady and the larger brown dog right next to her was named Tramp. This, no doubt, produced some wan smiles on those strangers' faces, and maybe even the affirmation kindly offered: "Of course they are."

To set the stage for the next dog saga, I begin by saying that cowboy stuff was very big in the fifties and it was television that fueled it. Although we were one of the last people on our block to get a TV, when our turn came to sit glued to the big wooden box with the little screen, it was shows like *The Adventures of Rin Tin Tin* and *Lassie* that held us spellbound. But much, much better, because it was so inclusive and roped in all manner of cowboy lifestyle for us to imitate, was *The Roy Rogers and Dale Evans Show*. This show had wholesome Roy Rogers for the boys, wholesome Dale Evans for the girls, Trigger for the horse lovers, and Bullet the German shepherd for the dog lovers. The jeep they sometimes ran around in was for the kids who, cowboy obsessed or not, still needed to see some wheels to feel happy. While each episode had it that with Trigger or Bullet's help, Roy and Dale always got the bad guys, the show wasn't officially over, and nobody touched that dial, until they sang "Happy Trails" at the very end.

Like millions of fifties kids, we bought the cowboy thing in every sense of the word, traipsing around in the cowboy hat, plastic gun, holster, and whatever else the allowance could muster up. But what also derived of this pleasant obsession was a love of horses. Indeed, through my mother's efforts, the three of us were already taking riding lessons and would get very proficient at it. The problem was, you rented horses by the hour. Wonderful as it was, it was also a sometimes event. More to the point, you couldn't take them home with you. But you could turn your dogs into horses. And this we did!

The game was simply called "Horses." To achieve some verity, we made bridles and bits for the dogs out of string. They coughed and strained against our efforts to get the bits in place, but this done, we'd trample down the hallway "on" our dog-horses to the hideout—the far end of the hall— where we'd tie the horses up to the banister, and sit down. But as the horses were the thing, our plots always quickly had us getting back to them and untying the reins. The dogs, happy to get moving again, tore down to the other end of the hallway, which was the town, where, of course, there was more tying up to the banister.

The division of horse material went this way: I got Moppet, no arguing here, because she was mine. That left Beau and the cat. Paula got Beau because she was the oldest. And my poor brother had to make do with the cat. The dogs put up with this nonsense. But not the cat! One false move with the string bridle and she was off, streaking down the stairs.

Loud complaints were called down to my mother in the kitchen that Paula and I were "hogging the dogs!" followed by the suggestion called up, "Let Brother have a turn with Moppet or Beau!" Which we didn't. If Brother lost his horse, he'd just have to play horseless. But with or without the cat, "Horses" wasn't rainy day entertainment. The sun could be blasting away outside and we'd be at this game in the upstairs hallway for hours. I'm sure this game translated well to our backyard, but I can't remember playing it there. What I do remember is the thrill of taking it to McKinley Park.

McKinley Park sits atop a hill in Bay Ridge. When my brother and sister and I were a little older, we began going there. It was small park, a ten-acre square, but it felt like the country to us with its long sloping hill, trees, grass, and paved pathways, and a little playground with swings and a slide. We didn't care about the playground and didn't stick to the paved walkways. The fun was off the pathways where we played "Horses," tearing down the well-beaten dirt paths between the bushes, designating some clump "the hideout," tying the dogs not to the banister, but to thick-trunked London plane trees next to real grass, dirt, pebbles, rocks, and twigs.

We would build on the sense of adventure and survival skills we learned here (don't loose each other; don't loose the dogs) to apply them on a larger scale when, sometime later, we decided we were not sufficiently appreciated at home (too much bickering, not enough TV watching, too much of a fuss made over messy rooms). We decided the solution to this lack of appreciation was to run away. The next morning, we packed my red wagon (that now bore the myriad scrapes of Moppet's toenails) with peanut butter and jelly sandwiches and a box of Ritz crackers. We leashed Moppet and Beau, and set out for the long walk to Shore Road, that stretch of narrow park that runs for miles alongside the Belt Parkway. Trudging along block by block, the three of us took turns pulling the wagon or sitting in it. The problem was, we ate the sandwiches and most of the crackers on the way there, so by the time we hit Shore Road and settled in under a clump of bushes, our rations were worrisomely low. Undeterred, we sat there eating the last of the Ritz crackers. By midmorning, this running away from home idea had lost its luster and we abandoned all thoughts of this new life for us under the bushes at Shore Road, and went home for lunch.

And then came the puppies.

I begin this saga with a statement that is as much an apologia as it is an explanation: spaying and neutering dogs was not big in the fifties. It was rare. Every now and then you heard how somebody's dog got "fixed" and now she couldn't have puppies. This declaration met with an exchange of regret all around. Nowadays, of course, the reverse couldn't be more the case. Now the onus is square and hard on the person who doesn't automatically spay or neuter the family dog.

But if neutering was rare, any discussion of sex as it applied to dogs—no less humans—was nonexistent in the fifties. Indeed, I clearly remember the girl in fifth grade who told me the facts of life. Being in a state of stunned disbelief, I uttered something like, "You're kidding!"

Until I remembered the vision of Moppet and Beau stuck together, end to end, in the middle of the kitchen floor (this event, of course, occurring the day the man came to fix the washing machine and my mother who was aghast but couldn't move them, spread out her apron in an attempt to block off the sight). A moment later, I connected this event to the litter of puppies that followed some two months later, which produced my second utterance: "My God, it's true!"

But it was common enough practice in the fifties that if it wasn't the family cat who showed the children the miracle of life, it was the family dog—minus, of course, the sex act that was the prelude to this miracle. Years later, there would be another breeding of another dog of mine. But this one was planned and executed at a kennel under the supervision of the breeder whose stud dog would be paid handsomely to mix his pedigree Great Dane genes with my pedigree Great Dane's genes. But in the fifties, accidents just happened. They happened when some little kid took the talk he overheard about Muffy being "in heat" to mean she was hot, so he took her outside for a walk to cool her off where, much to his horror, a stray male dog honed in on her scent and, despite the kid's screaming and arm-flailing, initiated doggy coitus in all of five seconds. Accidents also happened when a busy mother, who had all she could handle keeping track of three children, forgot to keep track of Beau for the five seconds that he got loose and found Moppet "in heat" in the kitchen.

So, real life imitating cartoon art, the Tramp we took in and opened our hearts to, thanked us for our largesse by impregnating the purebred cocker spaniel in a protracted sex scene in the middle of the kitchen floor.

While Moppet's puppies were a huge event in my life, there are gaps in my memory here. I remember what got her pregnant, but I can't remember her being pregnant. I remember the fact of her giving birth, but I can't see it in my mind. As to the puppies who resulted, except for one, I only remember them as a group. I can say that, unlike the cartoon Lady and Tramp who produced three little spaniel Lady's and three little mixed breed Tramps, Moppet and Beau's genes did the real life mixing that resulted in progeny who were a combination of their parents. All of them were black. Most had swatches of white down their throats. Some had a white "sock" or two. They all had long tails. All came with smooth little flop-over ears. And they were all as sweet as they could be. Which had my parents daily reminding me, "Don't get attached to them. Don't get attached to them." But of course I did, which made for the heartache I remember vividly when the time came to part with them.

But before this parting came my first example of canine motherhood. It was not the one I would try to model myself after, which would come some fifteen years later in the utter devotion I would witness in Della, my Great Dane. Rather, Moppet's take on the mothering thing was of the no-frills, no-nonsense order. That got the job done—no more, no less. So she fed her puppies, she cleaned them, she kept track of them. But not with the passion that flames in some dogs that you didn't know was in them—and they didn't know was in them—until the puppies arrive, and there it is, an all consuming love and fascination with their offspring.

But not Moppet. I didn't have to drag her away from her puppies so she could go outside to relieve herself. She was happy to have a break from the little critters. When we came back inside, she didn't rush past the cat to get back to her brood in the sectioned off area of the kitchen. She tarried with the cat. She took a look under the dining table to see if perchance there was a paper napkin that needed shredding. She gave a glance around the living room for her ball or any remnant of her former carefree days. Eventually duty called, or a puppy yelped, and she reluctantly took herself back to her brood in the kitchen and settled back into motherhood for this day and many more.

Then the puppies started to grow sharp little teeth. The weaning days were upon us. As Moppet didn't cotton to pain, she had definitive thoughts as to how to proceed. The next morning—I remember it with crystal clarity—she simply hopped up on a chair in the kitchen, her puppies madly yipping at her feet, there to stay until her brood got the idea the lunch counter was closed. This act of severance was delivered with glances in my direction that seemed to say, *Just let me tie up this last loose end and I'll be back with you.* Because, when all was said and done, Moppet's puppies were distractions to her, sweet and loving, but distraction nonetheless from where she really wanted to be: with me. Carefree, ready and able to be my companion again, to do what I did, to go where I went.

Moppet's weaning worked. The puppies leapt to the saucers of milk we put out and gobbled up the mashed up dog food, as Moppet watched from a safe distance. If they spied her and raced over to her, she raced for the chair. Despite the chair treatment, the puppies grew and prospered.

And what a happy crew they were, socialized to the nth degree by all our play with them as Moppet looked on, or joined in until it got too much for her and she sought out the chair again.

And so it went, this melee of puppy life, until the time came that they were ready to go out into the world, and they did, one by one, adopted by patients of my fathers, and friends of friends, until there was one last puppy. She had a white sock on one foot and I had named her Mitten. She stayed on with us for another week or two. When the day came to part with her, I woke up the way I went to sleep the night before: heartsick. She was adopted by a family with five children. I remember standing on the sidewalk outside our house as I watched the mother walk up the block, carrying Mitten, and I cried.

When I was twelve, we moved to Park Slope. This elegant neighborhood of glorious brownstone houses abuts huge Prospect Park with its three hundred fifty acres full of meadows, trees, grass, hills, and paths, with stone bridges, a huge lake, a smaller lake, and some connecting streams, an ice skating rink, and bridle paths. And all this wonderfulness was literally steps from our front door. The park was a paradise for Moppet and me, so much bigger than little McKinley Park, so much to see, so much to do. And we did it together, taking long walks across the open grassy expanse of the Long Meadow. Dipping into the woodland areas where the sporting dog in Moppet came rushing out to merrily chase a squirrel until it ran up a tree. She'd stand at the base of the tree and bark furiously, until she spied another squirrel and gave chase to this one until it too scrambled up a tree. And so it went, squirrel after squirrel, until her tongue was dragging. Then I would take her to the Paddle Boat Lake for a drink of water to cool herself off and calm herself down. She did get cooled and calmed, until she spied the ducks paddling around, which reactivated the sporting dog. Then the "takes to water readily" trait kicked in too, and in a flash she was in the water after the ducks.

Unlike most cocker spaniels, Moppet wasn't a great swimmer. She did a reasonable dog paddle. Her paddle got faster if there was something to swim after, but hers were not Olympic feats of water prowess, and the ducks knew it. They didn't take to flight at the sight of the little cocker heroically chugging through the water after them. They eased their speed up half a notch and easily outdistanced her without even bothering to look back. You had to admire her gumption, the big idea in her little head that her cocker spaniel feet could actually compete with those orange duck feet. But no matter, it was the chase that was the thing.

With the ducks now way in the distance, it was clear even to Moppet that this chase this day was over. So she gave it up and turned around to swim back to shore. When she came out of the water, it was hardly with defeat. Exhausted as she was, she danced around at my feet, so very proud of herself, so delighted with her performance. I leapt to praising her boundless spirit, put to these wonderful little contests—and she would have many more of them—in the woodlands and the Paddle Boat Lake of Prospect Park.

There's a well-known phrase among dog people: "A tired dog is a good dog." It speaks to the tonic that exercise is, how enough of it has the potential to transform a "bad" dog who chews rugs and tears up the sofa into a calm, well-behaved "good" dog. This, of course, applies to any dog. Now I offer up my own saying of a breed-specific nature: "The cocker spaniel who chases squirrels and ducks in the park is a happy dog." She has had the opportunity to play out who she is. This, just like the artist who needs to paint and the teacher who needs to teach, makes for cocker spaniel happiness.

While we're on the topic of sayings, there's that old one everybody knows: "It's not whether you win or lose, it's how you play the game." These, of course, are the proverbial words of wisdom offered up to the team that didn't win the game. If they don't fall on deaf ears altogether, at best they elicit a wan smile here and there, because even little leaguers know ours is a culture where winning is everything. But if you looked, as I did, at the defeated cocker spaniel who emerged triumphant from the waters of Prospect Park, you would know, as I began to understand, it *is* how you play the game. Be it the baseball diamond. Boardroom politics. Getting elected to something. Or chasing ducks.

Summer vacations provided more time to run around Prospect Park. We also took a few trips here and there. But the most wonderful trip we took as a family was to the White Mountains of New Hampshire to climb Mount Washington with the dogs. This wasn't the kind of mountain climbing where you bang the pick into a ninety-degree, sheer cliff and hoist yourself up. This was the hiking kind of mountain climbing. But you had to be in pretty good shape to do it because this hike wasn't a little meander through the woods. It went up, sometimes sharply, through fragrant evergreen forests, across streams, and over slippery sections of moss-covered rocks, and continued to go up, above timberline.

Posted at timberline, as all along the trail, were signs that warned hikers to turn back if the weather even hinted at a change for the worse. Mount Washington is famous for its quickly changeable weather above timberline that can turn even a hot ninety-degree August day at its base into freezing rain and blowing snow at its summit. The walls of the summit building display names, hundreds of them, of people—many seasoned hikers; others, people just like us—who did not heed these warnings, and perished. So we read those signs. But the weather gods had smiled on us, not with sun, with something that made the experience all the more glorious: the clouds that had transformed a blue sky into a breathtaking expanse of gray, with winds that blew rolling sheets of chilling mist against our faces, transporting us into the otherworldliness of this mountain whose summit for eons has lived, except for rare clear days, in the clouds, as close to heaven as many of us will ever get.

We paused here, at timberline, where only low growing grasses that hunker close to the ground can survive, to don thick sweaters against the chill and gather our strength for the most difficult and thrilling part of all: the two hour ascent over the single file path atop piles of rocks covered with lichen, through the mist and clouds, to the summit building at the very top, where the highest wind ever recorded on earth blew.

So this all day hike up and down Mount Washington isn't for the fainthearted whose idea of nature is constant warmth and palm trees gently waving in the breeze. This is a place of rugged natural beauty. To really experience it—just like that walk down the street—you need a dog to show you the way. Which brings me to our guides, Moppet and Beau, who took to this mountain experience with total abandonment. They would run ahead of us on the trail, run back to check on us, then take off again to run on ahead. And back and forth they went all day long. By this reckoning, Moppet and Beau climbed up and down Mt. Washington two, maybe three times this day.

If Beau found all this most invigorating, Moppet was beside herself with joy. In no other place and at no other time in her life would I ever see her more in her element. The more nature came at her—wetting her, chilling her, giving her cool water to drink in its streams, logs to jump over, rocks to scramble up, fresh cold air to breathe in—the more thrilled she became. Aside from her love for me, I would never see Moppet more alive or more happy than this day when she and I and all of us left the world behind to climb Mount Washington and walk among the clouds.

The beauty of this place never left me. Years later, I would return, not with Moppet, but with Timber. Then, some years later, with Boo. Each time, I would take the same trail we took as a family when I was twelve. And each time, I would remember the first time I walked this, one of the loveliest places on earth, with Moppet, and how she loved it.

Our move to Park Slope also had me enrolling as a seventh grader in that small but mighty private school that was a short walk from our house: the Berkeley Carroll School. It is all the mightier these days, and considerably larger, but no longer all-girl, as when my sister and I attended. It was among all those girls that I met my lifelong friend, Jane. She was the sweetest girl imaginable. We lived three blocks from each other, and for the next six years we would merge our lives, walking to and from school together, playing on the same basketball and volleyball teams, going over to each other's houses for dinner. Indeed, to this day when I think high school, I think *Jane*.

She had a sprightly wire-haired fox terrier named Tippy whose great obsession in life was to gnaw on rocks. While he was more the family dog than hers alone, he was much treasured by Jane. Not so Beans, the Boston terrier who belonged to Patty, our mutual friend and fellow Berkeley Carroll classmate, who lived one house away from Jane. Far from treasured, this Beans of a terrier seemed more an aggravation to Patty and her family than anything else. Then again, the whirling dervish that he was (this dog couldn't sit still for a minute) was made far worse by his incessant snorting and wheezing as though he had not a bone but the whole chicken lodged in this throat, none of which served to endear him to any hearing or motion-sensing entity.

Loved or not, Tippy and Beans were in for a change. There were new waves rolling in at the shore of our world. And no small ripples were these. They were more like tidal waves, one after the other, otherwise known as the teenage years. For many of us, not so much Jane and I, but certainly Patty and the rest of our circle of friends, these teenage tidal waves would wash the childhood dogs aside in favor of burning new interests: record albums, movie magazines, shaving our legs, the right clothes. And riding the crest of these huge waves were the boys endowed with the power we gave them to carry us aloft on these waves, or bring them crashing down on our heads. To keep us afloat, or stave off the crash, we obsessed about how we looked. How big our chests were, or weren't. Whether our hair was right, or wrong. If we were too tall, or too short. Too fat, or too skinny. And then, if we liked some boy and wanted to invite him to the spring dance, came the emotional acrobatics about as purposeful as plucking petals from a daisy: he liked us, he didn't like us, he liked us, he didn't like us . . . the last pluck (a three minute phone call, a chance meeting on the street) catapulting us to the pinnacle of joy: we had a date for the spring dance. Or the worst case of dejection pimples: no date, or not the date we wanted. So the adolescent heads turned away—in some cases, spun away—from the faithful little companions who brought us to this stage in life: our childhood dogs who now waited like cast off teddy bears put high up on the shelf for the little girls we no longer were to come back and delight in them again.

But not Moppet. I was as up to my ears in this adolescence thing as anyone else, casting off all manner of old ideas that seemed so childish now, as fast as I tried on new grownup ideas to see if they fit me. But my love for Moppet wasn't something to cast aside or put up on a shelf because I had outgrown her. I would never outgrow Moppet. I didn't want to outgrow Moppet. So even as a few adolescent waves knocked me off my feet, they didn't wash Moppet aside, nor did I leave her behind. I brought her with me—and willingly she followed—into this confusing new world, because she was core. She was inside me. In my bones. In my heart. Filling it with the same joy and warmth and comfort I felt when I was six. Now I was sixteen. And we were still doing it: this shared life, now at this new stage, each still perfect for the other, each still grateful for the other.

As much fun as Jane and I had together, it didn't include trouncing through Prospect Park together with Moppet and Tippy in tow. Jane and I did high school. We did after school sports. We did the teenage thing together. But not dogs. Dogs I did with Moppet. So she still slept on my bed, still followed me around the house. We took all those little walks together down to Seventh Avenue to get a quart of milk or newspaper. And on Saturday and Sunday afternoons, we took our long treks in the park together, Where Moppet gave chase to another generation of squirrels and ducks as I stood watching, my appreciation for her not diminishing from the vista of my sixteen years, but in fact growing. She was to my teenage years what she had been to my childhood: the ground zero of things good, things reliable, things sweet, not to be let go of.

My seventeenth year, we rented a large, old farmhouse in upstate New York where we went on the weekends, and spent that summer. It wasn't surrounded by woodlands, had no mountain vistas or waterfalls to trek to. It was set among pastures and corn fields where my father turned into Farmer Gray, digging up a large plot behind the house that he turned into a vegetable garden of most respectable size, sowing the seeds that would reap a thousand tomatoes in the fall and bushels of homegrown corn.

It was here I first experienced what country people think nothing of: the sheer amazement first thing in the morning—or any time of the day—of opening the front door and letting the dogs out. By themselves. And out they went, Moppet and Beau, each day for their little country outings. Maybe down the shady tree-lined driveway. Or into a hot corn field to see what was doing there. Or perchance a trek into a cow field to get a close up look at those big black-and-white mooing things. An hour or so later, they about-faced and trotted back home, feeling every bit the free-spirited country dogs, with one more adventure under their belts. Of course, they couldn't tell us the nature of these adventures; we could only imagine them. But there came one summer day when no imagining was necessary.

Back from an afternoon outing of our own, we pulled up the driveway, got out of the car and proceeded to walk to the house, when we heard the sound of barking, some of it strangely hoarse, coming from the grassy area near the house, in the center of which stood one very large, old tree with a three-foot trunk. As we all approached, we saw who was making such a racket. It was Moppet and Beau, who had cornered a woodchuck right up against the tree. They were clearly exhausted, tongues hanging out from the effort of chasing the woodchuck down in the first place, then keeping him there, the two working in concert to cut off any avenue of escape, with Moppet so determined to hold her quarry against that tree that she had barked herself hoarse. But when she saw us approaching, she threw her exhaustion aside, and took up her barking anew with much fervor, zipping her head around toward us to make sure we were getting all this, her moment of greatest triumph.

The little cocker spaniel, aided by Beau, hadn't flushed out her breed's namesake, the woodcock, the bird, but a woodchuck. No matter. A sporting dog has to make do. After duly praising her, I called her and she came running over, exhausted to the bone, but flushed with victory, her triumph done, now ready to do what all good sporting dogs who've come off a long woodchuck siege need to do: come inside the house and have a good long rest.

I returned to school that fall. September turned into October and then November. On the twenty-second day of November, I was sitting in homeroom class with Jane, Ellen, Helen, Carla, and other classmates when someone entered the room and leaned down to tell our teacher that President John F. Kennedy had been shot in Dallas. A half-hour later came the news that he had died.

That weekend, the nation gathered around its televisions to watch the funeral cortege with that magnificent, black, rider-less horse make its way down Pennsylvania Avenue. We sat solemnly around the television in our living room like everyone else. Sitting close to me throughout was Moppet, very quiet.

Soon after the Kennedy assassination, age caught up with Moppet. Her muzzle, like Beau's, was graying. She didn't run to the front door to go out, she walked. That glint still came to her eyes at the sight of the ducks, but she no longer chased them. Moppet was growing old. My life barely begun, she was thirteen and nearing the end of hers—a truth so unbearable that I refused to fully acknowledge it, when, suddenly, she spiraled downward. Her hind legs dragged. She had difficulty breathing. Overnight her coat lost its luster. Hollows appeared above her eyes. The sudden onset of old age was so evident that even I couldn't deny it. Next came the quality of life talks that made me cry because it was all true, then the aching thoughts of how to let her die a peaceful death.

It was decided that instead of taking her to the vet, my father would prepare a concoction that would ease her out of life at home. She would go to sleep and never wake up.

I remember watching in the kitchen as he ground the sleeping tablets down to a fine powder, and mixed this powder with milk. I sat on the floor with Moppet, crying as she drank it; and I stayed with her long into the night, touching her, talking to her, as she grew weary, closed her eyes and went to sleep. Eventually, I dragged myself away and went upstairs, waking up several times during the night, then falling back to sleep exhausted.

When morning came, I woke up, and my heart instantly clutched with fear. I was already crying as I ran down the stairs and into the kitchen and crouched down to where she lay on the towel. Very still. My throat aching, tears pouring down my cheeks, I wiped them away so I could see her. Then reached out my hand to touch her. She didn't move, but her body wasn't cold. She felt warm, but she was so still. I touched her again, and then—I almost screamed—an eye opened. She looked at me and gave a little wag of her tail. My tears of anguish switched to tears of joy. She pushed herself to a sitting position, gave out a great big stretch, and sighed a luxurious yawn. With that, she jumped to her feet and bounded around the kitchen more youthfully than I'd seen her in years, looking for breakfast!

Minutes later, my father, mother, and brother poured into the room— also prepared for a funeral—and their grave faces switched to relief. Then came the laughter all around. The "lethal" concoction my father, the Great Doctor, had served up to put Moppet to sleep had only served up the best night's sleep of her life!

I reveled in this reprieve. It wouldn't change the inevitable: old age had Moppet in its grip. But she wouldn't die today. Indeed, she had riotously avoided it. There was this day to live, there was tomorrow, and there would be more tomorrows to come for her. What I felt this morning was a joy such as few I have known in my life.

I finished my senior year of high school, and Moppet and I had one more summer together. That fall, I went away to college in Pennsylvania, but I worried about her, my letters filled with "How's Moppet?" and "Take care of Moppet."

I was coming home from college one weekend. I remember the exact stretch of highway, near the Park Slope exit, when my parents, who had been carefully avoiding my questions about Moppet, now told me how her condition had suddenly and precipitously deteriorated, and that days ago she had been put to sleep.

My heart stopped. *She died? Moppet died?* Even though I knew it was coming, I couldn't believe it. It was too hard to take in. I don't remember walking up the steps to our house, or going into the house. Time stopped right there in the car, on the highway, when I learned that Moppet and I wouldn't have what I had wished so fervently for: just a little more time together. She was gone.

I returned to college and stepped back into the higher education I was there for, my thoughts ever returning to Moppet and the fourteen years we had together, wondering, hoping that whatever I gave her could possibly compare with all that she gave me. How she loved me at a time in my life when I needed it most, how much fun we had together, how sweet she was, how the ducks in Prospect Park might not miss her, but oh, how I did.

When your childhood dog dies, the curtain comes down on your childhood. It's not that I wouldn't go on to act childishly in the best and worst sense of the word. But the kind of innocence that is held together by words like "forever" was gone. For a long time I could only think of Moppet with pain. When the pain finally lifted, I got her back. She is still with me, in my heart, and now on these pages, where she leaps back to life.

2

Della the Devoted

When a friend once asked me in my mid-twenties, "Who was, or *is* there anyone, who makes you feel the sun rises and sets on you?" the answer that flowed out of my lips without a moment's hesitation was, "Della, my Great Dane." Were I to be asked the same question now, some twenty years later, the answer would still be the same.

It had been six months since Moppet died. Having rejected the rural college setting, I was now a sophomore going to college in New York City. More to the point, I was living at home and therefore able to bring another dog into my life. And oh, how I desperately wanted one. Moppet had opened my eyes to the world of dogs with such resounding success and joy that life without a dog felt flat, so lacking in color and substance. But I wouldn't get another cocker spaniel. Even as I was progressing past it myself, getting another spaniel felt too much like inflicting that "second sister" syndrome on some new innocent little creature who deserved an open mind and heart unencumbered by fruitless comparisons with her predecessor. So I started to look around, to take notice of other breeds. Nowadays, I wouldn't have to look far as Park Slope is a mecca for dogs and dog lovers. All I would have to do is walk twenty paces into the Long Meadow of Prospect Park and simply observe the dog show that takes place here, particularly on a Saturday or Sunday morning, for a show it is.

Hundreds, maybe even a thousand dog devotees gather here to exercise their canines in the off-leash hours before 9 A.M. While some of these dogs are wonderful mutts, the vast majority is comprised of pure-bred dogs. A small percentage of their owners come here, coffee mugs in hands, to leisurely stand around and socialize while their dogs exercise each other. But the exercise all around them so contagious, most people walk in chatty clusters from one end of the Long Meadow to the other, then turn around and walk back, as their dogs also enjoy this opportunity to socialize and stretch their legs. What, almost to the person, their owners avidly talk about is their dogs, *their* breed. Where they got the golden retriever, the West Highland white terrier, the French bulldog, the whippet, the Norwegian elkhound, the Vizsla. And where they got the Neapolitan or Tibetan mastiff and the other unusual breeds that also show up here in amazing numbers.

But not so in the late sixties. The dog boom of the nineties that would skyrocket this nation's numbers of dogs to an unprecedented fifty-eight million—that would term the nineties The Decade of the Dog, especially the *purebred* dog—was twenty years away. So there weren't, as there are now, at least six Great Danes romping in Prospect Park with their proud owners so eager to stop and talk.

In the late sixties (it would continue through the mid seventies), the mutt reigned supreme. The Age of Aquarius was suddenly upon us. It was Flower Power. Make Love Not War (made possible by the pill). It was Stop The War (the Vietnam war). It was all things antiestablishment: the government, corporate America, and what we now call family values.

Young people like me in their early twenties with traditional names like Mary and Jane and John and Richard were dropping out of college and deserting their parents' hard-earned suburban life to take to the streets of Haight-Ashbury in San Francisco and Greenwich Village in New York City, where they named their children Flower and River and Moonbeam.

While nothing said "establishment" louder than a corporate job and a bank account, so, in a far lesser but very visible way did a pedigree dog. They cost money. They were elitist. And so, according to your garden-variety hippie, were the people who owned them. For those inclined to dogs, nothing said "antiestablishment" better than a mutt; the scruffier, just like its owner, the better. It was the perfect accessory to the fringe, beads, bellbottomed pants, and long hair, and the beards sprouting on young faces. Many was the barefooted hippie who thought he had achieved Nirvana when he rejected the dog names of his childhood—all

those Spot's and Rex's—to call his dog, "Dog." Indeed, a call of "Dog!"
any Tuesday in the hot hippie hangout of Washington Square Park in
Greenwich Village brought fifty mutts running over.

So how did someone in a youth culture increasingly inured in mutt-
ism opt for a breed as patently noble as a Great Dane? It certainly wasn't
to make any political statement. Truth be told, the idea first came to
me when I saw the mudguards over the rear wheels of a truck with
the illustration of a Great Dane. From this meager beginning, I turned
to books. But dog breed books were hardly overflowing the shelves of
bookstores in the late sixties. It was one lonely book—and a general
breed book at that—that I came across. I read the section about Great
Danes and loved what I read. An excitement began to build in me. And
then, as though it were destined, mere days later I saw my first real life
Great Dane: a big fawn (tan) male, calmly walking down Prospect Park
West (the long boulevard-like street that abuts Prospect Park). The sight
took my breath away. The next moment, as I pried my eyes off the dog,
I recognized the man walking this magnificent canine. He was a doctor
friend of my family and could hardly wait to tell me all about the new
great love in his life: his Dane. His enthusiasm and what my own eyes
saw officially hooked me. It would be a Great Dane for me.

Years later, I would turn to the American Kennel Club for breeder
information. This time, I turned to the classified section of the *New York
Times* where, as my great good fortune had it, I came upon an ad placed
by a top breeder of Great Danes. I made the phone call, during which
she interviewed me as closely as I interviewed her. I explained I was
interested in a black Dane puppy, and a female. She informed me she
had a litter of "blacks" that would be "ready to go" (breeder jargon for
puppies at the adoptable age of eight or nine weeks old) in seven weeks.
I hung up the phone, my heart singing.

The next seven weeks dragged along like seven months. But eventually came the Saturday we took the long drive through New Jersey to the
breeder who lived and breathed Great Danes, her champion dogs regulars
at The Westminster Dog Show in New York City. Danes aside, she was
a consummate animal lover. Her expansive kennel overflowed with cats
coming and going, and the little pet dogs of other breeds precariously
underfoot as they sniffed at our shoes. Indeed, you had to look where
you walked in this place, lest you tread on some furry little something.
Even the air was alive with animal presence in the raucous squawking

coming from the collection of big birds in big cages placed here and there in her office. All this was the wonderful prelude to what we were here for: the Danes. And Danes, as the breeder set about giving us the tour, she had aplenty.

There were fawn puppies, brindles, harlequins, and blues, some taking their first steps in the outdoor pens. Others were strapping five-month-old pre-teenagers. Then she guided us over to the pen that housed the litter of ten black puppies "ready to go." It was among these puppies—I remember the moment as though it were yesterday—that I first laid eyes on and chose Della.

At nine weeks, she was a chunky little thing, already the size of a small, husky cat, and all black, except for a swatch of white that ran down her throat and neck, plus a few white toes on her left front paw. The "ideal" black Dane is solid black. These areas of white (quite common in black Danes) were not sufficient to disqualify her from the show ring, but were considered "not desirable." But I loved the white on her. It was a startling contrast to and set off her jet blackness. White or no white, just like her parents, whom I also saw, Della was magnificent. And so sweet, as she stood puppy hopping around with her littermates in the sun. I couldn't wait to touch her, hold her.

My choice officially made, we went back into the breeder's office and did the paperwork. Finally came the moment that had kept me up nights: the drive home with the chunky baby Great Dane sitting in my lap, who I would name Della from the first word of my maiden name, Del Nunzio.

Let's step back for a moment and take a look at her breed. The name "Great Dane" is a bit of a misnomer. That is, while they are indeed of "great" size and stature, Danish they are not and never were. The Great Dane, classified in the Working Group, was made in Germany. His ancient ancestors derive from the Irish Wolfhound and old English Mastiff. As a distinct breed, it has been cultivated for some four hundred years. Like all old dog breeds, it was developed to serve a purpose. Historically the Germans used the Great Dane (*Deutsche dogge*) to guard castles and to hunt that most ferocious and swift big game: the wild boar, which required a courageous dog of commensurate size, weight, endurance, and speed. He also served as a fearsome dog of war. His boar and war days long behind him, nowadays the Great Dane, affectionately termed the "gentle giant," is an elegant and esteemed companion dog.

His temperament is spirited, friendly, courageous, and dependable, but never timid or aggressive.

Male Danes measure thirty-two to thirty-seven inches at the shoulder and weigh between one hundred forty-five and one hundred ninety pounds. Females measure thirty to thirty-five inches at the shoulder, and weigh between one hundred and one hundred sixty pounds.

Danes come in a range of colors: brindle, fawn (tan) with a black muzzle, steel blue, black, and harlequin (white with jagged black patches). The color of a Dane is connected with its size: that is, harlequin Danes tend to be the largest. Less tall are the black and steel blue Danes. With the smallest—a relative term with this breed—Danes tending to be brindle and fawn. Whatever his color, his shedding short-haired coat is low maintenance, only requiring occasionally brushing.

This breed is characterized by a distinct, unmistakable, overall look of masculinity in its males, and an equally distinct, unmistakable look of femininity in its females. The most obvious characteristic that achieves this separation of the sexes is the marked difference in height. But height isn't the only definer of the sexes. A male Dane exhibits a larger frame and heavier bone (achieving what breeders call a boxy look, where the ratio between body height and length is a square), whereas a female presents with a slightly more elongated look. While breed books don't always mention it (but breeders know it well), this male and female distinction is also most apparent, or should be, in the shape of the head. The ideal male Great Dane's head exhibits, just like its body, that desirable boxy shape, as compared to the less boxy head of the female.

So here she was, the baby Great Dane in my lap, my arms around her as I gently stroked her soft fur and marveled at the brownness of her eyes, her expression so sweet, her puppy smell going straight to my heart. Fourteen years before, I had held Moppet in my arms for the first time. Even as I already loved her, I had no idea the happiness that awaited me. This time I knew. It was just a question of finding out who she was, this lovely puppy who now looked up at me as I talked to her. And so began our life together, which would span the next fourteen years.

Did Della's genes ring true to her breed? Was she the "gentle giant" so often attributed to the Great Dane? You will see that in some ways, she was the typical Dane. In other ways, she departed vastly from that norm to be very much her own dog.

As a puppy, Della was sweet and adorable, and big. It never ceases to amaze me that, except for toy breeds, who are tiny at birth, medium, large, and even giant breeds like the Great Dane all start out in life more or less the same size: about the length of a hot dog. But not for long. In mere weeks, the Great Dane puppy leaves the cocker spaniel or beagle puppy in the dust, to double his size, then triple, then quadruple it, as he grows and grows and grows.

Apart from the sheer amazement here, what I also discovered in short order is big puppies need a lot more care. Not because they do different things. They do the same things a cocker spaniel or Dalmatian puppy does, but they do it bigger. They don't tear up the shoe, the sofa is more like it. Or three sofas. When they pee, it's not a puddle to clean up, it's a small lake. This isn't paper-towel cleanup. It's bring on the mop. And keep it handy.

There's something else about this big-puppy thing: size does not equal maturity. That is, the first-time owner of a Great Dane (or any large breed) puppy must not equate the size and bulk of his lug of a puppy with the maturity of an adult dog. The ten, then fifteen, then twenty, then thirty-pound Great Dane is still a baby, doing what babies do. So patience and understanding is required. Della was no exception, but oh, was she ever worth the patience and understanding—and yes, the massive cleanups. The chunky, shiny black puppy growing before my very eyes was wonderful. A profound joy came back into my life.

The same fields in Prospect Park that Moppet had run through were now Della's fields, and she took to them with a puppy's enthusiasm, bounding around in the grass like a half-grown colt, as I smiled, watching her. We often meandered past the Paddle Boat Lake where Moppet had chased all those ducks. Della found them interesting enough to make her ears prick forward, but look with mild interest is all she did. Great Danes don't care about ducks. It was the ducks—no doubt thinking a baby horse had wandered off the bridle bath—who cared about her. There were also the other dogs we encountered. Not the herds there are today, just enough to let her learn how to be dog with other dogs, and she was sweet and good-natured with them.

And, yes, she was beautiful, even as a clunky puppy with big feet and big knee joints. When she walked, she picked up those feet like the thoroughbred she was. Her glossy black coat shined in the sunlight.

Just looking at her gave me pleasure, like looking at a great work of art. Looking at her, I might add, also gave Beau pleasure. His gait that had slowed suddenly found new zip. His tail that had sagged to a droop since Moppet died sprang back into its curl. She gave him a new lease on life.

She brought a new force into my life.

It had nothing to do with her beauty. It's true there was something in me at twenty (and, clearly, still is) that connects to and appreciates the purebred dog, and a beautiful one at that. Then again, all dogs are beautiful to me. If I had to choose between a roomful of people—all strangers—or a roomful of unknown dogs, bring on the dogs! But Della's beauty wasn't it. It was *her*. The strength of her character, her strong likes and dislikes, the look of absolute certainty that came out of her sweet but intense brown eyes. There was somebody home in that beautiful head, and that somebody only had eyes for me. I was the center of her life. It started from day one, that four-hour drive home from the kennel when she withdrew her allegiance from the littermates she left behind to ply it to me, taking in my scent, imprinting on my face and my voice, welding her even then great emotional self to me, a bond forged on the New Jersey Turnpike that would be lifelong.

So she looked to me in every way, of course to feed her, and take care of her, but far beyond this, it was her desire to be with me. This she felt with a fierceness, even as a little puppy. If someone was blocking her view of me, she peered around their legs so she could see me. If I left a room, she immediately got up and followed me. If someone else got to that room before her and inadvertently closed the door, she pushed the door open. There could be no barriers between her and me. When I had to be away from her during the day, she would yank my coat down from the rack in the hallway and sit on it, watching the front door until I came home. Because I was The One. The Only One. Everyone else in her life—which was also my life—was secondary, background to the one she loved with an intensity that was stunning. It came from the Great Dane with something as large as she would grow: her great heart that she had wrapped around me. This love, this devotion became a force of rock solid stability in my life like no other.

Her forcefulness had much to do with how smart she was. Della's level of intelligence was not typical of her breed, which I quickly discovered as I set about her housetraining and general training. Once again citing Stanley Coren's *The Intelligence of Dogs*, his ranking of the Great

Dane in the not exactly brilliant slot of number forty-eight hardly applied to Della. But his very important discussion of the differences in
individual dogs within a breed most certainly does, as Della's was a
superior intelligence. In a class of Great Danes, she would have been the
Dane who sat in the front row, the Dane who got the A's. This I attribute
first to her gray matter—she had lots of it—and second to her strong
desire to please. These two traits are a winning combination in any dog.
In Della's case, they put her trainability right up there with a German
shepherd, poodle, or golden retriever. Indeed, even as a puppy, she was
sharp as a tack, ready and very able to take instruction.

So training Della was an infinitely rewarding experience. While I
didn't have all the dog training books that exist now to guide me, I had
what I learned from raising Moppet, and this I brought to Della. It's true
her housetraining did initially lag; this I attribute to the fact that, excepting
weekends and holidays, I was not with her all day. I took her out in the
morning, left for school, then returned in the evening, with my mother
doing her best in the intervening hours. Nonetheless, Della eventually
got the housetraining idea so under her belt that each evening she waited
for me right at the front door, stood still as I clipped on that leash, and
ran for the curb to take care of business.

Where she really excelled was in heeling. This wasn't the classic
comedy routine where the big puppy, soon to be great big dog, drags
the hapless owner down the street. Della took to heeling in a matter of
days, walking not one foot ahead, or six inches behind, but right next
to me with such precision that even I couldn't believe it. Indeed, had I
not been so wonderfully aware of this lovely little creature at my side, I
might have forgotten she was there.

Similarly, she quickly learned a very crisp sit. From this, she learned
to stay. So focused was she, her eyes trained on me, ears pricked forward,
that wrinkles formed on her forehead as she waited for my signal to
"Come!" And then she came bounding over into my outstretched arms
as I hugged her and praised her, thinking *Whatever did I do to deserve
this wonderful creature?*

And all this came in a package that was growing larger every day.

Like all large breed dogs, a Great Dane doesn't sprout from puppy
to full-sized adult in a matter of months. It takes a female Dane at least
a year to attain full height (males two years, and beyond). The second
year, they do something equally wondrous: they fill out. Their chests

expand. This is when, particularly if they're properly exercised, they develop full musculature, the rippling muscles across the chest and in the shoulders, hindquarters, and legs.

I didn't know it with Della, but I know now that caution must be used in exercising a Dane (or any large breed puppy) its first year, and even well into its second year. This is because the bones, most critically the leg bones, are still growing. Moreover, they don't always grow evenly (when this happens, typically it's the hind legs that grow faster than the forelegs). Uneven growth aside, the point is that in this still-growing stage, excessive exercise can cause stress injuries to the leg bones and the joints above them. So the runner must not even think of bringing along his six-month or even one-year-old Dane for long runs, nor should his juvenile Dane ever run on hard surfaces like asphalt roads. At this stage, he must only run on soft surfaces like grass or dirt. Only when he's completely grown can he safely run on hard surfaces, and gradually build up to the long distance thing.

Some of these same injuries can occur for the same reasons if young Danes are allowed to roughhouse too soon with faster, stronger, heavier dogs. Juvenile Danes (under one year, some even up to a year and a half) have neither the coordination nor the agility to make the sudden stops and turns, or take the bumping and being knocked around, that happens with roughhousing. But they don't know this. They just want to have fun and crash around like any other puppy! Fun is fine. But when it turns rough, it's time to extricate the Great Dane puppy and go look for somebody else to play with, have fun with, learn how to be a dog with, but not get mugged by.

Further, whether the exercising occurs with dog or human playmates, the idea is to work the young Dane just long enough to have him nicely tired—which will build muscle and stamina—but never to the point of exhaustion. If he ends up exhausted, he went too far, and it is the owner's mistake. Much better and right on target at this stage is moderate exercise that brings on that nicely tired state mentioned earlier that will enable a young Great Dane (or young dog of any breed) to be the non-destructive, well-behaved good dog when he gets home. It will also foster something else very important: a nap. Just like human babies and growing adolescents, Great Danes grow when they sleep.

I must have done it right—the sleep, the no roughhousing, no marathon runs, and the rest of it—because Della grew up without a single mishap of any kind into a Great Dane of perfect proportion with rippling muscles and great stamina. And yes, of great beauty.

Della and I were crossing Prospect Park West one day, having just come from the park, when I noticed an older gentleman, about to get into a cab, looking across at us. The back door of the cab was open, and he had his hand on it, but he was waiting for something. Della and I crossed the street, and as we approached, he looked at us and smiled as he said, "Beauty and the beast." I instantly assumed the "Beauty" referred to Della, and told him, "Thank you. She is beautiful." He smiled again, this time a little quizzically, then got into the cab. I heard it pull away as Della and I continued walking. Then, as we turned down our block, I played back in my head what he'd said: "Beauty and the beast... Beauty and the beast." And then it occurred to me, did I get it wrong? Was Della "the beast" he referred to? Which would make me "Beauty?" To this day, when I think of the four words this genteel man, long dead, said, even though I know he meant to the contrary, I can't hear it or think of it as other than the "Beauty" referring to Della.

Something else refers to Della: Truth, the essence, the import of any given moment.

The ability to see truth usually only comes with pain. It's the by-product of events of extreme emotion—a funeral, a car crash, a medical scare—anything that's big enough or bad enough to quiet the clutter in our heads. We're suddenly clearheaded. We look up and see the beauty of the stained glass in a church window that yesterday was just pieces of colored glass. Our ears unclog to the mastery of some great composer and we feel what he felt when he wrote those notes. We look at the person gaily chattering away across the room and suddenly understand the loneliness behind all that chatter. We see a bird flying across a gray January sky and wonder, Is it hope that lifts his wings against all that grayness? But this new opportunity to see and feel is short-lived. Soon enough the fog rolls back in and we settle back into who we were before, as everyday life takes over again. And it will take some other momentous event to clear our heads again.

But not if we live with dogs! We humans can seek truth—and in the sixties, there were millions who so portended—in the musings of the great philosophers. We can seek meaning sitting on mountain tops eating a bowl of rice once a week—the sixties saw plenty of this, too. But it will never come close to what a dog is born with. It's in his head, it's the look in his eyes. It's how he reacts to the world. Without a filter. With no editing. He just gets it, intrinsically understands the essence, the import—and yes, sometimes the bullshit—of any given moment. I call these little moments of truth. And Della gave me a thousand of them.

I took occasional weekend treks to rural upstate New York with friends to visit their hippie friends cloistered in the leaky geodesic domes who had "gone back to the land" (and were crushing it with every step of their bare feet). And here they sat, a dome full of identically clad people, all droning on in identical language about non-conformism. And there I sat, next to Della, who was inured to all these talking faces—she was just happy to be with me—when a gentle breeze caused the front door of the geodesic to open. She turned to look at it, then turned to look at me, our eyes met—and there it was, the most interesting moment, the only real communication in this room, that keyed on something as simple and truthful as a door opening.

And then there were the boyfriends. Or, potential boyfriends. Della was a force to be reckoned with here. It was get past "that dog of hers," to get to the girl. A challenge to be sure, because she had so much more sense than I did. First, she checked them over, making sure they posed no threat. After this, it's not that she was nasty to them, she just wasn't particularly impressed with them. I should have paid more attention to Della, I should have done what she did after the safety inspection: turned around and walked the other way.

There were also the encounters that looked casual: the fellow who tried to stop me on the street with the seemingly innocuous, "Do you have the time?" or "Do you have a match?" But it must not have been the time or a match they were after because when I tried to stop walking to answer, Della didn't stop. She kept walking, taking me with her.

Which brings me to Della's level of protectiveness. Her sheer size, plus the fact that she was black, was deterrent enough. Who in their right mind is going to argue with or take on a black dog the size of a small pony? Nobody. But was she the "gentle giant" so often attributed to the Great Dane?

While the giant part certainly applies, she was only gentle as long as x stranger or x situation fell within her idea of normal. But let someone on the street look one second too long in my direction, or let the hat on that person's head be crooked one centimeter off normal, and those ever vigilant antennae on her head flashed the warning to the intense brown eyes, which instantly zeroed in on the offending person or object. And they stayed there until the perceived threat was halfway down the block, now deemed the safe zone.

This behavior, plus her willingness to escalate the staring tactic into outright defense, is hardly typical of the relaxed laissez-faire attitude of most Danes. It was exceptional, just like the dog from whom it originated.

So walking the streets of Park Slope at any hour of the day or night with Della was akin to having a police precinct at my side. So, too, was walking in Prospect Park. Had anyone been watching twenty-something me walking through the woods at dusk and thought he saw an easy mark, this notion was instantly dispelled a moment later when the huge black dog walking at my side emerged from the shadows, her eyes already on him. While this individual may have given me a start, his was the pounding heart in this scenario. He was the one with the challenge: how to move away as quickly as possible from her, and keep moving. This level of protection would never spiral into chaos. It was completely under control. Della would only use her size and her teeth if she had to. Which she never did. Because she never had to. The mere sight of her sufficed.

Did Beau ever come with us to the park? In the beginning he did, but a year or so later, it was just halting walks down the street for Beau, as he had to be at least fifteen years old now. When Della was three, there would be one final walk for Beau when, the hollows now deep above his eyes, his body weak and gaunt, he went with my brother to the vet. When the vet asked him point blank, "Can't you see this dog is dying?" my brother agreed to have Beau put to sleep on the spot. When he came home, my mother would tell me later, he sat down in the living room and cried.

Then came Della's puppies. Unlike Moppet's, they were hardly an accident. It was now the seventies. The idea of not bringing unwanted puppies into the world was already catching on, and I took it perhaps even more seriously than the average person, as few things left me feeling more dejected than the sight of a stray dog on the street.

But Della was an exceptional Dane, inside and out. Hers were superior genes that deserved to be passed on. Further, it was summer. I was out of school and could therefore devote myself to this project. Then, too, I had a special interest: although the breeder would handle the selling of the puppies, one would go to my parents. This idea—two Danes in the family, Della plus one of her progeny—was thrilling. All this I carefully thought out, spurred on by what would make it possible: Della, four years old now, was due to come into her next heat. But I wouldn't mate her to just any Dane. I would, as dog people say, Do It Right and take her back to her breeder.

I called the breeder and explained my intentions. She agreed with all of it, and told me she had an exceptional stud in mind whose pedigree would be perfect to mix with Della's. Then, we went over the timing, the window of opportunity in the latter days of a heat, when the bleeding stops and a female is fertile and therefore receptive.

Three weeks later, we were back on the New Jersey Turnpike with Della luxuriously stretched out across the back seat, using my crushed lap as a pillow for her head and shoulders.

The breeder was ready for us. She had the apples (I'll explain later), and the stud dog was waiting in the wings. One call over the intercom, and that stud, a magnificent jet black Dane with rippling muscles, was brought in by an attendant. Indeed, the dog ran into the room. Just as the breeder said, this "boy" was a real pro. He took one look at Della, gave two sniffs to the air, and the next minute, he was ready to get down to business.

Not so Della. With the first touch of one of his front paws to her hindquarters, she turned around and gave him such a *And what do you think you're doing?* look that his ardor instantly wilted, and he fast removed that paw and stood there so dumbfounded that we all had to laugh. This pro of a show dog stud may have fathered ten litters with ten top females, but he never met Della. In or out of heat, she was no pushover, no placid female Dane. Her take on this high-priced Price Charming with ten blue ribbons to his name was the respect given a cockroach. Even so, he knew what he was here for. So he tried again and again, giving the nudges to her neck, then the test-the-waters paw strokes to her rump, all systems fired up and ready to go. But each time, she shot him withering looks and he backed off. After ten minutes of rejection, he was ready to leave the room altogether.

"Talk to her," the breeder suggested. "Keep her head occupied while we try to get something going at the other end." I did, using phrases with key words like: "Do you want some *dog food*? Do you want some *water*? Wanna go for a *walk* in the *park*?" which got Della's mind into happier places. At the same time, the breeder encouragingly patted Della's rump, and entreated her crestfallen stud to try again as she plied him with her own cheery words like: "Good boy! Come on! *UP!*" Until finally, suffice it to say, a union occurred.

Now, with the dogs cojoined, is where those apples came in, which the breeder passed around, apple-eating her idea of a pleasant activity to accompany—or was it to offset?—the stunning vision of these two giants of dogs engaged in serious mating. So we all chomped away as we waited for Della and her one-time Prince Charming to disengage. Some twenty minutes later, as I recall, the date was over. The stud was led away. We took Della home.

Soon after, I set upon cleaning up the front room of our basement, removing the old trunks and boxes, to make way for the birthing and puppy room that would be Della's and my living quarters when the time came.

Then I played the waiting game. Dog gestation is sixty-two days, two months in other words. But by day thirty, there wasn't even a hint of the puppies growing inside Della. She was still as sleek as a gazelle, not an inch added to her waistline. I already knew nature's design has it that when dogs mate, puppies invariably follow. God knows, Moppet had certainly verified this singular fact. Nonetheless, when no change whatsoever evidenced itself in Della, I began to wonder, Did the mating not take? Would Della, being the exceptional Dane she was, prove exceptional here, too?

I called the breeder, who told me with total confidence, "She's pregnant," and then went on to explain, "Nothing happens the first month. It's the second month when things start happening. You'll see. Just wait."

I didn't have to wait long. Seven days later, week five, Della's trim waistline disappeared, as her abdomen began to swell. The pregnancy, plus her usual hearty appetite, now had her gobbling up her food and drinking tons of water and needing to go out to relieve herself several times a day. These frequent walks did not bother me. I had willingly and happily committed myself to Della's needs; my time and energy belonged to her. We still went to the park each day, too, but the last two weeks I didn't let her run off leash. Her belly was so big I couldn't rid myself of the thought of those puppies jostling around inside her. Instead, we took long vigorous walks together through the Long Meadow to keep her emotionally happy and physically strong. But the moment she seemed to be tiring (which was probably more in my head, than the fact), we turned around and headed for home.

The last seven days or so—I had wondered when this would happen—the lunch counter on her underbelly came to life, swelling up, getting ready.

As we approached her due date, Della was the picture of robust prenatal health: still graceful, still as beautiful as ever, but very big in the abdomen. Now people stopped me on the street to ask, "Is she going to have puppies?" And I'd answer, my heart both thrilled and a little apprehensive, "Yes, she is."

I now set about putting the finishing touches on our puppy room. I put out stacks of old towels and newspapers for her. And brought down a cot, an end table, and a reading lamp for me.

I called the vet to remind him that Della could give birth any day now. As arranged, he wouldn't be there for the birth, but would be on alert and available should any problem arise.

The next day, Della went into labor. I was sitting at the kitchen table reading, she was laying on the floor by my feet when I looked down and realized her breathing was different: deeper, stronger. Then a restlessness came over her. She got up, walked around a little, sat down, then got up again. Then she started pacing around. I ran into the hall and called up to my father on the second floor, "It's starting!" He and my mother hurried down.

I took Della outside to relieve herself at the curb. When we came inside, I brought her directly down to our puppy lair. Soon after, the contractions that at first only she could feel, began to roll across her abdomen with increasing strength. She lay down on her side, groaning and straining. Giving birth is an earthy and stunning process. It's a rich palate of blood and fluids, primordial and beautiful, as the internal hurricane that birth is takes over, not bent on destruction, but creation. I watched enthralled as Della labored and strained, but fearful too because I couldn't help her. She didn't need my help. Instinct was guiding her. She pushed hard with the next contractions, and the first puppy came. She knew exactly what to do. She turned around, cut the placenta with her teeth, severed the umbilical cord, and immediately began licking and cleaning him. A moment later, he started breathing—and there he was, this tiny little miracle, Della's puppy, just born. She nosed him and licked him over and over until he was dry. A half hour later, the violent contractions began again. I whisked the first puppy out of her way as she labored to deliver the second puppy. Twenty minutes later, the third arrived; fifteen minutes after that, the fourth. And so it went, the intervals growing shorter with each puppy, until there were ten of them. I returned all the puppies to her and she licked and inspected every single one until she lay back exhausted and began nursing them with total serenity.

And so began the example of motherhood I would years later attempt to model myself after. Unlike practical little Moppet who found motherhood such a chore, Della had to be dragged away from her puppies to relieve herself at the curb—that's as far as she would go in the early weeks—to tear back into the house and run downstairs to nurse them, clean them, tend to them anew. And it wasn't just the superb care she demonstrated, she reveled in them, she loved them. The two solid black males, the four females who looked like little replicas of herself, the four males with just a trace of white on their chests. All of them she treated with absolute fairness. Not three licks for this puppy, two licks for that one; each puppy got his equal share of Della's loving mothering. I watched all this, mesmerized by such care, such love. What I also witnessed was the meaning of the word devotion, which isn't the sublimation of self to another, but the full force of self brought to another. Della had already given this to me. Watching her now give this devotion to her ten puppies—and seeing them thrive on it—was stunningly beautiful.

On day eleven, their eyes opened. Now they weren't staggering around in the dark for her when they sensed her presence, they could see her! Now when she returned from the short walks in the park I forced her to take, they ran over to greet her. For just a moment, she would stand there—outside the cardboard fence I had erected so that she could come and go, but her puppies were safely contained—as though she were counting them to make sure all ten were here. Then would she hop over the fence to greet them right back, licking them and nosing them. First things first, she would lie down on her side and nurse them. The nursing done, she would play with them. She let the whole pack crawl all over her, some managing to climb up her belly, then sliding down the other side. Others played with her big feet. There was always one gleefully gnawing away on her tail. If all these little paws on her felt like the puppy massage from heaven, she got a blissful look in her eyes when they would crawl around her face, stumbling over her eyes, sliding down her nose. She was the lioness with her cubs, the magnificent Great Dane giving her puppies a perfect start in life.

When they grew sharp little puppy teeth that to any other dog would have signaled weaning time, she ignored the pain and continued to nurse them, so totally dedicated was she to these puppies, her ten little sacks of gold. When their little nails (growing as fast as their sharp teeth, despite my efforts to clip them) started making red scratch marks on her belly, she still nursed them. But I couldn't ignore the toll this dedication was taking on her. It was time to intervene on Della's behalf.

In the seventies, commercial ready-to-go baby puppy food didn't exist. You concocted it yourself. I hit the kitchen and, like a mad scientist, began mixing the Pablum, carefully cooked ground beef, milk, vitamins, and other myriad ingredients as instructed by Della's breeder until I had homemade puppy gruel. I poured it into a large low bowl and carried it down to the basement with a cheery, "Come and get it!"

The first days the puppies waded and slide around in the stuff, getting more on them than in them. And there was always the puppy who had to do his serious thinking standing in the middle of the bowl. Della would come in the room to check on them, see her brood covered in this muck, and, one by one, she would lick each and every one to its former pristine state. Then, eyeing the messy bowl, she'd lick it clean too (I think she even developed a taste for the stuff). With everyone and everything back in order, she would start to lie down to nurse them, but I'd tell her, "No, Della. Go. Out!" She would reluctantly leave the room, to wait right outside in the hall.

With Della kept out of the room at feeding time, the puppies quickly got the idea that the bowl, not their beautiful mother, was now food. So four times a day I'd bring it in, filled to the brim, and they'd run for it and line up around it, all legs and bodies in the right place—outside the bowl—as ten shiny little black heads reached in and lapped up all those breakfasts, lunches, dinners, late night snacks.

With the puppies now eating on their own, Della's milk supply dwindled down. Even so, she still nursed them. I'd wake up late at night to little suckling sounds, look over, and there she was in the dark, on her side, feeding her puppies. Then, some ten minutes later, there would be silence.

With this real food started the real work for me. That is, while they were still nursing, Della took care, as all mother dogs do, of the non-liquid part that came out the other end, which is of a most inoffensive, edible nature. But this abruptly ends with the ingestion of real food.

Now what came out the other end was the same thing a grown-up dog does, and there were ten little behinds doing it. And they didn't do it in unison. There was no such thing as collecting up the soiled newspapers, putting down a fresh layer, and being done. I'd no sooner take away one section of soiled newspaper and put down fresh paper, when three little puppies saw how nice and clean this section of newspaper looked, and ran over to make their deposits. If I didn't immediately get to it—and often I didn't because it wasn't possible—the next second, it never failed, some puppy would inadvertently back into it. Then, playing around with his sister, another puppy would run through it. And somebody else would fall into it. So there were papers and puppies to clean.

So day and night I fed Della's puppies, and cleaned Della's puppies, gave them water, and changed the newspapers, all the while thanking God for the always ample, in every way, *New York Times*.

When I wasn't tending them, I played with them, these ten sweet little creatures, who grew bigger every day, who had come to associate people with all things good. Paula (home from college for the summer) and I would enter the room, call out "Puppies! Puppies!" and they'd come running over. We'd sit down in the pen with them, and they'd jump all over us, crawl into our laps, tumble off, and run back to crawl up again.

One day they all got loose. They were bigger now, the size of small cats, but very husky and strong, when, much to the amazement of four puppies playing against the cardboard fence, it gave way! Before I could stop them, they zipped out of the pen and out the door and ran down the hall—with me giving chase—to the laundry room at the opposite end. Here, like a bunch of kids in a toy store, the four of them grabbed socks and underwear and anything else that happened to be on the floor, and gleefully ran around the room with the socks and rags hanging out of their mouths. As I struggled to contain the mayhem here, the rest of them were escaping from the puppy room into the hallway, some happy to run up and down it, while others ran straight for all the fun in the laundry room.

Figuring that the only way to end this carnival was to fix the puppy room fence, I sprinted back—being careful to not step on anybody— quickly repaired the fence, then tore back into the hall where puppies were now running around every which way. I gathered them up by the armful and returned this bunch to the pen. Then I ran back to collect more and return them. Last, I headed for the laundry room, where I plucked an old rubber soap dish out of one mouth and stopped the tug of war two puppies were having with a washcloth. Then, with one last trek down the hall with three puppies in my arms, I had containment. All ten puppies were back in their pen, exhilarated with their adventure, as the hallway lay strewn with chewed socks and underwear and whatnot.

The opposite of puppy mayhem was when they would all fall asleep together, using each other as pillows, their legs and tails intertwined, ten little bellies rising and falling as they made a quilt of collective peace and contentedness.

Other times, they fell asleep on me. I would sit on the papers with them, play with their soft ears, and massage their fur, when there would come the big puppy yawns with pink outstretched tongues. They would fall asleep in my lap, all trusting and little, and these moments I understood what Della had known all along: the incomparable sweetness of these days.

Della was the lioness with her cubs. She loved them and protected them with everything she had. To go against her wishes was to incur the wrath and teeth of the lioness.

Della guarded the puppy room like Fort Knox, so to keep from unduly stressing her I only allowed a few visitors into her sanctuary. One of them was the doctor friend with the huge tan Great Dane. He only lived a few blocks away and had been telephoning to come over and see them.

He was a jovial fellow who enjoyed his cocktails. Indeed, he and his wife were regulars at the dinner parties my parents hosted, which would go long into the night, the gaiety and laughter rising with the flow of martinis, with his voice always booming above the rest.

So over he came one Saturday, so excited at the prospect of finally viewing Della's brood that my mother graciously mixed him a martini to enjoy right along with it.

I put Della in the kitchen, carefully pulled the sliding gate closed, and down the basement staircase we all went, with me leading the procession. No sooner had our guest stepped off the bottom step into the hallway, when Della (who had knocked down the kitchen gate) tore down those steps and bumped into him so hard she knocked the martini right out of his hand. There she stood, eyes glaring, ready to knock all of him down if he proceeded one inch farther in the direction of her puppies.

The apologies flew fast, but he took it all in stride. I don't remember exactly where I took Della to protect our amazingly still-happy guest, but it was someplace ironclad, like the fourth floor bathroom, with the door shut. When I came back down to pick up where we left off, there was no small trepidation in his voice as he asked me not once, but three times: "Are you sure she can't get out?"

When the day came to part with the puppies, I was a wreck. It was one thing to know this day would come, quite another to experience it. I trusted the breeder to screen the applicants as carefully as she had screened me. And oh, how lucky were the people who got these puppies. Their mother had been extraordinary. Exceptional, also, was their bond with humans who they saw as wonderful entities who were all about love and care and fun. But now they had to go out into the world, as all young creatures must, to live their own lives. I prayed they would go to good, decent people who wanted them for all the right reasons, and who would take care of them and love them as their mother and I had. The breeder assured me this would be the case. But even with all the assurance in the world, it was still an act of faith. It started with letting go. And so I did, nine times, as I handed all but one of Della's puppies over to the breeder, and left with my heartache to get back into the car for the long drive home.

No room in a house would ever look as empty as the puppy room in the front basement room of my parent's house the night we came home. The hour late, I went downstairs, alone, to stand there, overwhelmed by its stillness.

But motherhood hadn't ended for Della. There was Morgan, the male puppy I gave to my parents. For the next twelve months, he would grow up right alongside his mother. This sweet big lug of a boy Great Dane, who adored Della, and she, him, would grow up to be the love of my mother's life.

At about this time, my parents purchased Calendar House, a big old brick farmhouse, with much early American history attached to it, that sits on a bluff in the countryside of upstate New York. On summer weekends, Della and Morgan turned into what my mother called "the baronial dogs," cavorting on the grounds together. Winter weekends, mother and son sat like majestic bookends on either side of the huge fireplace.

At the end of that school year, my college career was suddenly over. I had majored in journalism. For a year I plied my skills at a publishing firm in New York City, but my heart wasn't in it. I gave some serious but brief thought to going back to school to become a veterinarian, but even though I was well versed in biology and zoology, I knew I'd get straight Z's in the math and chemistry. More importantly, I knew I could never deal with the blood and guts part of medicine, never neutralize myself to the suffering. But I was twenty-one and had to do something to support myself. So I turned to what had increasingly become a passionate interest and topic of intense study: plants. The question now, how to work it into a business. And so was born The Village Green Garden Shop.

It stood on Union Street right off Seventh Avenue in Park Slope, and was a stellar garden shop that would be glowingly written up in the *New York Times* and *New York Magazine* in the course of its eighteen years. The big front window was a veritable jungle, planted with lush dracaenas and ficus trees, mixed in with Chinese evergreens and flowering spathe plants and Calatheas and Marantas. Interwoven throughout was a thick grape vine where myriad species of bromeliads grew in utter splendor, next to living pale-green Spanish moss that hung down in wonderful drapes. Covering the ground was a lush carpet of baby's-tears. Into this tropical wonderland, we introduced a mix of colorful finches and parakeets who flew around free, a pair of Jackson's Chameleons, plus delightful little green tree frogs (who "barked" after this vivarium received its daily misting), and a toad or two.

In the center of the shop stood a large concrete pool with a huge lava stone planted with rabbit's foot ferns. A gentle cascade of water trickled down the rock through the ferns to the water below, where goldfish shimmered around. Farther into the shop was a custom-designed butternut wooden counter. Then, a step up led outside to a wooden deck under an arbor covered by a grape vine that produced myriad clusters of green grapes in late summer. Off the deck was the sunny garden, stocked with flowering annuals and perennials, and small shrubs and trees, where two more concrete pools were stocked with more goldfish and water lilies.

But the real beauty of this place was that Della and I weren't separated all day. I could bring her to work with me! I could be with her, and she with me, in this, our "work" home, where she plied those protective instincts of hers with stunning judgment and dedication. Indeed, word got out fast—to the few who needed to know—that this friendly neighborhood garden shop wasn't the easy target for a robbery that it looked to be. It housed a huge black dog. One wrong look at its owner (or her staff) would bring Della from her bed behind the counter to her feet in an instant, brown eyes blazing.

What also needs mentioning here is that I had married. Against my mother's words of wisdom *in retrospect* to "Never marry a man whose face you can't see," I had married a man with a beard. Then again, these were the early seventies, when all manner of young men sported foliage on the face. He also came with a German shepherd who was so high-strung and neurotic, he literally couldn't be walked on a leash. (Interestingly, his littermate, whom I met once, was so screwed up he growled when he was happy.)

As I now lived on the south side of Park Slope, but still only two blocks away from Prospect Park, these were the years that, as pre-arranged with an early morning phone call to my mother, Della and I would walk into our end of the Long Meadow and keep walking. My mother would enter her end with Morgan and keep walking. Then, some-where in the middle of the Long Meadow— the distance between them half a football field—the dogs would see each other and thunder across the meadow for each other, jumping around with joy, mother and son reunited. Della and I would see my mother and Morgan to their house, then walk down Eighth Avenue, then Union Street, to work.

Life gives you things as surely as it takes other things away. Four years later, when Della was nine, two things happened. The first was lovely. Her name was Timber. She came to me as a half-grown adolescent dog of most unusual linage: her mother was a malamute; her father was half Siberian husky, half Alaskan timber wolf. Della now had a sister, and I had another dog, this very confused little wolf hybrid who, as will be told, would need a lot of loving care to help her grow into the extraordinary creature she would become.

The second thing was terrible: Morgan died. He was six, and had been afflicted with a kind of arthritis in his back that nowadays could be treated with any number of drugs. But these drugs didn't exist in the late seventies. Morgan was suffering horribly and was mercifully put to sleep.

The taking away far from done, a year later, my father died. It was a beautiful day, the first warm day in May of 1978. I was standing at the counter at The Village Green, advising a lady on what to plant in her window boxes, when the call came from my mother that my father had collapsed in his office. I left the store immediately to go with my mother to Victory Memorial Hospital, where my father was pronounced dead of a heart attack, at the age of fifty-nine.

What followed was a dark and terrible time. Rumor has it that "work will sustain you" through such darkness. It didn't. It was Della's love, her constancy, her rock-solid devotion that sustained me as I struggled to come to grips with the turmoil within and around me after my father died. She was the anchor. She got me though it. And I loved her for all this with a fierceness as great as any feeling I have ever had for anyone.

It was also Della who gave me the emotional strength to do what I should have done much earlier. Three months after my father died, I left the bearded man to walk out the front door at eleven o'clock at night with two things: Della and my purse. And I continued walking, down Eighth Avenue in the dark, with Della at my side, to live with the man whose face I could see, and whose heart I could see—because he had one. His name was David. I soon married him, and have spent my life with him in a house on the other side of Park Slope.

In my haste (haste makes for bad decisions) to break loose from my old life and begin this new one, I didn't lay claim to so much as one floorboard of the house that my ex-husband took as solely his. But some months later I went back for something of far greater and lasting value to me: Timber. Della was reunited with Timber and on they continued, together, in their lives and mine.

Della's forceful character continued to spin out stunning lessons for me, most especially regarding determination and perseverance. Examples of them happened in our work life at The Village Green, they happened at home, and they happened away from home. One of them had happened years before, when Della was only two. I'll start with it.

It was my twentieth birthday. I had flown back to JKF Airport after a weekend visit in Ohio with my very pregnant high school friend, Jane (who would give birth to her son, Hank, the very next day). I had just entered the terminal and begun looking for my mother in the hundreds of people milling about, when way in the distance, at literally the opposite end of the terminal, I saw scores of people suddenly step aside—like the ocean parting—to get out of the way of something. A moment later, I saw what that something was: Della! My mother had brought her along to surprise me. Loathe to leave her in the car in the parking lot, my mother had brought her into the terminal. They had been standing near the front entrance, when Della spotted me in the distance and leaped forward, snapping the leash right out of my mother's hand, to run for me, zigzagging through the throngs of people who scrambled to get out of the way of this black gazelle of a dog running past them. When she reached me, she leapt up into the air, almost knocking me over, and jumped around me with joy. At this point, some of the startled faces observing this scene began to smile, as this was a reunion at JFK like few others.

Later, there was the day, when, believing me to be at my mother's house, Della managed to slip out the front door to take herself down ten Park Slope blocks (no doubt quite a sight, this huge black dog, alone, on a mission), negotiating cars, intersections—only she knew what else—to arrive five minutes later at my mother's front door. Here—as my mother's neighbors who saw Della, but were afraid to approach her, would later tell me—she waited for about ten minutes, barking at the door. When I didn't answer it, she left the house and took herself across Prospect Park West to look for me in the park. When her search there didn't locate me, she went back to take up her vigil at my mother's front door. When my mother came home twenty minutes later, the call came to my house: "Della's here."

One frigid January morning I arrived at The Village Green a half hour early with Della, and made the fateful decision to indulge myself in a big hot breakfast at The Purity, a simple fare restaurant around the corner on Seventh Avenue. My coat on, I gave Della's head a pat, and gaily headed over for that breakfast. I came back twenty-five minutes later to a horrible sight: Della in the front window, laying there like a watchful panther, smack in the middle of two years' growth of now flattened baby's tears, with crushed prayer plants and tattered bromeliads all around her. For reasons only she knew, she had chosen this day to claw and push her way into the front window to watch for my return. And it got worse; when she saw me, she jumped to her feet, dancing around with joy, her tail whipping back and forth as she whacked and destroyed more plants. It was a disaster. Fortunately, no birds got out.

Another time, on a late fall night when Della found herself left in the back seat of our car in the parking lot of a marina in Staten Island, watching me walk away from her into the pitch-black darkness of this strange setting was more than she could bear. Thus, she attempted to go through the barrier that separated us: the car itself (fortunately a real wreck). She applied her jaws, backed up by those neck muscles of hers, to the upholstery. Once she succeeded in removing this, her teeth scrapings on the car casing would bear testimony that not even steel had the power to deter her determination to reunite with me.

This powerhouse of determination and perseverance was also a creature of habit, and little games.

Where Ozzies, a favorite coffee bar, now stands on the corner of Lincoln Place and Seventh Avenue, there used to be an old drugstore with original wood paneling and big wall mirrors so old their edges were faded and mired with cracks. On the scuffed squares of black-and-white linoleum flooring stood two long aisles of display racks that were stocked with rows and rows of ancient cosmetics, faded boxes of perfume, rabbit-eared Hallmark cards, and cheap drugstore toys from the fifties. Loathe to install air-conditioners, the owner let two old ceiling fans push the hot air around in the summer. Through this store that even in the eighties was caught in a time warp, padded a German shepherd. On our walk to and from The Village Green, Della and I passed by this drugstore, where she and the shepherd did what was their twice-daily ritual: their simultaneous lunges at each other by the glass front door. Far from happenstance, these lunges were carefully planned and executed. As we walked by each morning, the shepherd was right there at the front door, waiting for Della. As we approached, Della was equally ready and primed for him. As we passed, she would lunge at him at the same moment he lunged at her.

Her lunge completed, Della and I continued down Seventh Avenue to turn up Union Street to start our day at The Village Green. I can only assume the shepherd took himself back behind the drugstore counter, there to stay until, some eight hours later, his internal clock said it was time to pad back down the aisle to take up his post at the front door and wait for Della to walk by. Which she did. And they did their simultaneous evening lunges. Then home we went, and back down the aisle he went.

Five years came and went with the two of them jumping at each other, every morning, every night, six days a week. By now, the shepherd was old, his lunges slower, more like half-lunges. But not about to give up whatever he got out of this game of mutual ambush, he kept it up for another year, as did Della. Then, one morning on our way to work, we walked by and Della looked at the doorway, ready to jump at him, but he wasn't there. He had died. For many months after, Della and I would pass the glass drugstore door and I'd see her head turn to look for him, and dare I say, the disappointment on her face when he wasn't there. He had become a fixture in her life. Then one day she did the something that marked the finality of his death: she stopped looking.

A year later something happened in the park that portended the future. It was a hot August day and the park was deserted. Della and I were coming back from one of our long walks and were nearing the end of the Long Meadow by Grand Army Plaza, when Della suddenly stopped walking. She stood there for a few moments, then lay down in the grass, on her side. Stunned, I crouched down next to her. Was it the heat? Or had she stepped on something? I picked up her feet and started to check her pads for anything lodged in them, when a voice called out, "Is something the matter with her?" I looked up and saw a fellow who was sitting on a park bench and had witnessed what just happened. His intentions may well have been the best, but the park was so deserted, we were so alone, that something in me chose to minimize it. "No, no, it's alright," I called back. "She's just hot." I turned back to Della, gently stroking her neck. Her eyes were open, and she looked back at me, but there was distraction in her gaze. She lay here for some ten minutes, when whatever it was, was over. She got up and walked home, as fine, as normal as ever. But years later when I thought about this hot August day, I realized that it might have been a heart attack that happened to Della in the park, one big enough to stop her in her tracks, but small enough that she could walk away from it.

Della was thirteen now, an extraordinary age for an extraordinary Great Dane. Her muzzle was completely gray, she had myriad benign mammary cysts and patches of scaly skin on her abdomen and legs. But like a great love finally showing the signs of age, it wasn't apparent to me. She was still beautiful to me. She was still amazingly youthful to anyone else observing her. Her skin fit like a glove over the rippling muscles. She still moved like a graceful gazelle. She was fit and strong as ever. But not forever immune, as none of us is, to the inevitable.

Her fourteenth year, age caught up with Della. Overnight, she began to weaken. Her hind legs, always so strong, so powerful, began to drag when she walked. We still went to work together; she loved to go to work with me. She couldn't bear to be left behind, and I couldn't bear to leave her. So we walked the four blocks very slowly, and I remember the feeling in my throat as I gestured to people to please move out of her way because she couldn't move out of theirs. On our way home one day, her hind legs, which had progressively weakened, began to wobble. It would not get better. She could no longer go to work; the four-block walk was too long. When I took just Timber to work now, there was the plaintive look in Della's eyes as she stood on teetering legs in the living room watching me leave. But she knew I would be back. And I was, every night at seven, to hug her and be what we had been for fourteen years: together. When July turned into August, I was so relieved. The store was closed for the month, so there was no need to leave her. The days were ours.

We had just began these days together when her hind legs gave out. She could no longer walk. David helped me set up her station in the bedroom, with pillows and soft blankets to cushion her. Here she lay, her head alertly poised above her shoulders—with the bedroom door left open—so that when I wasn't with her, she could see me, and she followed me around the apartment with her eyes. When I felt her gaze on me and hurried in to thank her, her ears went flat with affection as I hugged her, my beautiful sweet Della.

She was *all there* in her head: her personality, the force of her character, the intelligence in her eyes. But in the ensuing days, her body tumbled to ruin. Her muscles atrophied from disuse until even I who couldn't bear to believe it could no longer deny it: There was no hope, no turning back the clock. Della was dying. But how, I agonized, do I choose the day, the hour, to end the life of such a dog? How can I let go of her? *You steel yourself*, I told myself. *You love her enough to give her the final act of love.*

David and I decided—we made the phone calls to arrange it—that we would take Della to the vet she knew upstate near Calendar House, where she would be put to sleep, and then buried at Calendar House.

That Saturday morning, with the van pulled up right outside the house, and a soft bed of blankets in the back ready for her, David and I went back inside to get Della. She had sensed we were all going someplace and she wanted to go, too. As we went into the bedroom to pick her up and carry her out to the car, she did something extraordinary. After weeks of laying there in the bedroom, barely able to move anything but her neck and head, Della got up, and on frail and shaking legs, she slowly walked through the apartment. Then—our hands right there to catch her, lest she fall—she walked out into the hall and farther on into the vestibule. She stopped at the little step in the vestibule, her legs shaking. David and I helped her up it. Then she walked past our little front garden, through the gate, and onto the sidewalk. David rushed ahead to open the sliding door, as I guided Della, her body wobbling, over to the van, where she stopped. We lifted her up into the car and placed her onto the soft bed of blankets behind the front seat.

Drained by the effort of walking, she slept for much of the three-and-a-half hour drive. But now and then I would feel her eyes on the back of my head and turn around, and she was awake, looking at me. I smiled at her, reached down to pet her, then turned back to the road ahead so she wouldn't see my tears.

Our sad drive ended in the gravel parking lot outside the vet's office. We parked in the shade of a tree, and left Della briefly to go into the waiting room where a number of people were waiting. The staff was expecting us; they knew we were not going to bring Della in. As arranged, the vet would come out to the car to tend to her. The receptionist said he would be out in a few minutes.

We hurried back outside to the van, where I got into the back with Della, and sat, with her head and neck cradled in my arms, as I talked to her. When the tears started to roll down my face, I wiped them away, steeling myself to keep the anguish off my face and out of my heart, too. She could read my face. And she knew my heart. She had helped build it. *Only think of her*, I told myself. *Only think of her, and let these moments, her last, be what she deserved: calm and peaceful.*

A few minutes later, the vet came out and stepped over to the open side door of the van. When Della saw him, she weakly lurched at him with the little strength she had, even here, even now, trying to protect me. "No, no. It's okay Della," I said, reassuring her, petting her. "He's our friend. Our friend." She trusted me, and I felt her body relax as she took her eyes off him and returned them to my face. With the syringes in his hand—the first one to sedate her, the second one to stop her heart—the vet looked at me. "She's ready," I said, as Della gazed calmly into my eyes, and I held her and smiled at her, gently stroking her neck. As the vet reached for her front leg and slipped the first injection into her vein, I told her, "Good girl, Della. Good girl." He withdrew the syringe, and waited a few moments. Her gaze still on me, I told her, "I love you, Della. I love you," as he began to inject the second syringe. Her eyes were where they had been all her life—on me—when she peacefully closed them and died.

Then, as she could not hear me, I cried.

We drove to Calendar House, and over to a grassy plot near the garage my father had built one summer. David did most of the digging. Della had loved this part of the grounds; she had played here with Morgan, and she and I had often come here together. We wrapped her body in the white sheet we had brought with us, and carefully lowered her body into the ground under a pine tree that still grows there. In the years since, when I go to Calendar House, I go out first thing in the morning, coffee cup in hand, and stand here, this place of hallowed ground, where Della lays.

3

Timber: The Glory Years

To say Timber, my extraordinary wolf-hybrid, was the most beautiful dog I have ever seen doesn't even begin to describe her: the yellow eyes in the white face mask, the pelt of blended white and silver and gray that covered her back, her white throat and feet and tail, and her thick luxuriant fur that smelled of wildflowers. If she was lovely on the outside, her *inside*, her temperament—which made her spectacular beauty so approachable—was Spring itself: sweet and sensitive. While, unlike Della, she didn't live to please me, she pleased me in every possible way, as to live with Timber was to live in a state of grace.

As already related, this one-of-a-kind, lovely creature entered my life, when Della was already nine, through sheer accident as a half-grown, adolescent dog of most unusual lineage: her mother was a registered malamute; her father was half Alaskan timber wolf and half Siberian husky. To understand how these components came together to make the extraordinary dog Timber was, I will stop here to describe the malamute, the Siberian husky, the timber wolf, and the wolf hybrid.

First, the Alaskan malamute. This giant Arctic breed (classified in the Working Group) was named after the Mahlemuts, an Inuit tribe of northwestern Alaska, and was traditionally used as a sled dog. He stands twenty-three to twenty-six inches at the shoulder, weighs seventy-five to one hundred twenty-five pounds, and has a compact, strong, muscular body. He has a thick, heavy coat of medium length, with a dense, woolly undercoat that is one to two inches in depth when in "full coat." His plumed tail is carried in a gentle curl over the back. While malamutes come in various colors that range from light gray through the intermediate shadings to black, they always exhibit white on their underbodies, legs, feet, and distinctive facial mask. Their eyes are brown and almond shaped. While many malamutes sport amazing blue eyes, any eye color other than brown is a disqualifying fault in the show ring. As for temperament, while the malamute is friendly and good-natured, he can also be domineering and challenging, which makes him notoriously stubborn and most uncooperative with regard to obedience training. (Hence, Coren's ranking of the malamute in the not very impressive number fifty slot.) He has a "high-prey" drive that can prove troublesome in households with small pets. While he doesn't bark, he is highly vocal and best known for his howling. Because he singularly lacks the traits of protectiveness and aggression, the husky is not a good watchdog. Further, his independent nature does not make him a "one-man" dog.

The Siberian husky (also classified in the Working Group) was bred in Siberia and was traditionally used as a sled dog. This medium-sized, highly athletic dog measures twenty to twenty-three inches at the shoulder, and weighs between thirty-five to sixty pounds. He has an undercoat that is thick and soft, with an outer coat that is harder and straighter and grows right through the undercoat. Like the malamute, the husky sheds copiously year-round (especially in the spring), and therefore needs regular brushing. This high maintenance is nicely offset by the fact that not only is the husky fastidiously clean, he is free from the offensive body odors that many dense-coated breeds ferment. His furry tail is carried in a gentle curl above the haunches when at attention, and falls down when in repose. His almond-shaped eyes may be brown or blue, one of each, or parti-colored (brown mixed with blue).

Like the malamute, the husky, while naturally friendly and gentle, can also be challenging, independent, and obstinate—none of which makes for easy obedience training. Thus, Coren ranks this breed in the also not too impressive number forty-five slot. Like the malamute, he lacks the protective and aggressive characteristics that make for a good watchdog. He rarely, if at all, barks. Instead, he howls and yips like a wolf. He has that same high-prey drive that makes him a threat to small animals, including small dogs and, of course, cats. Above all, the husky's independent nature—which can even cross over to a diffidence in regard to his owner—does not make him a "one-man" dog in any sense of the term.

The timber wolf (Canus lupis), also known as the gray wolf, is the largest member of the dog family (Canidae), which, of course, includes the domesticated dog (Canus lupus familiaris). His habitat is forested areas in all of the Northern Hemisphere. In the United States, outside of Alaska, the only substantial numbers of free-ranging wolves occur in northern Minnesota. While they can reach three feet in height, the average timber wolf stands between twenty-six to thirty-two inches tall at the shoulder. Adult male wolves can weigh as much as one hundred twenty pounds, but they average between ninety-five to one hundred pounds. Adult females can weigh one hundred pounds, but average between eighty to eighty-five pounds.

The pelt color of the timber wolf spans the full range of shades from white to cream-colored, buff, tawny, reddish, gray to black; but gray is the predominant color, hence the animal's other name, the "gray wolf." The pelt color—just as with malamutes and huskies—is determined by the color of the outer or straight "guard hairs" that grow right through the undercoat, which is short and dense and highly insulating.

The timber wolf has pointed ears and a tapered muzzle. Where the domestic dog's tail is held high and often is curly, a wolf's tail hangs. His legs, built for fast and far-ranging travel, tend to be longer than the legs of dogs, this feature promoting not just speed, but the ability to negotiate the deep snow that seasonally covers much of this creature's geographic habitat. Besides getting around extremely well on land, the wolf does equally well in water and is known, even in winter, to plunge into frigid waters to swim after prey.

In addition to the howl for which he is most famous, the timber wolf emits a wide range of vocalizations that include whimpering, whining, growling, yipping, squeaking, and, yes, the occasional bark.

Well-documented is the fact that the basic unit of wolf society is the pack. Within this pack is a highly structured social order that is based upon dominance, with the highest-ranking, most dominant "alpha male" (who breeds with the highest-ranking, most dominant "alpha female") leading and guiding the pack. Below this alpha pair are mature subordinate dogs of both sexes who occupy the middle and lower ranks. Below them are "peripheral" wolves of both sexes whose low rank often places them on the fringe of pack society. Last in line are the juvenile pups who, even though they don't become part of the pack core until their second year, establish dominance among themselves through play fighting as early as three weeks of age.

What establishes and maintains the social order within a wolf pack—or quickly resolves most conflicts in a non-violent method when they do arise—is the high level of communication between its pack members. Fundamentally, it is achieved through postural communication ("body language") and myriad vocalizations. Postural communication (very similar to that of the domestic dog) is the deliberate placement and angle and movement of the head, neck, trunk, and tail to convey a host of information, including the all-critical dominance and subordination issues. But it also communicates the wide range of wolf emotions, including joy, anger, affection, rivalry, friendliness, tolerance, timidity, and helplessness.

This visual communication is greatly enhanced by the wolf's highly expressive face. Endowed with myriad facial muscles, he conveys intent and emotions (and subtleties and nuance therein) through intricate movements of the nose, snout, lips, forehead, eyes, and ears. All this is backed up with the vocalizations: the whimpering, growling, yipping, and howling.

As for temperament, while this highly intelligent and adaptable animal is one of the wildest and shyest in the Northern Hemisphere, he is extremely docile and friendly and affectionate toward fellow pack members. This ability to form strong positive attachments begins in puppies as young as three weeks old, but notably, these attachments are only to members of their own pack, not to wolves of other packs. As the puppies grow up, they shy away from and become increasing fearful of unfamiliar wolves. Indeed, in the absence of their own pack members, wolf puppies become extremely distressed.

Another defining characteristic of the timber wolf is his fundamental, deep aversion to fighting. Indeed, those aforementioned elaborate methods of communication function to avoid physical confrontation. Thus, actual fighting is rare; it is the tactic of last resort.

The most defining trait of the timber wolf is extreme fear—and therefore avoidance—of unknown entities and entities known to pose a threat. In wilderness areas where wolves have had even minor exposure to man, their reaction to the smell—no less the sight—of man is to flee.

Which explains why people living their entire lives in wolf country may well have heard the glorious howling of a wolf many times, but rare is the person who actually sees one.

Contrary to fanciful fables that have wolves adopting human beings, people have adopted wolves and raised them as pets, but with results—usually poor—that hinge, among other significant factors, on when the wolf puppies were acquired. Wolves are unlike dogs, who can be successfully adopted at virtually any age. The transition phase—the window of opportunity in which a wolf puppy can transition, to one degree or another, to humans—is short and starts very early. It is a mere twelve to twenty-one days after birth. Wolf puppies taken and tamed within this critical time frame can, to varying degrees, become attached to humans (and dogs and other animals) with whom they have daily and considerable contact. For puppies caught after three weeks—no less months later—the process of socialization is virtually impossible; they react with extreme fear to humans (and other animals), resulting in a wolf "pet" who remains essentially wild, unmanageable, and untrustworthy among humans. Nonetheless, people have adopted and sought to tame older juveniles. Their success, or lack thereof, hinges on the dedication of these humans to do what the adult members in this juvenile's pack would have done: give hours and hours of attention and affection every day to overcome the young wolf's aversion to humans and replace it with trust and affection. Which, given the nature of this shy and fearful creature, invariably does not make for a tame wolf, but sadly, just a captive one.

Next, with or without human prompting, dogs will breed with wolves—and vice versa—resulting in fertile offspring that are termed "wolf-dogs," or "demi-wolves." The "wolf hybrid" is generally defined as a dog with at least $1/4$ wolf in him. Native Americans supposedly crossed some of their dogs with wolves. Eskimos and other inhabitants of the far north have used quarter-breed and half-breed wolf-dogs in their sled dog teams. While the handful of modern-day breeders of wolf-mixes occasionally cross their wolves with German shepherds and Samoyeds, typically it is with malamutes and huskies. In some cases, these malamute and husky crosses can produce a dog that is visually indistinguishable from a full wolf. In any event, wolf-dog mixes show such a variety and range of temperaments and pelt colors and other characteristics that few generalizations can be drawn, except the most important one: The mingling of the wolf and dog is a roll of the dice that invariably produces a hybrid whose bond with humans is tentative at best.

Then there is the rare exception. Which brings me to Timber.

While the experimental nature of her deliberate breeding in the wilds of upstate New York could have resulted in the wolf hybrid not sure if she belonged on the rug in the cabin or living free high up in the mountains, Timber's genes produced a hybrid with the breathtaking beauty of a wolf, and a dog's trainability and capacity to trust and emotionally connect with humans.

But she didn't start out this way. The first time I laid eyes on Timber, she was a half-grown, slightly scrawny, seven-month-old dog who was so upset and confused, she wouldn't make eye contact and barely responded to her name. She had reasons to be confused. Days before, she had left the only life she knew—a very rural one—only to be plunked down in busy, urban Park Slope, that, pretty though it is, could not have been more foreign to her. More importantly, she had been suddenly cut off from the only people she knew: a reporter, with a wife and child, and another child on the way. When a job opportunity suddenly transferred them all to New York City, the reporter determined he couldn't do all three: a new job, a new baby, and this wild little hybrid. So Timber was put up for adoption. He contacted friends of friends, who in turn—knowing I had large dogs and a lifestyle that could accommodate a dog like Timber— contacted me. And so, one spring day in 1976, Timber was brought to me at The Village Green, where I first glimpsed this traumatized waif of a wolf hybrid who stood before me, eyes downcast, haunches hunched over with apprehension, as scrambled and psychologically fractured a dog as any I have ever seen.

Did I ever consider renaming Timber? Not for a second. It would have added to her confusion. She came with the perfect name. And kept it. She barely ate during the first days and lost more weight. She couldn't be walked on a leash. She didn't even know what a leash was. She was terrified of other dogs. After gradually accustoming her to the leash, the first time I took her to Prospect Park and some dogs ambled over to say hello, she turned and ran. She was abjectly afraid of people and dodged their attempts to befriend her. To work off her extreme anxiety, she engaged in some highly destructive behavior: she ripped down curtains and shredded them; she chewed through two sofas; she destroyed articles of clothing foolishly left within her reach. What she also did, because the concept of housebreaking was as foreign to her as that leash, was eliminate in the house as her need arose.

How this wild and unhappy little hybrid evolved into the extraordinary creature she became is a story of the unique mingling of the malamute-husky-timber wolf genes in her, in combination with the forces outside herself to which she was exposed. We will examine both as we watch her grow up.

The malamute and husky in Timber was reflected in a dog with these breeds' more than ample level of intelligence. But where both malamutes and huskies exhibit, as noted earlier, a strong independent streak in tandem with that intelligence that makes obedience training so difficult, Timber's malamute-husky genes skipped over this snag, producing a dog highly receptive to human suggestion and instruction. However, like everything else about her, she didn't start out this way. More than anything or anyone else, it was Della—her influence and her example—who got through to Timber. For instance, heeling. In a matter of weeks, Timber went from a dog who was all over the sidewalk to a dog who heeled perfectly. I used Della to show Timber what this heeling business was all about by walking Timber sandwiched between us. Timber quickly got the idea. She also got lavish praise for imitating Della. Far from the typical malamute or husky who finds praise trivial (and therefore moves himself not to elicit it), Timber loved it. Praise became a huge incentive for her.

Similarly, she learned the all-important come command that makes for harmonious human-dog relations, and at its extreme, can be a lifesaver for the dog. In the park, off leash, Timber ran through the fields and woods with Della and saw how she stopped dead in her tracks and came running back when I called out "Della, come! Timber, come!" In a matter of weeks, Timber was running back to get what Della got: the praise and hugs for being such a good dog.

Timber also stopped eliminating in the house. She saw what Della did at the curb; soon, she was doing the same thing.

She also learned to shake hands. Noting that Della, who I had sit right next to her, got praised *and* fed little squares of cheese when the paw came up, Timber started to do the same thing—the paw for the cheese—and enjoyed the game!

Like any malamute and husky, Timber loved the cold and snow, the colder and snowier, the better. Like both these breeds, she did the various vocalizations, including, of course, the famous howl. And how glorious, how lovely—and what fun!—it was to watch her and hear that howl when she wanted food or attention. When she wanted the leash put on her because it was time to go to the park and she knew it, she did a round of joyous howling to remind me. She also did a low, mournful eerie howl during those rare occasions when she was left home alone.

Unlike malamutes and huskies, who live with barking dog breeds and still rarely bark, early on, Timber, who took her cues from Della, added the bark to her repertoire. Now she barked (with a few howls thrown in) along with Della to alert me that the mailman was approaching. (It didn't work the other way around: Timber didn't teach Della to howl. Della didn't, she couldn't howl.)

Without a doubt, Della was the key to much of Timber's progress and happiness. Without her, Timber's story would read very differently. Timber saw how relaxed and confident Della was in the company of other dogs in the park. At this point, nine-year-old Della had even become, shall we say, a little overconfident. She didn't exactly bully other dogs. More accurately, she occasionally took a few liberties with them. If another dog's owner tossed a ball and Della got to it first, she took it in her mouth and tarried with it for a minute or two until she decided it wasn't that interesting after all, and dropped it. If Della stopped for a little drink at the Paddle Boat Lake and another dog approached with the same idea, Della eyeballed the other animal, who caught that look and waited to quench its thirst until Della had quenched hers.

Timber saw these things, and learned from them. Her other-dog confidence was growing. Then again, so was she. Her size had become a factor in her confidence and demeanor. She was no longer the timid, scrawny, scrambled egg of a dog. She was two years old, stood twenty-six inches at the shoulder, weighed eighty pounds, and was gloriously muscled under her thick fur. She had suddenly become a force in her own right for dogs in the park and on the streets to measure themselves against—and they resisted any inclination to test what their eyes saw.

With or without Della, the Paddle Boat Lake in Prospect Park now became Timber's private water fountain, too. When other dogs happened along and saw her drinking, they waited. But this is not to say she didn't play with other dogs. Indeed, it was this same new confidence that let her relax in their midst, enjoy them, and run around with them, and she was good natured and sweet about it. As for any other contest of dog wills, there weren't any. She was too big and too strong. She knew it. They knew it.

What human eyes saw was the gorgeous dog she had grown into. When we stopped on Seventh Avenue to look in a store window, Timber attracted little crowds. Strangers on the street would break off their conversations as they saw this spectacularly beautiful dog with the sweet face coming toward them. Many a hand would reach down and surreptitiously run its fingers across her back as she passed to see how deep that amazing fur was, or maybe just to touch something so beautiful. Many a person would stop to ask the question that would follow Timber around all her life: *"Is that a wolf?"* To which, depending upon who was doing the asking and where, my answer varied. If it was a fellow hiker on the trail up Mount Washington (more about this later), the natural setting tended to elicit the truthful answer. If it was a stranger on a city street, the answer was always, "No, she's a malamute." But fellow malamute owners, particularly those with dogs in tow, didn't always buy it. I'd see them look at Timber, then their dog, then back at Timber and see the unspoken conclusion on their faces: *That's no malamute.*

Of course, they were right. Timber had the pelt, white face mask, furry pointed ears, and powerful, athletic body all malamutes do. But she was three inches taller and at least five pounds heavier than the average female malamute. Then there was her tail. It didn't do the characteristic malamute curl over her back—it hung straight down like her wolf grandmother's. And yes, she was beautiful. But this wasn't what made those malamute owners, even as they walked away, stop to turn around to take another look. All malamutes are beautiful, but not like the dog they just encountered. It was Timber's spectacular beauty that made these people stop and look one more time at what got their hearts beating fast: the breathtaking sight of a wolf standing right there on the corner of Seventh Avenue and Union Street in Park Slope, Brooklyn.

Which brings me to the wolf in Timber. Was she a dog in wolf's clothing? Or a wolf in wolf's clothing? The answer is she was both. She was neither.

There is not the slightest doubt in my mind that, true to her wolf component, and particularly when she was young and so psychologically fractured, Timber could not have survived, much less flourished, in the absence of other dogs. The pack instinct was in her genes and in her head.

She needed other dogs, needed their company, needed to interact and socialize with them, and no human being on earth could have supplied this need. Della and, in the beginning, the German shepherd, became her pack. And so did I. I was the leader of the pack, then Della, then the shepherd, then Timber. Far from resenting the order, it suited her: she was the newcomer, the youngest, the least dominant. This was also the order in which she was fed, her water bowl filled, and her leash put on. Within this order of dominance, the pack functioned and she flourished.

There was only one area where, for a brief time, the order of dominance broke down, and it was at Timber's instigation. The first six months or so after she arrived, Timber would occasionally take to spending the entire night guarding the fifty-pound bag of dog food and cases of canned food. It wasn't that she was hungry. She was fed twice a day, and she gobbled up her food until she couldn't stuff in any more. This behavior wasn't motivated by an empty stomach. It was the wolf in Timber guarding the wolf's cache of food. She couldn't bury it, so she sat up nights guarding it. When Della or the shepherd dared to approach, more of the wolf came out: What moments before was a face of amazing sweetness turned into a sinister mask, her lips curled way above her teeth as her throat emitted a kind of low, guttural vocalization no dog produces.

The first time Timber let the wolf in her snarl at Della over the food bag, Della reacted not with anger, but amazement—you could see it on her face—then turned and walked away. She would continue to walk away, which was fortunate because Della didn't cotton to threats from any dog, and this newcomer was no exception. Soon after, any reaction on Della's part became moot as Timber learned there was no need to be the wolf where food was concerned. There was plenty for all.

Timber found pigeons most interesting, and she would leap into the air after low-flying birds. But as an unfortunate incident in Prospect Park showed me, she could chase down and catch little animals who could easily outmaneuver any regular dog. This was that "high-prey" drive. Malamutes and huskies share it, but timber wolves own it: they catch to kill to eat to survive. I had forgotten this, or didn't take it seriously, until it came rushing out to show me.

It was a lovely wintry day. A few inches of snow had fallen. I had taken Timber to Prospect Park and we were walking in that same area where Moppet had chased all those squirrels—but, of course, never caught one—when Timber spied a lone squirrel in the distance foraging in the snow for food. The next instant, she streaked after it, despite my cries for her to stop. The average dog, though maybe not the typical malamute or husky, would have been hopelessly thrown off by the deliberate zigzagging of the squirrel, but Timber knew exactly what she was doing. She anticipated the darts to the left and right of this frantic little creature as it tore across the snow, and each time the gap between them shortened. The next second, with the safety of a tree four feet away, the squirrel jumped for it, when Timber leaped high into the air after it. To my horror, she caught it in midair, shaking it and breaking its neck. When she hit the ground, squirrel in mouth, it was dead.

I ran over screaming for her to drop it. She clasped her teeth even tighter on it. This was no game being enacted in Prospect Park. The dog had come here to play. But it was the wolf who chased and caught and killed the squirrel—and now was going to eat it. My screams—and some pounding on her—finally got through to her. She loosened her jaw, and the poor little creature dropped to the ground.

I yelled at Timber to back away, and she did. The dog in her was back. It understood and cared how angry I was. The eyes that only moments ago had flashed their defiance were now apologetic and worried, and watching me very carefully.

I turned to the squirrel. I couldn't bear to just leave it there, so I gently picked it up in my gloved hands, carried it over to a little bed of leaves, wrapped its tail around its body, and took one last look at it. As we walked away, my wrath at Timber began to fade. There was no more reason to blame her for what happened this day than to blame a cat for catching a bird. She had only done what her genes had programmed her to do. The dead squirrel in the leaves was my fault. No other animal was ever harmed by Timber because I would never underestimate the wolf in her again.

On a lighter note, Timber loved the water, found it soothing and relaxing, and was the expert swimmer all timber wolves are. She cut through the water with not so much as a ripple and with such speed that she turned the head of many a retriever-owner who thought his breed was the one at home in the water.

She did much of her swimming in the Paddle Boat Lake. There was no need to flail my arms and make a lot of noise to alert the ducks. They knew her. They had sized her up just as they'd sized Moppet up. So they didn't gently paddle away, or speed-paddle away. Swimming was too risky. There was a wolf standing there. One look at Timber about to plunge into the Paddle Boat Lake, and its ducks took to flight, not to return until the wolf went home.

Timber loved the water so much that David and I made it a point to take her to the ocean in off-season when the beach was virtually deserted. She had never seen crashing waves before and found them fascinating. She played the game adventuresome dogs play: She ran up to greet a wave, then, as it started to break, she ran back up the beach as the water raced after her, only to turn around and run back to greet the next incoming wave. But she also swam in this water. Despite the waves breaking over her, she had the power and skill to swim in the ocean, even against its strong currents, until, afraid she might be tiring, we would call her. She would come out, the salt water falling in torrents off her thick coat, and stand there just long enough to shake herself off. Then back she went for more, as we stood watching, filled with such admiration and affection for the wolf who was strong enough to take on the Atlantic Ocean—and love every minute of it.

Moppet had started my rapt appreciation of nature. Della had sustained it. But Timber would take it to breathless heights.

On our walks to and from work, Della, in her all-business watchdog mode, tended to look straight ahead to check out people, occasionally glancing sideways, before turning her attention to who was behind us. Where she didn't look—because people aren't found there—was up at the sky. And neither did I. The buildings block the sky. But even where they don't, I didn't know to look. Timber did. Walking down Seventh Avenue to go to work, she would feel the white and silvery hairs in her luxurious fur wave. A breeze had come up. Her yellow eyes would look up—and I followed them—to its source: the wind pushing the clouds around in a gray sky, and the storm gathering there. And I saw the look in her eyes, the connection she felt, even here on city street, with the largest and most glorious expanse of nature on planet earth: the sky, in all its colors, its constancy, its changeability, and its moods.

When we took Timber to Calendar House and took nighttime walks through the pitch black darkness of the countryside, she would pause and gaze up at the stars, celestial bodies, and yes, the moon when there was one. She didn't howl at it, she just took long looks.

I have since looked out hotel windows in London and seen Big Ben lit up by the moon, and stood marveling in Maui at the deepest blue sky I ever saw. But you don't have to go anywhere to see and feel this beauty.

Just look up. It's there, anywhere, this lovely place, the sky that Timber first showed me when I was twenty-six, and I have looked at every day since.

And then there was the trip David and I and Timber took to climb Mount Washington. The last time I had been there, I was twelve years old. I so much wanted to take the same trail I'd taken then, but I couldn't remember its name or where it was. It took some questioning of forest rangers as I described the trail: the stream that rushed past, sometimes crisscrossed it, that led all the way up to the Lake of the Clouds Hut at timberline, then the ascent over rocks to the summit.

Our ranger friends listened carefully, but were still unsure, until I remembered something else: the Cog Railway and the log cabins for rent that were very close to the beginning of this trail. These two details proved the salient ones. "Follow the signs," they pointed in the right direction, "to the Cog Railway. It's ten minutes away. Your trail is there."

We jumped back into the car. Ten minutes later, we were there. The Cog Railroad was to the left. To the right were the little log cabins nestled in the woods. And straight ahead was the entrance to that wonderful trail up Mount Washington. But this time it wasn't the merry little cocker spaniel who would expand my appreciation of all this rugged beauty. It was Timber. The wolf had come home, if only for a visit, from whence she came: the wilderness. Where black bears still roamed. And eagles flew. Where nature, not traffic lights, dictated movement. Where the weather was at the whim of this majestic mountain that could turn even this, a hot sunny August day at its base, into hail or snow at its summit.

What a time Timber had here! She loved every foot of the trail, every log, every twig. She leapt over the moss-covered rocks and nimbly trotted across narrow little foot bridges as we climbed higher through the cedar forest. Many a moment, she paused to sniff an animal footprint in the fragrant, soft earth. We didn't know, even experienced rangers might not have known, the forest creature who had passed here, but Timber knew. She was one of them. When she wasn't reading tracks with silent excitement, she would run down to immerse herself in the stream that rushes by this trail, her fur fanning out in the water, her yellow eyes looking up at us on the trail, as we waited. She took just one more minute to revel in this cold, crystal clear water, then jumped out to run up the bank, run past us, and take up her position as leader, some twenty paces ahead of us. But she always stopped to turn her head and make sure we were there. If she followed a bend in the trail and more than half a minute elapsed without her seeing us, she would run back to reconnect with us, then race forward again.

At one point, we stopped above a waterfall to take in the vista of the valley below where the base station of the Cog Railroad now looked like a tiny toy. We broke out the sandwiches in our backpacks, and I fed Timber two of the bags of dry dog food I'd brought along. She gobbled them up. I gave her a third bag, and she ate it with dispatch. When she still stared longingly at our sandwiches, we gave her one of these too.

Refueled, we returned to the trail, with Timber running ahead, when a young couple coming down the trail encountered Timber coming up toward them. They stopped dead in their tracks—and so did Timber. When David and I came upon this scene seconds later, the young man, whose arm the woman now clutched, had just started to call out to us, "Is that a wolf?" when the wolf wagged her tail. We answered truthfully, as they marveled at Timber and petted her. There would be more question-and-answering when a half-hour later, a family with teenage kids encountered Timber. And then a very fit older couple. And then a bunch of college kids. Each time, there was awe and then amazement at how sweet she was, as she stood there, fanning her tail, her eyes smiling at all the touching. There were more Timber encounters when we reached timberline and stopped at the Lake of The Clouds Hut where hikers can sleep overnight in bunk-style accommodations or just come in and enjoy some very hearty meals. Some hikers were there, about twenty of them, and a lot of forks stopped in midair when the timber wolf walked in.

In typical Mount Washington fashion, above timberline, the hot August day we had started out in was quickly changing, with a mist and fog rolling in. Then, a cold rain began to fall. We pulled on our rain slickers and set our sights on the summit in the clouds ahead, the idea of a hard-earned cup of hot chocolate at the top gaining appeal. But it would not come close to the loveliness of the two-hour, sharp ascent over the rocks and through the mist to it.

When we reached the top, the old stone summit house I remembered, with its huge fireplace and so much history and character, was gone. In its place stood a modern facility—architecturally most impressive with floor-to-ceiling windows—replete with two gift shops, a bookstore, a cafeteria, and tables and chairs positioned near those huge windows.

But unlike the old summit house where dogs were welcome, posted on the thick glass front door was a sign showing a picture of a dog with a slash across it. I tied Timber up outside, near the door, and we went in for that hot chocolate. We had just settled into two chairs near a window, when the announcement came over the loudspeaker: "Would the owner of the . . . (there were several pauses) . . . wet malamute . . . ah, the husky? . . . the, ahhh . . . please tend to your dog?" While we appreciated the concern in this person's voice, there was no need for worry on Timber's behalf. I'd positioned myself so she was in my direct line of vision. Although the rain now had a punishing feel and look to it, Timber loved the rain, the harder the better. She had even turned her face up to it, letting it wash down on her, reveling in it.

An hour later, we began the hike down Mount Washington. When we reached the base at dusk, there was the regret this wonderful day was over. But Mount Washington was in my blood—and now it was in Timber's. She would come back here two more times with David and me, and each ascent would be as glorious, as wonderful as her first.

Timber also possessed a wolf's love of snow, which was especially evident in 1982 when a blizzard blanketed Park Slope with four feet of it and created the best snow experiences Timber ever had. The streets were impassible. Cars were hopelessly buried in five-foot snowdrifts. People had to shovel their way out of their front doors. For five wonderful days, Park Slope reverted to the look and feel of the turn of the century neighborhood it had originally been. The cross-country skiers came out in force. Where buses rumble, there was the laughter of kids being towed in sleds down the middle of Seventh Avenue. Huge snowmen and child-made igloos dotted the snow-covered sidewalks. But the jewel in this winter wonderland was Prospect Park, shimmering with acres and acres of pristine white snow where Timber was beside herself with joy. She tore around in it, jumped into it, played in it, rolled in it, threw it around, ate it. What she didn't do was tire of it. She would have never willingly left all this on her own. I had to drag her home every day.

There was another snow, this one years later, that fell in very late spring. The crocuses had already come and gone in the front and backyard gardens of Park Slope brownstones, so, too, the daffodils. Tulips were now rearing their heads through the warm soil, when an April snowfall came without warning and covered the tulips and sidewalks and rooftops with a foot of white, fluffy snow. If a manual on wolf hybrid ownership existed, events like this might have prompted it to say, "The caring and responsible wolf hybrid owner will make sure her hybrid gets any and every opportunity to play in snow, no matter what time of year it falls." I needed no prompting. I took out the winter coat that I had put away weeks ago, leashed Timber, and got her up to Prospect Park to partake of the winter wonderland it had been thrown back into. And it's good I did, because the next day the sun came out and melted all the snow, and by late afternoon, it was spring again.

These are the things that made Timber a wolf. The forces—inside and outside of herself—that made her a dog are just as remarkable.

Unlike any wolf hybrid—no less a wolf—who is useless to humans as a watch dog due to genetically determined behavior that chooses avoidance over confrontation, flight over fight, stand-and-fight as the last resort, Timber became a most effective protector with impeccable judgment that could distinguish the real from the imagined threat, and react accordingly. This behavior can only be attributed to two factors: First, it was yet another skill gleaned from Della's tutelage. Second, Timber sensed the humans in her "pack" had a need to feel and be protected by her. And she rose to the occasion.

Timber could not have had a better example of the perfect watchdog than that set by Della. As already recounted, Della feared and was intimidated by no one. What she also had was that all-important judgment: the ability to distinguish between the guy standing in a doorway, and the one lurking in the doorway. The one simply standing had no problem with Della. It was the lurking one who caught her eye and then, if he didn't move on, heard her growl. Had he made a move in my direction, he would have seen her teeth right before he felt them. Timber saw these things, and she learned. She had many opportunities to learn. There were the daily morning runs in the park with Della that ended in the walk down Union Street to The Village Green. There was being at The Village Green, except in August, eight hours a day, six days a week, seeing what Della did, and learning how to do it herself.

People already knew about the huge black dog at the plant store on Union Street. Now there was more to know: the second dog, the one who looked like a wolf, who was almost as big as the first dog. Word got out fast: If you had ill intentions, or even thought ill intentions, and the first dog didn't pick up on them, the wolf one would!

So Timber took up her guard-dog position right behind the counter with Della. When the bells on the front door rang, which signaled that people were coming in, Timber would sometimes take it upon herself to leave Della and step over to the counter where she would stand up—all five feet of her—with her hind legs planted on the floor and front feet poised on the counter, to take a closer look. If she liked what she saw—if the people looked okay to her, as virtually all of them did—she'd hop back down and join Della. If she didn't like what she saw, she stayed there, her yellow eyes following this person around. The people who needed to be intimidated, were. They about-faced and left.

The second thing that made her a superb protector was something, already stated, that was inside Timber: She sensed the humans in her pack had a need to feel and be protected by her. This perception was so strong, it overruled and canceled out that most fundamental, genetically dictated behavior of all wolves that is critical to their survival: the avoidance of confrontation; the take to flight, rather than fight and chance injury; the stand-and-fight as the last resort because it can mean death. What made Timber go completely against this grain to stare at questionable people, creating confrontation, and bare her teeth, threatening to fight, and made her once or twice lunge at someone, was her bond with the humans in her pack.

Which brings me to the real miracle of Timber.

Unlike the typical malamute and husky who prefers snow to his owner, unlike the average wolf hybrid whose attachment to humans is notoriously tenuous, and unlike the wolf who shuns humans altogether, Timber's genes produced a dog's capacity to bond with humans. And bond she had, deeply and profoundly and joyously, with us. And we to her.

At home, she would fix her gaze on David and I working in the kitchen, from her favorite place in the apartment: "her" blue lounge chair in the far corner of the bedroom. She slept in it, across from our bed, at night. She napped in it. Sometimes she just sat in it, wide awake, surveying the apartment from her blue "den" that housed her so snugly.

Whatever got her to her chair, she always settled into it exactly the same way: she hoped up, turned around, and laid down, facing outward, with her front feet, from the knees to the toes, dangling down. When she fell asleep, her head rested on her knees.

As David and I worked in the kitchen, many was the time we would look into the bedroom and see Timber there, in her chair, watching us. Then came the words of affection we called over to her, followed by something far more beautiful: the look on her face when she heard them. When we left the kitchen to sit in "our" chair, the sofa, in the living room, Timber couldn't see us. The next moment, she'd vacate the blue chair to come into the living room after us, nudging one of our hands with her paw, to get it on her head, to get what she wanted far more than that chair of hers: our touch, our affection.

When I took Timber to the park to run through the fields and woods, as much as she loved them, she didn't keep running. She'd stop, her eyes turning back to make sure I was there. But she didn't always trust her eyes. She'd run back, even when I didn't call her, to reconnect for just a moment using what she trusted more, her nose, which she used to sniff my hand. Smell was absolute truth for her. Only then could she run joyously forward again.

In the beginning, the high level of Timber's training was inspired by Della's example. But after Della's death, it continued. Timber learned to heel off leash. She learned to back up with a mere wave of my hand so indicating. But the most amazing example of this new learning was with food. In the kitchen, a foodstuff that would not have been good for a dog would occasionally fall to the floor without our knowledge. But Timber would see where it landed, walk over, give it a sniff, then take it. Now aware that something had fallen—and that she had it—I'd tell her, "No, Timber." Then I would reach down and—her teeth on the food, her taste buds already activated, her throat ready to swallow it— open her mouth and take out whatever it was. And, willingly, so gently that not so much as a tooth ever grazed my fingers, she let me, because I had trained her to do this. She also did it to please me, because what I wanted mattered to her, because she loved me. It was a love as strong as any dog's. Indeed, this feeling, and the learned behavior it fostered, was all the more remarkable because it came from the dog in the wolf who once sat up nights guarding her food.

So strong was Timber's capacity to love and feel affection that it extended beyond her core "pack" to fan out to the deserving, beginning with little children. She adored them. She wasn't the big bad wolf of their "Little Red Riding Hood" fears. She was the big sweet wolf who wagged her tail when they came running over, and let them pet her. She loved all these little hands on her, and even let them play with her fluffy tail, something many a dog can't handle. Children gazed straight into her eyes and Timber returned that gaze, as she saw in them what they saw in her: a gentleness, born of innate, amazing sweetness.

She also liked her vet, Dr. Wasserman of The Heights Veterinary Hospital. He adored her and thought she was wonderful, as did his associate, Dr. Turoff, and their staff. When they heard Timber was in the waiting room, here for some shot or another, they didn't wait to see her in the examination room. They came into the waiting room to greet her. And she greeted them right back.

They had never treated a wolf hybrid before; they have never treated one since. At her first visit, the wolf part of her made them a little leery; eyes checked to be sure a muzzle was handy. No need, they fast discovered, for worry or restraints. She beguiled them with her gentle ways as surely as she beguiled anyone who came into close contact with her. She tolerated the shots and whatnot with good nature. If she didn't like whatever happened, the moment it was over, all was forgiven and she was slowly wagging her tail back and forth as they petted her and marveled at this disposition as lovely as any they had ever seen.

Then there was her weeklong stay, one August, at a boarding facility on Cape Cod. The cottage we had rented didn't permit dogs, so we boarded Timber at a kennel with indoor and outdoor pens that was run by a couple, their two teenage children, and additional summer help. But Timber didn't stay there during the day. Every morning David and I would have a quick breakfast, then go over and pick Timber up to take her out with us for the day to go swimming in the ocean, or hiking through the pine-barrens, or meandering through the towns of Wellfleet and Provincetown, and then return her at dusk to her keepers for the night. They would be waiting for her, not because the hour was late, but because they were so glad to have her back! They had come under the spell of her sweet ways and wanted to spend every minute they could with her.

So every morning when we came to pick her up, it was the same thing: "Do you *have* to take her out today?" "We *do*," we'd told them, apologetically.

But they made do with the little time they had with her, which to our initial amazement, included bathing and completely drying her everyday right before we came to pick her up. Indeed, Timber was never cleaner, her fur never fluffier, her whites never whiter, than these seven days on Cape Cod!

So they'd bring her out every morning, dazzlingly laundered. We couldn't imagine how they even found the time to do it. The place was filled with dozens of dogs. These people had their hands filled as it was. Further, with all the swimming she did, Timber came back at night just as clean as she started out. There was something else behind the daily bathing of Timber that didn't take long to figure out: bathing her meant touching her, getting close to her.

Then, there was the morning we drove over to pick her up—having planned an afternoon of letting her swim in the freshwater ponds that dot Cape Cod—and the place was closed. Like vacationers sometimes do, we'd forgotten what day it was. Posted right there, just as on their business card in my pocket, was the sign in the grass that reminded us: Closed Sunday.

We turned and walked back to the car, dejected. We couldn't believe it: *No Timber today?* I can't remember what David and I did this day, but then, as now, I have a very good idea what Timber did. Her keepers, when they weren't tending to the other dogs in the kennel, probably took her inside the house with them and took turns playing with her and gave her treats to eat and took her for lots of little walks. And then they pretended she got dirty so they could give her another bath.

When the week was up and we drove over to pick Timber up, these people were ready to pay us to let her stay on just one more day. But she had to leave, and so did we. So they all came out and walked us to the car, and hugged Timber goodbye and told us to "Please come back anytime" as they hugged her more and finally let go of her so she could hop into the car. And they stood there, watching her in the backseat, as we drove away.

This ability to connect with people—and they to her—would take Timber to places and experiences few other dogs have.

It was a Monday; I had brought Timber into Manhattan so she could run in Central Park, where David was going to pick us up after work. Walking down Fifth Avenue toward the park, she attracted the usual little crowds of people. The only way to deal with it was to keep moving, which we did. Then a woman came up right alongside us, extremely polite, but insistent as she posed the question: "Is that a wolf?" When the wolf, seeing I was engaged, calmly sat down and waited at my feet, she really wanted to know the answer.

I started to go into the she's-a-malamute thing, when the woman pulled a business card from her brief case and explained she was an animal agent, that Timber was "extraordinary." And if Timber was what she thought —a spectacularly beautiful creature who looked like a wolf but was trained like a dog—she would like to represent her, get her work in photography and commercials.

My initial response was, "You're kidding." She wasn't.

Two or three months down the line, I finally found the time to visit her office in Manhattan and let her have that "interview" with Timber that she'd been requesting. Here, beyond that first impression on Fifth Avenue, she saw Timber was trained to an amazing level, with a beauty— she took lots of Polaroids—that was breathtaking. We also had The Talk in which I explained that Timber would not be interested in any job anyplace, anytime unless it was not only safe, but also something that would be pleasant and fun for her. No need to repeat this. The agent got it the first time. The last detail: No one but I would handle her.

She called with various work projects. Some of them I turned down on the spot; they didn't fit my work schedule. Others weren't right for Timber; the hours were too long. Or I didn't think she'd like the location. Or it was an unacceptible product being pushed; in one case, fur coats for a print ad with a model so adorned, walking a wolf on a leash. "Not possible," I explained. "Timber doesn't help sell fur coats."

But then came the work that was right for Timber: a science-fiction book cover that needed a photograph of a wolf in its layout. A year later, she did another book cover that also needed a wolf. These photography sessions, shot in studios, required that she obey the stay command, standing there and not moving. And then take further direction to angle her head one-way, then another. Or, look in one direction, then switch to another. But never flinch, never move, never look or get bored, but stay "crisp," be the "vibrant wolf" all afternoon long.

It may sound like nothing, but thousands of dollars—photographers' fees, their assistants' fees, the lighting people—not to mention the client's satisfaction, ride on the ability of the dog model to deliver the goods, over and over.

Four years later came the most interesting work Timber ever did. A popular British rock group entitled "Lone Wolf," needed a beautiful lone wolf on its album cover. The photograph would not be shot in the wilds of Canada or Alaska with the early morning mist rising up from a meadow around her, but in New York City. The concept: a lone wolf walking across the deserted intersection of Madison Avenue and 51st Street, with the steam from the manholes underfoot rising up around her, at daybreak.

We took a cab in and arrived at four A.M. The barricades were already up, closing three blocks of Madison Avenue off to cars. Some two dozen people—the photographer, his assistants, lighting people, production assistants—were milling about. When Timber stepped out of the cab, the milling stopped as heads turned to look at her. The photographer came running over, thrilled with how she looked. And equally concerned with the question it all comes down to: "Will she do it?" Not just in the rehearsals—he knew the drill, he'd worked with animals before—but when it counts: when the camera starts clicking.

I had him show me exactly what Timber needed to do, which was to stand motionless at one corner of the intersection and slowly walk forward on a diagonal, over the manholes, through the rising steam, to the opposite corner.

I walked Timber through it several times, let her feel the steam, see it couldn't possibly hurt her. Meanwhile the photographer, anxiously running his hands through his hair, squatted down to check various angles, as his assistants laid out his cameras and various lenses and rolls of film. An hour later, at daybreak, the shoot was ready to start.

I took Timber over to the far side of the intersection, and told her to stay, then unclipped the leash and took off her collar. They didn't want a wolf on a leash. The wolf had to do it herself, which she did, and not with verbal commands, but with the hand signals she already knew. She stood there, her eyes trained on me, and I walked away from her to position myself directly behind the photographer, who was prepared to walk backwards, as was I, as Timber walked forward.

At his mark, my hand, which had been raised to keep her in the stay position, now switched to not just the come signal, but the come slowly signal. She started to walk slowly forward, over the manholes, the steam rising up around her, as the camera clicked away and the photographer, beside himself with joy at what he saw through his camera lens, exclaimed, "Beautiful! Perfect! Fantastic!" And she continued coming forward, over more vents, the steam rising through her fur, as the photographer backed up and kept shooting, until Timber was at the other side of the intersection.

She did it over and over, six rolls of film's worth. When it was finally finished, the photographer ran over and hugged her, telling her, "Thank You. Thank you. What a dog!"

The shoot wasn't over. We all piled into vans and headed for the next location: the Brooklyn Bridge, where the crew hauled out all the camera equipment and the rest onto the pedestrian walkway. They couldn't close the Brooklyn Bridge, but it wasn't the bridge they were after. It was the pedestrian walkway. The photograph on the back of the album cover was to be a lone wolf walking across the deserted Brooklyn Bridge in the early morning hours. Thus, there couldn't be other people—or bicyclists, or dog walkers—in the shot. The production assistants either stopped people (most of them very happy to watch, even from such a long distance), or let the hurried ones walk through (which meant the shoot had to stop) until the walkway was clear again.

When everything was set to go—the tripod set up, the camera attached, and the photographer poised behind it—I took Timber about five hundred feet away, took her leash and collar off, and motioned her to stay. I then walked back to join the crew surrounding the photographer and stood directly behind him, as Timber stood waiting for my hand signal, eyes sharply focused on me. The distance between her and us was far too great for verbal commands. Even if they had been possible, the humming of cars on the roadway below would have blocked them out.

She stood there, waiting. When the photographer told me, "Now," I signaled her to come slowly. They didn't want her to run. It was essential that she come forward slowly. She did just that, as the camera started to click away and the photographer intoned, "Fabulous. Fabulous. Keep her coming."

Then, when she was half way to us, he quickly asked me, "Can you make her stop?"

I changed my come-forward signal to the raised-palm stop position. She stopped.

He grabbed another camera and shot half a roll of her at this distance, then said, "Make her move again? Come forward now?"

I signaled Timber to start walking again. She did, and kept walking forward as the camera clicked away, and—as my hand signal didn't change—she continued walking forward until she was twenty feet away from the camera. Fifteen feet. Ten feet. Five feet. Then, as I still hadn't signaled her to stop, she walked right up to the camera lens where the photographer was now screaming, "Fantastic!"

As successful as the film shoot was, five, six, seven rolls of film is never enough. Like the first location, they did it over and over, changing cameras, adjusting the lenses, switching angles, stopping to discuss how the light was changing, what the wind was doing. Each time they started up again, Timber did exactly what they needed her to do.

When it was over, the photographer loved Timber in the sense of how professional she was and the pictures she'd given them. As the crew set to folding the tripod, putting all the cameras back in their cases, and gathering up all the empty coffee cups, the photographer came over, gave Timber a final pat, and asked me, "Can we drop you off somewhere?" I thanked him for the offer, but explained Timber and I had other plans. We walked across the bridge together into Brooklyn Heights, then took the long walk up the hill to Park Slope and home, the "working dog's" day done.

I received a few checks that paid for a lot of dog food, but what did Timber get out of all this? For her, it was an adventure, new places, new people, new experiences, and the pleasure of taking instruction and being lavishly praised by me. But did she *need* to walk through steam vents and get to know the Brooklyn Bridge so well? No. She did it for me, because I asked her too. And she trusted me—because I was trustworthy—to only ask her to do what I knew was right or interesting or fun for her.

What was always absolutely interesting and fun for Timber were occasional romps through Central Park, especially the time we came out of the park and walked past the Plaza Hotel, then across to the cobble stoned plaza with the water fountain, where—before I could stop her—Timber suddenly jumped into the fountain, splashing around with absolute joy! Crowds of tourists—even hard-core seen-it-all Manhattanites—gathered to watch, smiles on their faces, as the tourists pulled their children in close so they, too, could see the big beautiful dog cavorting in the fountain outside The Plaza Hotel.

What all these observers couldn't possibly know was the inner beauty of this lovely creature. How she taught me the meaning of grace through the art and beauty of her graceful ways. How she taught me subtlety and nuance by how sensitive and attuned she was to everything and everyone around her, to voice tone, to facial expression, to the slightest change in body language, to the very feeling in the air. Watching her, being with Timber, was hearing the sound between beautiful notes; it was sensing the quickened heartbeats that transform a string of words into poetry. This is what the beautiful dog who attracted the crowds outside The Plaza Hotel gave me every day.

A few months after the swim in the fountain, two new members joined Timber's pack. The first was Twinkie, a gray-striped, pink-nosed, sweet little cat. I had wanted a cat for years, but the squirrel incident ever etched in my mind had driven the wish away.

Then one cold January day, as I waited on the sidewalk on Seventh Avenue with Timber, David went into a Korean fruit and vegetable store near home for some cantaloupe and came out saying, "There is the cutest, most remarkable kitten in there. You've got to see her."

I went in and took a look, and there she was, as sweet and adorable as David had said. And smart, too. Her kitten-mates were here and there, shivering in corners around the store. But not Twinky. She had positioned herself right in front of an electric heater behind the counter and sat there, the heat blasting at her with such force it flattened the whiskers on her face. And she sure was cute. I made a little sound and she looked up at me with such bright little eyes, it was hard to walk away from her.

I went back outside where David waited, eyebrows lifted expectantly. "I'm right," he said. "She's special, isn't she?"

"God, yes," I agreed. "She's adorable. But what about Timber?"

The answer to that question made us walk away.

But I thought about it overnight. *Maybe if we were very careful, if we kept them in separate rooms in the beginning.* But then I saw the squirrel, and the little kitten left my mind.

The next day, we ran out of coffee at The Village Green and I left the shop to go to The Leaf and Bean, a gourmet coffee and tea emporium a half-block away on Seventh Avenue. But I walked past it and went into the fruit and vegetable store, three stores down. I recognized the Korean fellow behind the counter from the day before and started to ask him, "Do you still have the little—" when I looked down at his feet and there she was, right by the heater. He reached down to pick her up and said in halting English, "You want?"

"Yes!" I said.

He handed her over. On the way back to The Village Green, carrying my precious cargo, I actually remembered to pick up the coffee.

When David called later to see how my day was going, I told him, "Guess who's here?" He knew in an instant. "You went back? You got her?" he laughed.

"I did!" I told him.

As it turned out, all my fears about Timber were for naught. She'd changed, or matured—who knows what it was. The point is, she couldn't have been nicer or more gentle to this meowing little newcomer, who had added one kitty's worth to her pack.

The pack was soon to add yet another new member. I was pregnant.

When our daughter was born in March of 1984, far from resenting this intrusion as many, even the nicest dogs will, ten-year-old Timber factored Lexie into her pack as one more person to interact with, one more entity to give and receive affection from. She was lovely with the little baby Lexie was. When Lexie became a toddler and glommed on to Timber to stabilize her, Timber let her, and walked ever so slowly around the apartment with Lexie hanging on to her ears, her face, whatever she happened to grab. Timber didn't put up with all this manhandling, she loved it.

As for the half-eaten sandwiches Lexie was wont to walk around with, taking a bite now and then—Timber never touched them. She knew they were food—just like what occasionally hit the floor in the kitchen—but it was food in Lexie's hand. Maybe for long distance sniffing, but never for the taking. Then there was the time we'd given Lexie a slice of cheese to eat. Typically, she'd taken a nibble here and there as she played with a toy, then put the toy down—but not the cheese—to go look at a book. Then some time later, she came over and started telling us about the book, with hand gestures—as Timber stood watching—that had the hand with the cheese waving it literally under Timber's nose. This was too much, even for Timber. She reached forward, and ever so gently, with a touch as light as a feather, she took the cheese out of Lexie's hand (Lexie didn't even know it was gone!) and ate it.

From the first moment she was born (even before it) I had fallen hopelessly in love with the child who "fed" Timber the cheese. I poured everything I had into this exquisite little girl so wonderful that if nothing else in my life ever went my way, it wouldn't matter. The best thing

I would ever do—and have ever done—is Lexie. Giving birth to her, loving her, taking care of her. I had never changed a diaper in my life until I changed hers. I never knew I could endure a thousand nights of interrupted sleep and still be able to smile—until Lexie. Then again, I had had the teacher extraordinaire: Della. Her example was right there with me. Her patience I now sought to emulate, and her exceptional care of her babies. Her joy in her offspring I didn't have to emulate; it was already in me. David and I rearranged our lives and the furniture in the apartment to accommodate Lexie's needs. We turned my old office at the store into a baby room. And yes, I would nurse Lexie probably longer than any mother in modern history until she made the choice: off Mommy, time for cups and glasses.

Timber didn't take a complete backseat to Lexie, or find herself suddenly ignored, which can happen to even the most loved dog when a baby arrives. But motherhood had turned my life hopelessly, irrevocably— and deliriously happily—upside down. There weren't enough hours in the day to do it all: a baby, a husband, a business, writing my first book, and this wonderful dog. What I tried to do, wherever possible, was blend some of Lexie's and Timber's needs together.

Before going to work in the morning, it wasn't always the big run in the park that Timber was used to. Often it was the walk—with Lexie in the stroller and Timber trotting alongside—down Prospect Park West to the Third Street Playground that is just inside Prospect Park. As the playground prohibits dogs, I tied Timber on a long leash to the chain-link fence. Then Lexie and I went in and played on the swings as Timber sat contentedly in the shade, watching us, her ears pricking forward when Lexie shrieked with delight at something, then falling to repose as Lexie took to quiet play in the sandbox. So Timber got the walk from our house to the playground, then the walk from the playground to The Village Green to start the workday, with a little time in the shade in between.

But with unfailing regularity, the three of us took what we called "The Timber Walk," where we entered the park at Grand Army Plaza, but didn't turn left for the Long Meadow. Instead, we strolled along this winding path that is just inside the park where the (even then) huge ginkgo tree stands, enjoying the sun-dappled shade of this leafy glen. Then the shade gave way to sun as we continued on past the tiny playground for babies, and up the little hill in the cool shade, to turn out of the park at the Third Street entrance some ten minutes later. This taste of the park under our belts, we made our way to The Village Green. But we took our time, pausing to look at the delightful front gardens and the many petunia- and geranium-filled window boxes courtesy of the many avid gardeners in Park Slope. (Indeed, I recognized many of the plants in these well-tended gardens and window boxes. They came from The Village Green, and here they were in all their splendor, where I could admire how they had spread and grown up.) All this we took in, until we turned down Union Street for the store, where Timber and I went to work, and Lexie ran into her playroom for her toys and books.

To be sure, it was a tamer existence than the one Timber was used to. But there were Monday mornings or afternoons when David, often off from work himself, got Lexie all to himself. And I got Timber all to myself. I'd throw her leash on, and we'd tear up to the park and off we'd go through the Long Meadow for a real run! Or to the Paddle Boat Lake for something she hadn't had in a while: a swim! Or into the woods for a while, just her and me and the birds, where we'd just walk together.

These Mondays reminded Timber I was still hers. And they reminded me she was still mine.

Then—no doubt it was her hybrid vigor—Timber had never been sick a day in her life, she got an infection that almost killed her.

As we walked to work this day, I noticed that her hindquarters looked a little hunched, as though her back legs hurt. With Monday three days away, and David's work schedule impossibly busy, I called a mobile vet service that had been recommended to me. They came, they examined her, and then they misdiagnosed her. They thought the tenderness in her pelvic area (she yelped when they palpated it) indicated a bladder infection. They injected her with an antibiotic, gave me some tablets to administer orally, said she would be fine in a day or so, and left.

A day or so later she wasn't fine. She was worse, now clearly hunched over with pain.

That night, David and I took her to The Heights Veterinary Hospital where Dr. Wasserman examined her, didn't like what he saw, and admitted her on the spot. A half-hour later, he put her under general anesthesia and performed an emergency hysterectomy to save her life. This was no simple little bladder or urinary infection. It was "pyometra," a uterine infection, which was so advanced that when Dr. Wassmerman opened her up, Timber's uterus was so enlarged, so infected, so filled with purulence, it was on the verge of rupturing. Indeed, it was just beginning to rupture as he went in. The surgery had, he said, "gone well," but she was very sick. They were administering intravenous antibiotics to ward off any further infection in her abdomen, and they would, he assured me, keep a close eye on her.

When I called the next morning from work to check on her, she was "still very sick, but holding her own." When I called later that afternoon, there was no change. The next morning, David and I went to see her. She had stopped eating and drinking water. Lack of food wasn't the important issue. It was fluids, the dangers of dehydration. They were now administering intravenous fluids, in addition to the high-dose antibiotics. We petted her and said cheerful things that made her eyes brighten and tail wag, until our time to visit was up and we had to leave.

The next day, her condition suddenly turned critical. The fluids were still an issue. But this isn't what deeply troubled Dr. Wasserman; it was Timber herself, the look in her eyes. An indifference to life had set in. He urged us to visit her right away. No need. We were leaving the house to do just that when he telephoned.

When we arrived and went in to see her, Timber was lying on her side in her pen, tubes coming in and out of her, so weak she could barely pick up her head. We softly called out her name and gently touched her. She opened her eyes, looked at us, and the tip of her tail gave the faintest wag, then it fell to stillness as she closed her eyes again.

I left crying, my heart now filled with a terrible fear: *Was Timber going to die?* In between this devastating thought, my self-recriminations flew: Why hadn't I seen it sooner: the infection? How could I have trusted a vet service that came recommended, but recommended or not, *I* didn't know them. *How could I have trusted them?*

"She's in the right hands now," David assured me. It was true. The Heights Veterinary Hospital people were all pulling for her, doing everything they could for her, most especially, Dr. Wasserman. He lived above the office, and throughout these days would go down periodically through the night to look in on her.

We were prepared to visit Timber first thing the next morning. Then at midnight a call came from Dr. Wasserman that started with two of the most beautiful words I have ever heard: "She's better." He'd gone down only minutes before to look in on her, and she was responsive. She looked at him, let him feed her. She had come back from the brink of death.

Three days later, we brought Timber home and she bounced back to health. Of course, there would be no puppies for Timber. Then again, even when we had occasionally discussed it, who could we have mated her to? A malamute? A husky? Another wolf hybrid like her? That was just the point: There was no malamute or husky or hybrid like Timber. She was one of a kind. Now the puppy issue was moot. But we didn't care. We had her. That was all that mattered before she got sick. It was all that mattered now.

The years went by. Lexie turned three, then four, and started pre-school at the Berkeley Carroll School, the very same school I had entered as a seventh grader. The school had vastly increased in size since I'd attended. Preschool through fourth grade was housed in the two buildings on Carroll Street that the school had expanded into years ago. Now, every weekday morning, Timber took the ten-minute walk with me down Seventh Avenue to Carroll Street to get Lexie to school. Once there, we dropped Lexie off, then headed up to Prospect Park where Timber got back all those before-work runs in the park. We took full advantage of them, enjoying every minute, refreshing ourselves with the air, the trees, the grass; on a sunny day, a gray day, a rainy day—it didn't matter, it was all wonderful. Then a look at my watch told me it was time to leave the park and turn down Union Street to go to The Village Green and start our workday.

At this point, many people came into the shop to see Timber, as she had developed a not so small following in Park Slope. Most people still thought—because I stuck to it—that she was a malamute, albeit a most remarkable one, who was so sweet, so nice to them, that they would stop by, and bring their children or friends along, just to say hello to her.

Timber was happy to see them. She'd come to the counter, jump up, hind legs on the floor, front legs on the counter, and let them pet her, as her tail fanned back and forth. To some of these admirers—long-term customers who I had come to know so well they felt like acquaintances, whose affection for Timber was so deep they deserved to know what she really was—I told the truth. Which caused them to marvel at her all the more.

What I didn't reveal, because I didn't want to think it or remember it myself, was Timber's age. When anyone asked—at The Village Green, on the street, in the park—how old she was, I told them she was six. For seven years she was six, even as she had turned seven, then eight, then nine, ten, eleven, twelve, thirteen. Now she was fourteen, and still "six." But she looked six! She was as healthy, vibrant, and beautiful—again, that hybrid vigor in her—as ever, even though, the year before, in her thirteenth year, Timber became deaf.

Much as it is with aging humans so afflicted, it was a gradual process. I would call out her name, and she wouldn't respond. When I said it louder, she heard me and came trotting over. Three months later, a loud call got no response. When I shouted her name, she turned her head, heard me, and over she came. But six months later, not even shouting turned her head. Timber couldn't hear anything; she was deaf.

At home, or at the store, I tapped the floor with my foot to get her attention. She felt it. The next instant, her eyes were on me. Here is where her great sensitivity, and how attuned she was to body language, gestures, and facial expression, that so graced my life, now served her so well as I worked out an intricate system of gestures and hand signals to communicate very effectively with her. What the spoken word had achieved, I now communicated with gestures that conveyed a litany of words, ideas, and emotions that Timber instantly grasped. The wave of my hand to beckon her to come because we were going to go to the park. The wait signal in the hall because I couldn't find my keys and had to go look for them. When I found them, my *Okay, let's go!* gestures got her dancing at the front door. And out we went to the park to have the wonderful time we always had, with her eyes, as she ran around, regularly checking in with me, looking for any signals of what she might need to know. This is why I used those hand signals on Madison Avenue and the Brooklyn Bridge. Because Timber couldn't hear. But she was so adept at visual cues, I knew it wouldn't matter. And it didn't. The ironic fact, of course, is had she not known hand signals, that shoot on the Brooklyn Bridge would not have been possible.

But the year before, when it was clear she was loosing her hearing, it seemed such a terrible loss. I felt so sorry for her. But she didn't care! Life was still beautiful to her. When I saw this, it didn't matter to me. There were still years of life in store for her.

She passed her thirteenth year. Now she was fourteen. There seemed no reason why she couldn't continue on, until, one day, walking home from The Village Green on Seventh Avenue, I saw it: a slight weakening in her hind legs. Over the next days, it worsened. Then she began crying out with pain.

We took Timber to The Height's Veterinary Hospital. Dr. Wasserman had retired by now. His associate, Dr. Turoff, who had also known Timber for years, had taken over his practice. He examined Timber, listened to her heart, her lungs, and found no problem there. But I saw the look on his face as he examined her hind legs, hips, and lower spine. Old age had finally caught up with Timber in the serious degrading of the bone of her hip joint and lower spine that had now turned acute, causing pain. While the painkillers we left with would alleviate her suffering, there was no cure. As with Della, there was no turning back the clock.

For a few days, the pills eased the pain a little. She walked stiffly around the apartment. Then the pain rose right through it, making her cry out, and afraid to move. I doubled the dose. She still cried out. I tripled it. One day she was slowly walking for her blue chair in the bedroom when her back legs completely gave out. She collapsed to the rug at the base of our bed, and she could not get up. Her back legs were paralyzed. She lay there, taking short breaths, in terrible pain. Before this, she had been taking food and water.

Now, she stopped eating. Then she refused water. The next day, she did something that devastated me with its terrible implication: she turned away from life. No longer even cried out, even as she was wracked with pain. The end was near. She knew it. My heart grave, the only question now was, Could we let her meet this end in this terrible pain that nothing would stop? Or do the right thing, that final act of love, have her put to sleep.

I had been speaking with Dr. Turoff all along. This night I called him and made arrangements to bring Timber in the next morning and have her put to sleep, as she could not, she must not, endure that pain another day.

On top of this was an awful coincidence. Lexie was turning five the next day. Weeks earlier, we had planned a party for her. Even as Lexie wanted to talk about her party, she would interrupt herself to ask us, "What's the matter with Timber? She hurts ... doesn't she?" We couldn't tell her the dog whom she adored, from whom she had learned the word "dog," was suffering so terribly that she would die on Lexie's birthday. Instead we told her, "Timber does hurt. We're going to take her to the vet tomorrow, in the morning."

"Will she be all right? Will she get well?" Lexie kept asking. We lied every time we told her, "Yes, she will."

That night, I called my friend Brigitte. Her daughter, Alice, and Lexie were good friends. They'd known each other from birth up, and Brigitte and I occasionally babysat for each other. I asked her if she could possibly take care of Lexie at her house for a few hours the next morning. When she heard the reason why, Brigitte was so sorry; she liked Timber very much. "Would you like me to come over and pick Lexie up?" she offered, trying to lighten the burden of the next day. "Thank you, but no," I told her. "We'll drop her off in the car."

The next morning, David and I took Lexie to Brigitte's house to play with Alice, then turned around and went home.

The appointment was set at 9 A.M. with Dr. Turoff. To spare us the distress of having to walk through the waiting room, he told us they would leave the back door unlocked.

We carried Timber out of the house and into the car. When we got there, twenty minutes later, the back door was slightly ajar.

I held the door open as David carried Timber inside and into an examination room. Dr. Turoff was waiting for us with one of his attendants, the fellow who was always kind but said few words.

David gently eased Timber down on the table. I stepped over to her head, talking to her, as David stood next to me. Even here, in so much pain, she gazed up sweetly at me, as I stroked her head, and talked to her, telling her how good she was, and that she was going to be all right. Dr. Turoff shaved a few inches of fur off the inside of Timber's right front leg. The little fluff of white fur rolled over onto the table. When the attendant reached for it, I told him, "No. Please. I would like it," as I clasped it and put it in my pocket. Turoff now prepared the two syringes: one to heavily sedate Timber, the second that would stop her heart.

He stepped over to Timber, then, his face so sad, he asked us, "Are you ready?" David looked at me. "Yes," I finally said.

As Dr. Turoff slipped the needle into her vein, I looked into Timber's eyes and gently stroked her head as I told her "Good girl, Timber. Good girl. I love you, Timber." A few moments later, her body, which had been so tight with pain all these days, began to relax. I smiled at her through my tears. Her pain was over. Dr. Turoff waited, then slipped the second injection into her vein that would stop her heart. I petted her and touched her, as did David, looking into her eyes. For a moment she was still there, in her eyes; then, my heart reeled as her gaze froze, and her head slowly came down to rest on the table.

How do you walk away from such a dog? It is not possible, yet you do it because you must. I stroked Timber's neck, then leaned over to smell her lovely fur one last time. The fragrance of a field of wildflowers rushed through my heart. David took my hand. As we started to walk away, I stopped and looked one more time at the most lovely creature I have ever known.

I completely fell apart outside on the street, and in the car as we drove back to Park Slope. Then, I pulled myself together. I had to. Lexie was waiting for us at Brigitte's house. Her guests were due at home in two hours. Had it been anyone else but Lexie, I could not have done it: push my grief aside and put on the party. So I got the smile up on my face and kept it there. It was there when we picked Lexie up. It was there when we got home and the doorbell began to ring.

We did the party, an afternoon gathering in the backyard garden with my mother, Paula, and Brother; Brigitte, her husband Chris, and Alice; and a bunch of Lexie's other friends and their parents, who were also our friends. When Lexie opened up her presents, and made a wish and blew out the candles on her cake, I was very happy for her as I watched her enjoy every minute of what she deserved: a happy birthday.

That night, after Lexie was asleep, I sat outside in the backyard in the dark and cried out the sorrow that was inside me.

We didn't tell Lexie right away about Timber. Knowing how upset she would be, we didn't want her to associate her birthday with Timber's death. We deliberately let some time elapse to separate the two events. When she asked about Timber the day after her party and in the ensuing days, we told her she was still at the hospital, and would have to stay there a little longer. Lexie went along with this explanation.

Ten days later, a Friday, with the weekend ahead to give her time to grasp it and come to grips with it before she went back to school, David and I sat down with Lexie on the sofa and told her the truth and our reasons for withholding it. Tears streamed down her face. "Timber's dead?"

We explained the details she needed and wanted to know: what happened at the vet, and that Timber had died very peacefully. Lexie understood it, agreed with the rightness of it, and then she cried.

For many months, I could only mourn Timber. Then, over time, and with reflection, this sadness came to be replaced with a glory in her and her life and how blessed I had been to know her. For Timber was enchantment. She was a creature of the wilds, the rustling of wind through tall trees, who graced us with her very presence for the fourteen years I call "the glory years," when a sliver of the moon came down from the heavens to live with us, accept us, and, most amazing of all, given who and what she was, love us.

4

A Rottweiler Named Boo

O ne doesn't speak ill of the dead" is a saying—invariably reserved for humans—whose message is clear: To recall fault in a deceased one would spoil his memory, this constituting the somber transgression of disloyalty. But herein lies the conflict for me because, with all due respect for most of the deceased humans in my life, it is not they but my dogs who have been the unwavering paragons of nobility, the pillars of loyalty, the great communicators of so many things of value, each dog offering his or her particular take on these qualities, that has lent color, substance, reliability, warmth, love, and truth to my life. Thus my profound gratitude for Moppet, Della, and Timber. And my great reluctance now to "speak ill" of, to find serious fault with, the dog you are about to meet. Which brings me to a rottweiler named Boo. And explains why I need this lengthy apologia to bring myself to be able to say what still feels like a betrayal: that much as I loved him, Boo and I were a mismatch. He was the one hundred-twenty pound tank of a rottweiler who lived to pulverize so much as a whiff of danger. I was looking, certainly for a dog to protect me, but also for what I'd found in the dogs before him: a new puppy to wrap my heart around. But Boo had his own ideas.

But first things first: while they now constitute a large presence in the parks and on the streets of especially the larger cities and their suburbs (the American Kennel Club cites the rottweiler as the fourth most popular breed in the United States today), I got Boo when *nobody had a rottweiler*. And I'm not talking about the horribly overbred, wobbly-footed, spindly rottweiler that looks like a fat Doberman pinscher, the rottweiler—with rare exceptions—that you see today. No, this was a real rottweiler, a German-bred tank of a rottweiler with the strength of an ox, and a head chock-full of brains that was so broad we used to joke you could arrange a table setting on it. Set into his highly expressive face were two intense little brown eyes that fed him his particular take on the world.

The year was 1989. The Village Green was in full swing, Lexie turned six, and it had been five months since Timber died. These months were a sad and strange time, my life filled with a terrible stillness every day that I woke up to the house without Timber and came home to the house without Timber. Traces of her, most especially her leash and food bowl, had not been put away, as this act would have documented that she was really gone. Rather, I put them aside. Adhering to my philosophy that each new dog who entered my life deserved an open mind and heart, when the time finally came that I was able to fully embrace a new puppy, I deliberately looked at the other end of the dog spectrum and discovered the rottweiler.

I didn't discover this breed on every street corner or running in packs in the park. Eleven years ago, there wasn't a rottweiler to be seen. It was an obscure breed that, absenting the few who showed up in major dog shows, only existed in the back pages of dog magazines where breeders advertise, and rottweiler ads filled all of one inch of advertising copy.

Thus, as with the few other late-eighties, early-nineties rottweiler owners, it was the film *The Omen* that gave me my first peek at this most imposing dog. Then, there was the one lone "rottie" who showed up in Prospect Park and whose owner spoke so highly of his dog, how courageous he was, and especially, how intelligent. Very encouraging words, these. Time to hit the dog breed books.

They talked of the rottweiler's ancient origins, and how, because its ancestry is not fully documented, the rottweiler we know today is presumed to have descended from one of the "drover" or herding dogs indigenous to ancient Rome, most likely the Italian mastiff, a heavyset rugged dog possessed of great intelligence and a strong guarding instinct. The Romans used this rottweiler-mastiff as a herd and guard dog, and for hunting large game like lions and wild boar. When the Roman armies set out to conquer the ancient world some two thousand years ago, this early rottweiler marched right alongside the legions as a war dog, draft dog, and stock dog who drove and guarded the herds of cattle needed to feed these marauding armies. At night, these same dogs stood as sentinels over the camps.

In A.D. 74, one legion's long trek across the Alps marched it right into the successful conquering of the ancient city on the Neckar River (in what is now southern Germany) that the Romans would call Arac Flaviae.

For the next two centuries, cattle raising flourished in Arac Flaviae, and so did the numbers of rottweiler-type dogs necessary to guard and drive the herds to market. Then, circa A.D. 260, the Romans were ousted from Arac Flaviae by the Germanics, but not so their dogs. Cattle raising and trading remained the mainstay of this city, guaranteeing the need for the rottweiler. Some four hundred years later, Arac Flaviae was renamed not after the dog, but the red tiles ("das Rote Wil") of the Roman villas that were unearthed in A.D. 700 in an excavation to build a Christian church.

Rottweil's dominance as a trade center for cattle only increased through the Middle Ages. So did the concentration of butchers plying their trade within this city and the proliferation of the Rottweiler Metzgerhund (the "butcher dog" as he was now called) to drive the cattle to and from market, or haul the beef products to local destinations. This dominance of the beef industry and the dog who made it possible continued right up to the middle of the nineteenth century, when the driving of cattle was outlawed in Germany, and the donkey cart and railroad replaced the dog cart and the dog who pulled that cart.

Without a raison d'etre (as, historically, dogs belonging to the working classes had to earn their keep), the numbers of rottweilers dropped precipitously. Indeed, by 1800 the breed almost became extinct, only to be rescued in 1901 by enthusiastic breeders centered in Stuttgart who, seeking to improve the strength and courage of the drover dog that the ancient Romans held in such esteem, now bred the 'butcher dog' of the Middle Ages into the rottweiler we know today. This rottweiler functions as a police dog, an esteemed watchdog, and a companion dog.

The rottweiler's medium-large, robust, thickly muscled body is black, with clearly defined rust markings on his face, body, and feet. His medium-length, coarse coat sheds, but is low-maintenance, only requiring occasional brushing. The male rottweiler stands twenty-four to twenty-seven inches at the shoulder, and weighs between ninety-five and one hundred thirty pounds. A female measures twenty-two to twenty-five inches, and weighs between eighty to one hundred pounds. (This is another breed in which males have a look distinctly masculine, and females have a distinctly feminine look.) The ideal temperament of a rottweiler (classified in the Working Group) is a stable, well-balanced dog of extreme courage and intelligence, with an inherent desire to protect home and family.

It was this description, and the very words the dog-breed books echoed—courageous, exceptional trainability, well-balanced—that drew me to the rottweiler. Notably, it was also the "esteemed guard dog" in the rottweiler that got my attention and held it, as the late eighties and early nineties seemed fraught with crime, particularly in the cities. While pretty Park Slope was an oasis of civility and stability, it was not immune to the pervasive climate of fear that was bolstered by the occasional act of local crime. And I was in a business where anyone could walk through our door. So yes, I wanted a dog who would be protective at work and at home. But equally important and attractive to me was that "high level of intelligence" attributed to the rottweiler, which Stanley Coren aptly documents in his ranking the rottweiler in the number nine slot, a veritable dog genius.

These days you can hail a breeder of rottweilers as easily as you can hail a cab. Eleven years ago the information I received from the American Kennel Club listed all of six breeders, five of them in Ohio.

With a six-day workweek that couldn't accommodate a jaunt to the Midwest, I turned to the source the brought me Della: the classified section of the Sunday *New York Times*. Here I came across an ad for a litter of "rotties" bred on Long Island, the town a mere hour away. While the ad raised the unmistakable flag of "backyard breeder," I thought, "One never knows, there could be quality there." In any event, my bright idea was, we could make a family outing of it, take a little drive to suburbia, have lunch, and in the process check out some puppies.

Thus, one morning David, Lexie, and I set out for our first in-person look at rottweiler puppies. And cute they were, all nine of them. Most pleasant, also, was the woman and her two children happily cavorting in the grassy backyard with this pack of rambunctious puppies whose outgoing and friendly behavior said, "No people-shy puppies here!" Far from it, this was as fully socialized a bunch of puppies as one could possibly hope for. Unfortunately, as I had anticipated, the problem with them was quality. That is, sweet as they were, these nine little puppies were, even to my inexperienced eye, a far cry from the standard set for the rottweiler, their slim bodies more Dalmatian than boxy rottweiler, with small, slim heads to match. In short, no "type" rottweilers here; they were clearly the progeny of a very amateur breeder. But such a cheerful, forthright amateur breeder, the woman even producing a Polaroid of her female in the act of doggy coitus with the father (the "papered" rottweiler down the road) to authenticate the male parentage of this lively brood now amiably set about tugging at the laces of our shoes. I thanked her with utmost sincerity for her hospitality, told her we would have to think about it, shook her kids' hands, gave several puppy heads a pat, and we piled back into the car.

My next inquiry, this one also from a newspaper, took me from friendly backyard breeder to not-so-friendly basement breeder. My phone call was answered by a gruff voice, bellowing against a crescendo of barking in the background, that made no attempt to disguise its annoyance (a very bad sign) at my various questions. But he was quick to get down to the meat of it: that he had rottweiler puppies, adolescents, adults, male, female, "You name it, I got it." Clearly, a puppy mill. Not the infamous mills in the Midwest with the rows and rows of dog crates surrounded by weeds and rusty car wrecks where at least the sun is known to shine on this misery. But an urban puppy mill. A basement puppy mill, with subterranean rooms no doubt running full speed, this guy, through coincidence or cunning, on the cutting edge of mass production of the breed that would burst on the scene some eleven years later. I couldn't hang up the phone fast enough.

Thinking that finding the right breeder, or any breeder of merit, was turning out to be much harder than I had anticipated, I was about to take another look at those Ohio breeders, who now didn't seem so remote. Then David, fresh from research at the library, handed me a sheet he'd xeroxed out of a very current dog-breeder magazine. And there it was, the name of a breeder not west of the Mississippi or just south of the Great Lakes, but in Catskill, New York, some two-and-a-half hours from New York City. Even better, her ad read like the real thing: a nice sprinkling of Ch's (short for champion) preceding the sire and dam's registered names, and the expected whelping (birth) date of the offspring of this champion parentage.

Ten digits later, I was on the phone with this breeder who was German and a very serious breeder of rottweilers for some twenty years. She did not have puppies "ready to go," but she did have the "just whelped" litter. With a directness that spoke more to efficiency than friendliness, she invited us to drive up and see them. I explained we would be at Calendar House the following weekend and would drive across the river and arrive at noon on Saturday.

The following week, we turned off a picturesque country lane and pulled into her driveway, then instantly slowed to a crawl to avoid mowing down a man (her husband) leading a lively troupe of slung-low-to-the-ground dachshunds, their "personal" dogs. We crept down the driveway that ended with their house to the left and the kennel dead center. And an impressive sight it was: tidy flower beds in the front of an expansive country kennel with twenty-odd dog pens that each opened out into sizable outdoor runs. The car doors opened, and our feet had no sooner touched the driveway gravel when the voice on the phone turned into the woman emerging from the kennel who I would know for the next six years: the breeder with the most magnificent rottweilers, now barking furiously at us, that I would ever see outside of a dog show ring.

Thus I met Laura who, much like her dogs, was fearless, large and broad of bone, short on pleasantries, and long on directness. She set about showing us around, constantly performing other tasks as she talked to us: one hand pouring huge spadefuls of kibble into one dog's bowl, the other hand picking up the hose to wash down the concrete flooring in the neighboring dog's pen. All the while, she explained, as we followed her from one area of the kennel to another, how this "bitch" or another was strong on x trait, and this "dog" was strong on y trait. Soon enough, she dropped the kennel talk to refer to them as she really thought of them: as this "boy" or this "girl." Those moments when I managed to tear my eyes away from her magnificent dogs, I leaned in close to listen, understanding precious little of what she was saying, but utterly convinced of what mattered: she knew what she was talking about.

At the end of the tour, Laura allowed us to view the just-whelped litter of puppies, an honor offered with much instruction. "You can't touch them," she said as though all three of us were children. "Your hands have germs. You must stand," she pointed to the viewing distance five feet away, "*there*."

We dutifully stepped back, and waited as she picked them up, one at a time, little handfuls of newborn rottweiler puppies, soft little brown bodies *the length of hot dogs*, sleepy and acquiescent in her broad hands. "And would one of these be ours?" I ventured. She leaned down to return the last puppy to its littermates, straightened up, and said, "Yes."

I reminded her that we were looking for a male. She said a male would be "available," meaning we didn't choose which one, she would choose. Not about to argue with her (and poking David to remove the look I knew was on his face), I agreed. We wrote her the check for one hundred dollars that would hold our puppy, and made arrangements to come back in eight weeks.

Eight weeks later, we were back on the Taconic Parkway headed north.

Laura was ready for us. She had the paperwork laid out, including the sheet that listed the dates and nature of the puppy shots Boo had already received, plus the schedule of inoculations to follow for the next four months. She also had his AKC registration papers all set to go, another sheet that covered recommended diet, and as I recall, she also provided us with a small bag of the food Boo was used to in order to carry us over until we got our own supply.

Finally, she left the room and brought him to us: only nine weeks old, a little butterball of a chunky puppy with soft black fur and bright little eyes—our baby rottweiler.

So began my life with Boo, a life in which, just like the dogs before him, he would teach me far more than I would ever teach him; indeed, his would be the most searing lessons any dog would ever teach me. But thoughts of how he would develop and where he would take me were the farthest thing on my mind. My thoughts this hot July afternoon as we turned back onto the woodsy lane and headed for home were utterly absorbed with the enchantment of this moment: the longed-for puppy. Not in my lap where I had envisioned him, but in Lexie's, as days ago she had explained it was important to her that she be the one to hold him. I was even gladder now that I had granted this request. I saw the smile on her face as she looked down at him, the first puppy in her life, her little hands gently stroking his head and the soft puppy fur across his back as she talked to him, telling him who she was, who we were, and that this car ride was nothing to be afraid of.

It didn't take days or weeks to begin to find out who this little baby rottweiler was. The seeds of personality, already sown, were sprouting up before our very eyes not ten minutes into the drive home as Boo began to squirm with growing discontent against Lexie's hands. It wasn't that she was doing anything wrong. She knew the difference between hold and squeeze. It wasn't how she was holding him that was making Boo struggle; it was being held *at all*.

"He doesn't want to sit with me. He's upset," Lexie said, turning around to me in the back seat. "Maybe you should take him?"

I reached between the two front seats as she leaned around and carefully passed him back to my hands that could barely wait their turn. But far from calming him down, Boo's reaction to the bigger, more experienced hands now on him was a bigger struggle to get them off him.

Thus, not one half-hour into our life together, little Boo and I were already engaged in our first deadlock: the baby rottweiler with, even then, his own ideas that ran contrary to his safety and well-being. So he squirmed against my hands like a baby seal caught in a net, his aggravation mounting with each passing mile. Taking David's suggestion that sitting on the upholstery next to me might better suit Boo, I gently placed him on the seat, a foot away. But he continued to agitate, the space between us still too close. In a moment, he was headed for the edge of the seat, struggling, despite my efforts to gently pull him back, to reach his destination: the floor that offered what he needed and wanted: seclusion and isolation. The floor still not good enough—my hand accidentally brushed him when I pushed a box of tissues out of his way—this little tug of war finally ended when he stubbornly scrambled under the car seat beyond where my hands could reach, there to stay for the next sixty miles.

Did it matter? Did it change the thrill I felt two and a half hours later as I carried this puppy into the house for the first time? It did not. Dogs, cats, birds, people, if there's a brain in there, sooner or later it reveals the character of its owner. In higher-order animals, it's stress—the right stress and the right amount—that eradicates the choice of whether to be or not be oneself. The stress Boo experienced this day in the car revealed something unmistakable about who he already was under his soft baby fur. In the trauma of leaving his littermates behind and the newness of everything around him, this puppy did not feel comforted in the slightest by the loving clasp of human hands. It was too confining, too much contact.

Even so, I felt such pleasure as I lowered Boo, sleepy and disoriented from the long drive, onto the rug in the middle of the living room where he stood, so tiny. But he was quickly coming to, his brain, like a computer just switched on, starting to spew out data, like his amazement at his new surroundings, its objects, its smells—all very different stimuli from his familiar kennel digs. But first things first—he did it so fast I never saw it coming—a little pee on the rug. He was, after all, despite his big ideas, just a puppy, the little rottweiler after all his trails and tribulations, finally home.

Unlike Moppet and Della, it wasn't I who named Boo, but Shawn, my Village Green cohort and dear friend. Shawn was from North Carolina, where Boo was a popular southern nickname. The first time she said it, it rang true for the little rottweiler who had been nameless for three days. And Boo he became.

The next weeks were filled with the hard work that comes with a new puppy. And indeed, I had forgotten just how much work was involved. Yes, I had been immersed in dogdom since age six, but the last puppy I'd raised was Della, some eighteen years before. Fortunately, the parenting skills had been nicely brought up to snuff by Lexie's arrival.

But at ten weeks of age, her feet could not walk her right up to the edge of a deck or run her into the path of an oncoming truck. Boo's could. His feet worked, and they were directed by a head full of curiosity about everything, especially, of course, the dangerous stuff.

If this sounds rigorous to the perspective first-time dog owner, it is rigorous, these early days and weeks. Good things usually are. But there's nothing to think over, nothing to decide, as you simply do it. You answer the urgent middle of the night calls. You clean up the messes. You switch your life around as required. In short, you do whatever is necessary to fulfill the commitment you made as protector and nurturer of this new life. And you do it willingly and happily, cutting no corners, because no corners should be cut. You can't build a sturdy house—or a sturdy dog—on a shaky foundation. Any adopter of an older dog can tell you, you can try to fix what needs fixing later. But if you have a puppy, it's so much easier to get it right from the start. The reward? The wonderful dog to emerge.

But puppyhood is hardly something to rush through. It's too much fun, and, as any puppy-to-dog owner knows, it flies by soon enough. Rush through it and you'll miss out on it. The attitude I tried to remember with Boo was: Savor these moments. Take mental (and actual) snapshots. Even so, it seemed that one day he was a tiny creature mightily engaged in figuring out the world and his place in it; then I blinked and he was a huge, strapping rottweiler who, as far as he was concerned, had it all figured out. And I was left to ponder with amazement, and yes, some regret, How did we get here so fast?

Thus, as I write this some ten years later, I draw upon those mental snapshots I took of Boo. There was the night he first came home, when he first learned the word "cat" and that it referred to Twinkie and Snowball (our newly adopted kitty), those two sleek creatures with the long tails emerging sleepy-eyed from the bedroom. Mighty glad they were to see us, their tails held aloft, both emitting those little greeting sounds cats make to their favorite humans, especially when they've been gone all day. Then they saw him: the little black figure on the rug, who stood mesmerized by these two apparitions. The cat brakes when on. The high tails instantly dropped. The sleepy eyes jumped awake.

Boo did what virtually any red-blooded dog would do. He chased them, charging forward on stubby puppy legs, full speed ahead. (This was the first time I saw him run.) The cats instantly about-faced and ran, their flight only stopping when two arching soars landed them to a sliding halt on the kitchen counter, there to survey the little black mass now in the kitchen, too, madly trying to catapult himself onto the counter.

There was no mistaking the conclusion simultaneously reached on the cats' faces, as no creature I ever met conveys utter dismay more effectively than a cat. It's not so much the stiff body language or the flattened ears. It's the *look* in a cat's eyes, like dark look in the two pairs of eyes trained this night on the baby rottweiler.

But no creature I ever met conveys the (very gene-related) irresistible urge, the fun, the thrill of the chase better than the dog. This tiny rottweiler no exception. A first rate demonstration it was: not a second's hesitation, good puppy speed, then once the cats were treed, no signs of letting up. In so doing, Boo discovered what all dogs discover: *it works.* You run forward, the chasee runs away. And there's power here, too: to affect things. You act. They react.

Thus, not five minutes into his time home came closure to the issue I had mulled over in the preceding weeks: Would Boo, only half their size, need protecting from the cats? Or was it the other way around: Would they, twice his size, need protecting from him? I already had my answer.

Which raised new questions: How quickly and to what extent would Boo learn to put a lid on, or at least curb, the cat-chasing thing? How soon, in other words, would he learn to make the distinction that virtually all dogs make between outside cats, considered fair game by even the most mild-mannered dog, and his own off-limits house cats? These were little issues compared to the larger ones to come: How quickly would he learn to curb any negative behavior dictated by not just his dog genes, but his rottweiler genes? And square on target: his male rottweiler genes? And bull's-eye: this particular male rottweiler's genes? These issues would rear their heads soon enough.

Here's another mental snapshot taken in the backyard at home two weeks after Boo arrived. We were in the backyard, white impatiens all along the side fence, azaleas and forsythia against the back fence. A huge ailanthus tree from the neighbor's yard looked down on this little scene replete with baby Boo in a sprawl on the cool slate patio near the house. He was lazily taking it all in. The wind chimes gently ringing in the soft breeze. The sparrows chirping away in the tall branches of the ailanthus tree. And the faint music of a radio playing. These were sounds now so familiar to Boo they were lulling him to sleep, when there came something new to his ears: the metal-scraping sound of a window closing. Boo was instantly on his feet barking. (This was the first time I heard him bark.) But with such fervor, these gusts of barks, that his little feet bounced on the ground, bobbing him up and down like a little jack-in-the-box.

This snapshot evidenced something I already knew about Boo: How smart he was. Had this been an audio version of "What's Wrong With This Picture?" he didn't have to mull it over or replay the tape. He had the answer in a second: the metal scraping was the "wrong" sound that didn't belong in this picture.

But far from the typical puppy response to a strange sound—instantly seeking the security of my legs, or high-tailing it into the house—this puppy retreated not. The window closing had awakened the guard-dog genes in the baby rottweiler who now, all seven pounds of him, stood firm, defending his territory—the house, the yard, the shrubs, me—with the ferocity of a lion, albeit a tiny one.

"It's just a window, Boo," I told him, gently stroking him. "It's okay!" But clearly it was not okay with him. He heard something that alarmed him and no amount of reassurance was going to convince him otherwise. In situations of perceived threat—real or otherwise—Boo trusted his own ears, his own instincts. There was nothing to do, as his little racket continued, but pick him up and carry him into the house.

The next snapshots are quick ones that show Boo doing what is typical of all puppies, rottweilers included. Boo peeing all over the rugs as though they were patches of grass in desperate need of watering. Boo depositing little brown mounds over these same rugs at amazing frequency. Boo chewing on everything—the sofa, chairs, rugs, table legs, us. Boo getting into things he wasn't supposed to: Who knew he would find the contents of the lower kitchen cabinets of such interest? Boo getting out of things he wasn't supposed to: Who remembered a puppy could slip out the front door with such stealth and speed?

The cure for this doggy mayhem was the same thing that works with all puppies: law and order. This was not accomplished with a crate, as crates still weren't the big thing they are these days (because they *work*). Eleven years ago, only breeders and other dog professionals knew the virtue of crates. Regular people like me resorted to the next best thing: a schedule, a regime based upon careful observation that noted, for instance, Boo's need (like all puppies) to eliminate after eating or upon awakening from a nap. Thus, right as he started that little circling thing, I whisked him pronto to the newspapers (or to his spot in the backyard), waited for him to take care of business, then praised him as though he had just painted the Mona Lisa. Boo was housebroken in two weeks. He was a rottweiler down to his toenails.

To stop Boo from chewing on everything, I carefully watched as he approached a dining table leg, then delivered a sharp "NO!" that stopped him dead in his tracks. I followed this with praise for sparing the table leg, then immediately offered the right thing to chew on: one of his toys.

To stop his attacks on our shoes, socks, and other objects casually dropped on the floor, we put our things away. When the sock didn't find its way to the laundry bin and he made a beeline for it, Boo got the "No!" treatment instantly. Thus, the differentiation constantly offered between his stuff (Go ahead and have fun!) and our stuff (Absolutely off limits). In short order, he understood. But there would be notable exceptions to his ability to quickly grasp what was "explained" to him and then adjust his behavior accordingly. So, yes, he stopped chewing on forbidden objects, but he continued to chew on us, his sharp puppy teeth directed at attacking the socks and shoes on our feet, and when we made the mistake of not wearing them, the skin of our feet. And no amount of "No!"s or pushing him away could deter him. Our resistance, the defending of our flesh, only made him renew the game with more determination.

The fact is Boo could not be trained out of this behavior. It only stopped when the teeth themselves solved the problem some two months later. They fell out, to be replaced by the Rocky Mountain adult teeth that, thank God, did not have this maniacal need for chewing.

Eventually, Boo's cat-chasing thing got better. That is, he only chased the cats if they moved quickly, "quickly" defined as anything above a slow walk, with sideward glances, carefully watching him. But if their anxiety got the better of them and they attempted something as foolish as a mad dash across the room, he was after them in a flash, my shouts of "No, Boo!" utterly ignored. Thus, when the ante—the cat speed—was upped, Boo, at twenty weeks and beyond, instantly regressed to the mind set of the eight-week-old puppy who first chased a cat.

The remedy here came not from Boo but the cats, who changed their behavior, favoring the off-limits-to-dog heights of the kitchen counters, the seclusion of the fireplace mantle, or the maze of chair feet under the dining table when their assessment determined Boo was in one of his cat-chasing modes.

Did I make a mistake here? I did. You don't give a dog the upper hand where cats or anyone else is concerned. You nip that behavior while still in puppy bud. I had ignored the advice I would later know to give—get it right from the start—because I was too enthralled and impressed with Boo, and too inexperienced with this breed to know that control once relinquished to a rottweiler, even one this young, is not easily reclaimed. You give it, you lose it.

In between attempting to enforce those few rules he could not abide was the wonderful stuff: easing him into his new life with all the patience and encouragement he deserved. And most especially, enjoying him.

The only flaw in this happiness was something about Boo that set him apart from every puppy I ever met. Boo was not a puppy who thrived on love and affection, being held, petted—the stuff most puppies live for. Far from it, a pat here and there was about all he could tolerate before the squirming started, followed by (before they fell out) the application of the sharp puppy teeth to the offending hand to make clear the message he first demonstrated on that ride home: that this little boy was different. He was not a hands-on puppy, he was a hands-off puppy. Love, the giving and receiving of affection—when and if it occurred—had to be on his terms. And his terms were sparing and stoic. Anything more upset him, unnerved him, caused him psychic and literal discomfort. It was too confining, too much contact.

It was a stunning revelation to the person who had had a veritable love fest with Moppet, Della, and Timber. And it drove home one of the first lessons Boo taught me, that just like these dogs, love comes in many sizes and shapes. But the differences in style of love, for dogs and humans alike, must never be allowed to obscure the love itself being offered. As are not all the same. We are who we are. And we love not according to some rulebook, but as we feel it. Boo did not feel it the way Della or Timber did. It was simply not in him. Thus, I had to readjust my heart where he was concerned, and this adjustment did not come easily. I had to work at it, switch to different channels, as it were, to find Boo's wavelength, and then fine-tune myself to it so I would not fail to pick up his rare transmissions from the heart. Even so, these transmissions often came with the static of ambivalence. But it made them no less precious. And something else of no small import: Had I not made this adjustment to Boo, I would have missed out on him, on who he was and the love he did have to offer. This was not something I wanted to do, as loving my dogs is very much a part of the why I have always had them, even if, as in Boo's case, that love came with a caution warning.

But when he was asleep, I didn't have to curb myself. I could adore him, revel in his puppyness, put my hands around his round little belly, pick up one of his hind legs, hold it in my hand, and gently put it down. I could lift his soft little ears, roll them around in my fingers and marvel at them, the fur so fresh, so new. When he was asleep, I could give him all the physical love and affection he couldn't handle awake.

With August fast coming to a close, The Village Green with its glorious yard was soon to reopen where Boo, just like the dogs before him, would accompany me six days a week. Thus, the dog area behind the counter had to be puppy-proofed, the lower shelves cleared of fertilizers and sundry plant supplies; in short, anything that could harm him. He would need structure here, too, a schedule to accommodate his needs, such as hourly treks to the yard so he could relieve himself, and time for fun and play in the yard. He would also need a good supply of squeaky toys for his active mind, chew bones for those busy teeth, bags of dog food, his food and water bowl (cleaned to a pristine state), and his bed, the big green-plaid one from L.L. Bean that still had Timber's fragrance on it.

When September rolled around, Boo took up his place at work. He was fascinated with the plant deliveries coming and going; customers coming and going, so many of them with small children in tow; the flurry of the UPS man's regular stops here; the mailman's daily visit; friends stopping by to say hello. And he fast learned the rhythm of life here: that relative calm could instantly give way to much hustle and bustle on both sides of the counter, then return to that calm, then jump back into high activity as the ringing of the bells on the front door signaled the arrival of the next throng of customers. He also learned the significance of this ebb and flow: that in quiet moments, I could play with him or take him into the yard for little runs on the bark chips. But when we were busy, he had to be a good boy and entertain himself behind the counter with his bountiful supply of squeaky toys. Many a customer made a purchase this fall against the squeaking backdrop of Boo's feisty chewing on those toys.

Here, just like home, there were instances in which Boo revealed who was really inside that puppy fur. At least five times during his first day at The Village Green, I carried him out to his designated bathroom-spot in the yard, a low traffic corner, where I gently put him down on the bark chips and waited as he squatted and took care of business. Next he had a few moments to walk around while I picked up whatever had resulted. Then, our mission accomplished, I reached down, scooped him up, and carried him back inside the shop to his area behind the counter. In addition to the bathroom runs, he also had several opportunities to run around the yard with no goal except his enjoyment. The end of this, his first working day at The Village Green, I carried him home thinking, *This is working. He was safe and happy. Everything went well.*

On day two, an hour after opening, I carried Boo out into the yard, placed him on his bathroom spot, and waited. Like clockwork, the little fellow squatted and produced a dropping on the bark chips. This done, he had the few minutes to walk around as I tended to clean up. Then, a minute later, he saw me start to lean down to pick him up and, clever boy, he knew what came next. But he'd spied a much better place to go than back inside the shop. So when my arms reached for him, he scrambled away from them and ran forward to where he did want to go: into a small crevice in the large pile of ornamental rocks for sale on the ground under a two-tiered display rack filled with chrysanthemums. And here he lodged himself, the upper half of his body firmly wedged into this small space, his rear end and hind legs sticking out.

I tried gently tugging on his legs to pull him out. It only had the effect of making him cram himself even tighter into the crevice. So there we were, Boo's head and torso exactly where he wanted them to be, in the cool dark solitude of his newly discovered—and not to be relinquished—little cave, and me staring at his protruding little black behind and legs wondering: *What now? Do I risk hurting him and drag him out? Or let him be?*

It was déjà vu: the little puppy crammed under the car seat all over again. This time with an audience: the dozens of people who came and went through The Village Green this late morning and early afternoon. The scenario went something like this: customers would enter the shop, do the usual looking around, then step out onto the deck and into the yard. Here, they engaged in the extremely pleasant experience this outdoor shopping area provided, strolling around in the fresh air and sun, pausing to look at this or that. Then, their eye was caught by the fetching display of chrysanthemums, where they noticed—not everyone, but a good number of them—the other display: the little black rear protruding from the rocks under the mums. Which brought them, concerned citizens that they were, quickly back inside to me and Shawn, with their anxious words: "There's something furry outside . . . an animal. It's stuffed in the rocks under the rack . . . where the mums are. But it's not moving."

"Yes, we know," was my response. "It's our new puppy. He likes the rocks. Likes to sit in there. A little quirk of his. But thank you for telling us." Some people let it go at that, others went back out to take another look.

You never knew what you'd find at The Village Green. One year, there was the sudden appearance in the lushly planted front window of myriad uninvited little brown mice running up and down the vines, scaring the finches and parakeets. Then there was the huge black panther of a dog—otherwise called Della—who wreaked heart-wrenching damage on this *no longer* lush planting. Then there was the female Jackson's chameleon who chose Mother's Day to give birth to twenty baby chameleons in the front window, and then—with a dozen horrified customers looking on—proceeded to stalk down and gobble up every single one of them before we could get in and stop the carnage. So why not, this crisp fall day, *half a puppy* protruding out a pile of rocks in the back garden?

Suffice it to say there was nothing to do but wait for Boo to come out. Which he did, three hours later, nicely rested, extremely pleased with himself, and ready, because it was *his* decision, to come back inside.

On day three, Boo rejected something any other dog would have treasured: the L.L. Bean dog bed I had meticulously vacuumed and carefully positioned in the dog area behind the counter so that Boo would have the perfect vantage point from which to survey and be entertained by the activity around the counter. His bed was also strategically placed so that, particularly as he grew up and attained his full size, our new canine guardian would be in full view of the public.

His first two days, absenting the second day's stint in the cave, Boo seemed to like his bed. He hopped around on it. He plopped down on it to gnaw away at his chew-toys. He pounced on the squeaky toys caught in its folds. And sometimes, when he just sat there thinking things over, I had to smile because he looked so little in the middle of it. He also fell asleep on this bed, usually on his side, his little legs sticking straight out, his round belly rising and falling. So when Boo and I arrived at the shop on day three, I gently placed him down on his bed, handed him a dog biscuit, and walked away with total confidence that he was fine. When I came back a little while later to check on him, he was sitting on the floor next to his bed.

"No, no, Boo," I laughed, picking him up and placing him back on the bed, "Here's where you sit," I said, patting the cushion encouragingly. "And look," I placed some toys right next to him, "how nice this is!" But no sooner did I take my eyes off him than he promptly ambled off the bed to plunk himself down on the floor. It went back and forth like this over the course of the day: I'd place him on the bed, he'd promptly remove himself to the floor. Indeed, this bed-floor tug of war would be a regular thing over the next weeks, months, and years to come.

My insistence on that bed was hardly to thwart him. My concern was for that issue of no small clinical import for any puppy destined to become a heavy, large-boned dog: his joints. To protect them from deleterious impact on hard surfaces that causes those large hard calluses you see on the elbows of so many heavy-breed dogs. It was also to prevent the nasty complications that can arise: the bleeding from those calluses, the very difficult to cure infections in those calluses. And arthritis from joint trauma that can hang on for years.

But Boo didn't care about joints or health, he cared about comfort. For him, this soft wonderful bed did not constitute comfort. What suited him was the opposite of soft: the hardness of the floor, which, at The Village Green and at home, this rottweiler would seek out all his days.

From his position, Boo made it his business to sift through the sights and sounds around the counter. What was he screening for? Irregularities: the person who looked too tall, spoke too loud, moved too fast. Any of which brought him barking to his feet, his toys instantly forgotten, to scrutinize the source of this irregularity with the very same skill he first demonstrated when he heard that window close in the backyard at home. But now he was perfectly willing to escalate his tactic. If the offending individual did not lower his voice or slow down his movement, Boo ran forward, his barking now furious and unrelenting. People's reaction to this mini policeman were of the "My, what a feisty little puppy!" order. But no one took him seriously. Six months later, everybody would take Boo seriously.

While Boo could run around the yard at The Village Green and the garden at home, walking on the streets, in the park, or anywhere else frequented by other dogs was still weeks away. Not one toe of his feet could touch the world at large until the shots to protect him from all doggy pathogens were complete. Conventional wisdom has it that the rottweiler's immune system matures more slowly than other breeds. Thus, Boo needed not the usual three months of puppy shots to protect him, but four months.

This, of course, flew in the face of his need, like all puppies, for socialization, his deliberate exposure to other people, places, dogs, cars, traffic—all the sights and sounds of the real world. What's the safe distance for this doggy education? In his owners arms. So, in addition to carrying him to and from the store each day, I carried him into this larger world. I took him down bustling Seventh Avenue so he could see for himself how dogs, just like the humans walking them, come in all sizes and shapes and colors; some outgoing and friendly, others reserved and quiet, and everything in between. I made sure to stop so Boo could lean down and get a closer look at these furry faces and sniff noses with those dogs so inclined. He was enthralled. When little kids spied the small black bundle in my arms and rushed over to investigate, Boo reveled in their attention.

As thrilled as Boo was with every bit of our see-the-world excursions, the fact that he had to experience them from the confines of my arms was maddening to him. Thus, these outings were also wrestling matches. As Boo struggled to free himself, I struggled just as hard to keep a hold on this squirming little black bundle who had started out at seven pounds, but quickly grew to ten pounds, then fifteen, then twenty. When Boo hit the twenty-five pound mark, it was like hauling around a huge sack of potatoes. But here's the important distinction: A twenty-five pound sack of potatoes, burdensome though it may be, doesn't attack you. It doesn't have teeth to direct its frustration at its carrier's neck. Staggering around the streets with the sharp puppy teeth at my neck, I began to pray for the day Boo's puppy shots would be complete and free us both from our tribulations.

Thus, the regular visits to the Heights Veterinary Hospital to get those shots completed, and our regular exposure to the merry pandemonium this and any veterinary waiting room presents. For me, the centerpiece of this experience, of course, is the dogs. Large, small, furry, smooth, long tails, no tails, purebred, mixed breed—it matters not. Despite the best efforts of their owners, the adult dogs in the know are in various states of agitation: panting, circling, whining; with one or two so stressed out, they are yawning their exhaustion. Guaranteed distraction, if only momentary, from this anxiety? The cats in the carriers. All the little faces with the triangle ears peering through the grills, some with looks of resignation at this awful confinement. Others so upset they manage to hide themselves under the little towel. No kitty apparent in there, just unearthly sounds coming from the carrier, making all the dog ears in the room prick up, eyes darting around looking for its origin, and when sight reveals nothing, upturned wet noses sifting the air for clues. Until the door opens and all eyes—dogs' and owners'—automatically turn to see who's coming in now. And everybody shifts over to make room on the bench, as the newcomer sits down with anxious dog or cat in tow. The conversations that were threading around the room, exchanges that started with openers like, "How old is she?" followed by the polite correction that the "she" is a "he," now pick up again, drawing in the newcomer.

I pause here to say that there's something about the waiting room of a vet that restores my faith in human kind. Of course, it has much to do with the hands stroking all those furry heads, the comforting words being offered, the fact that these people are here in the first place tending to the needs of their pet. Heartwarming as these things are, the little miracle is what happens to people in this room, the camaraderie that occurs, the easy connection each person feels and makes with the person sitting next to him or her. The source of this camaraderie? It is the bond with the dogs at the end of those leashes, the bond with the little faces in the cat carriers. It is the animals who engender this human connection that breaks down the barriers between people and makes stranger so eager to talk to stranger.

Nothing enlivens this dynamic, or makes one feel more part of it, than the presence of a puppy, like the one that was now sitting—make that squirming—in my lap, no doubt wondering what all the fuss, what all the panting and meowing was about. He thought this was a terrific place, all the activity, the people and animals coming and going. Indeed, I thought his little head would burst with all these sights and sounds. With him thusly engaged (and my hands mightily engaged in preventing him from hopping down into the thick of all this wonderfulness), I happily fielded the inquiries that came our way: "How old is he?" Quickly followed by "What is he?" But no sooner was the breed question answered, than it was our turn to go in.

Far from being anxious, Boo found the adventure only continued in the examination room. It including mention of "How nice to see (me) again, looking so happy" (that is, not utterly devastated as I was six months ago when I was here to have Timber put to sleep). And words about "how sweet" Boo was (a parent of a new puppy can't hear enough of this). And what a "nice example of a rottweiler" he was (this also falling on appreciative ears). Then came the examination itself, followed by whatever shots we were up to. Boo's reaction to all this? It was the second half of the vet adventure. Not the crowd in the waiting room, but something even better: Dr. Turoff, whom, for reasons known only to himself, Boo fell in love with! Thus, he didn't resist being gently plunked down on the scale that would weigh him. He didn't do the squirming act when Turoff examined him. And he barely felt it when Turoff slipped those needles in.

Boo's regular meetings with his beloved Turoff finally ushered in the last day I had to carry around my twenty-five pound lug of a puppy, and salvation came in the nick of time, as one more day, one more pound, and I would have had to haul him around in a wagon. He received his last shot, and what a thrill it was for me—and instant relief for him—to lower him to the floor and clip that leash on his collar. Then, with Lexie and David holding the door, Boo ambled up the step that led to the sidewalk and walked out on his own four feet into the world that was waiting for him to partake of it. And partake he did, at breathtaking speed, with me running to keep up with him, the mental snapshots clicking away.

The time had come for Boo to learn housebreaking. No more newspapers. No more whisking him to his bathroom spots at home or at work. It was time to acquaint him with something all city dogs need to learn: the curb: what it is used for and, further, it must not, as so many dogs do, be confused with something very close by: the sidewalk, where people walk. Thus, at the appointed hour, whether at home or The Village Green, on went the leash and out went Boo for his practice sessions in the "big boy" bathroom, my hope being that the same precision elimination applied to the newspapers and backyards would now be transferred to this new locale. Did he get it? He got it with lightening speed, with such fervor, this use-the-curb, not-the-sidewalk idea, that he would practically pull my arm out of its socket to get to that curb. Did he, still a juvenile, have the occasional mishap in the night, typical enough of any puppy, or make a little puddle on the floor at the store because customer traffic delayed my tending to his needs? Did the bladder or the will that controled it give out before he got out? It did not. This was a rottweiler who, true to his breed, possessed an extraordinary capacity to instantly grasp what was required of him and then summon amazing self-discipline to adhere to the newly learned concept. So much so that even then, as a half-grown puppy, as in the years to come, on those rare instances (I can count them on one hand) when Boo did have a mishap indoors, I never pointed out the transgression. I knew with utter certainty that it was not his fault, that it must have had some clinical basis. Either he'd eaten something that didn't agree with him, or he was reacting adversely to some shot. As this was a dog who would rather die than eliminate in the house.

Next, we moved into the next basic of dog training: heeling. Boo didn't have, as Timber did in Della, another experienced dog to show him the ropes. But, true to his genes, this juvenile rottweiler didn't need a demonstration to show him what was required. All it took was one or two corrections with the leash on our walks to and from the store before he marched right alongside me, like the little soldier who whizzed through boot camp, the drill perfectly understood long about the second day, the drill perfectly executed from that day forward. And indeed, this chunky puppy (now the size of a hefty boxer dog) trotting alongside me with such precision caught the amazed eye of many a dog owner, especially the harried ones being dragged helter-skelter down the sidewalk by dogs who didn't have—or hadn't been taught—clue one about heeling. Something this puppy already had down pat.

The next subject in his schooling was the sit command: the application of the doggy rear to the floor, the ground, the sidewalk, the whatever. Not achieved with the pleading string of "Sit-sit-sit-sit!!" And when this fails, the wrestling act, the human madly pushing away on the rear end, the dog resisting with equal determination. The goal is one sit command delivered in a normal voice, promptly followed by the act. Again—no surprise—all it took was one or two practice sessions at home and the store before Boo got it. He plunked that rear right where it belonged and kept it there until my cheery "Okay!" released him.

Smart dog, I thought. *Very smart dog.* It's one thing to read about the intelligence, the trainability of the rottweiler, quite another to experience it, to see it in action, the look on his face, in his eyes as he understood, then instantly put that knowledge to action.

The sit under his belt, we moved straightaway into its logical extension, the stay: the park yourself and don't move until told to do so. We practiced this one at home and at the store. Each time, I'd start with the sit, then walk away from him; at first only a few feet, then five feet, then ten, then fifteen, all the while, at this early stage, repeating the stay command. Then I'd stop, turn, and face him, always waiting several moments (so he wouldn't confuse my standing still as the automatic conclusion to his stay) before issuing the "Okay!" to release him, instantly followed by "Come!" Which brought him running across the floor or yard to me and to the praise I couldn't wait to give him.

Now we moved into the down command: the all-fours on the floor and keep them there until released. He got this one with lightening speed, and he would hit the floor with such zest—like someone pulled the rug out from under him—that I did very few downs with him, concerned his instant collapse to the floor would damage his joints,

Next, the up command: the hop up, jump up on whatever—and its equally useful converse, the off command—the hop off, jump off whatever. As the store's layout offered ideal places to practice them, we did the training demonstrations for these brother-sister commands here. Thus, I'd wait for a lull in customer traffic, go to Boo, clip his leash on, and lead him over to the big slab of slate that artfully substituted for a step and led out to the deck. With the slate step right in front of him, I told him "Up" and moved the leash over the step, gently urging him up. Then, the off command, the angle of the leash urging him to do the reverse, to hop back down, followed by new praise. In three days, at the stroke of one "up," this boy was hopping onto decks, hopping into cars, hoping onto benches in the park; and equally conversant in its opposite, he was hopping off decks, off logs in the park, off anything I asked.

"Shake Hands" was mere child's play for this rottweiler. In one training session, those paws came up with a *pow*. Further, if I didn't instantly clasp the offered paw, Boo zipped it down and shot up the other paw.

Then there were the myriad other directives, like "go downstairs," "move" (out of the way), "get back" (back up), "go" (walk forward), "stand" (don't move), "be quiet" (stop barking), "stop that!" (whatever the offending act was), which Boo quickly assimilated and put into action. Further, he could put together two, even three directives. I could tell him to "Go upstairs and sit down and stay there" and he would dutifully walk up the stairs, sit down on the landing, and stay there until I released him.

The lesson his wonderful brain did not grasp? The aforementioned "we do not chase cats" did not compute in Boo's brain. While he did manage to tone down the frequency and strength of the assaults on his own house cats and our store cat, Mama, Boo would chase any other cat all his life. In the park, he discovered squirrels, and found them thrilling subjects for the chase as they ran like hell to get away from this dog thundering through the woods in hot pursuit. And while I knew that, unlike Timber, he lacked the speed and agility to actually catch one, it did nothing to quell my anxiety—or the yelling that accompanied it. But no reason to tar and feather the fellow.

Not so the following. Young Boo—and older—had a special hobby he saved for the wee small hours of the night when the rest of us were fast asleep. Garbage Parties: the expert manipulating of the kitchen trash receptacle's lid as though he had not paws but hands to raise that lid. This achieved, he dragged out every ounce, every shred of refuse—the more disgusting the better—to strew it across the kitchen floor. This abundance laid out over a five-foot radius, he now went through it, gobbling up ex-food stuffs of such a revolting nature, the miracle was that none of it ever did him in. Was he sorry when I came out in the morning and my jaw dropped? Sure he was sorry. He didn't enjoy the expletives and dirty looks I shot his way. And I put him in a sit-stay to make sure he got the full measure of my disgust as I set about gathering the heavy duty tools: the shovel, broom, dustpan, reams of paper towels, and oceans of disinfectants to clean it up. But was he sorry enough to not do it the next time the garbage party spirit moved him? No. The parties continued. So I escalated my tactic. I bought a different refuse can, the step-on-the-pedal-and-up-pops-the-lid kind. No good. He just stepped on the pedal and up popped the lid. I tried moving the can around. He found the new locations and proceeded accordingly. *Is this dog smarter than I am?* I wondered. *Am I some kind of moron who can't outwit her dog and make her garbage stay put?*

Salvation came in the form of bricks—three of them—applied to the lid to weigh it down, a charming accessory to any kitchen trash receptacle that prompts one's guests passing through the kitchen to wonder *Who lives here? What manner of people are these?* When our trash receptacle with its three-brick lid surfaced in polite conversation, my explanation was simple: We had a rottweiler named Boo who loved Garbage Parties. The only way to stop him? Apply the three bricks to his head or apply them to the lid. Much better the lid.

Cats, squirrels, and garbage aside, young Boo's brain connected with everything else I asked of him. But as exciting as his formal schooling was, it paled in comparison to the real joys I hadn't experienced in nine months: a dog, this dog to share my life with. To join me for the ten-minute walk each weekday morning to take Lexie to school. With Lexie dropped off, he and I headed for Prospect Park for our regular hour-long trek through the park before going to work. The same walks I had taken with Timber were now Boo's walks: his time and mine to take in the trees, grass, birds, squirrels, and, of course, the other dogs. And although I have to think hard to remember the days—as they were numbered—when Boo could run free with other dogs, I do have snippets of memories of him ambling good-naturedly up to a fellow canine, ready to play and roll around in the grass with this new doggy friend. Then he'd jump to his feet and chase his little pal around. Then the roles would reverse and he would be the chasee. And so it went, these carefree spontaneous encounters with no goal but a good time had by all. When the hour was up, we would leave the park and head straight to The Village Green, where Boo would flop down behind the counter, nicely tired out and ready to start his workday.

A month or two down the line, when Boo was nine months old, we had cause to visit the Heights Veterinary Hospital. This time, he wasn't a squirming puppy sitting in my lap in the lively waiting room. He was a seventy-pound strapping rottweiler who heard the "sit" command, immediately parked his rear end right next to me, and was using every ounce of self-control to keep it there. Despite the lady who sat down right next to us with the cat carrier, its occupant howling away inches from his ears. Despite the dog who got away from his owner and ran across the room to merrily touch noses with Boo, something that would have brought any other canine springing to his feet. But this exceptional self-discipline and subjugation of his will to mine was witnessing its last days. There was change in the wind. The gentle breezes of puppyhood were soon to shift. Adolescence was around the corner, not here yet, but fast approaching, something innocently forecast in the course of this visit.

It started with Boo bounding down the hall to greet his beloved Dr. Turoff, who responded with many affectionate thumps to Boo's side, sending Boo into delirious tail wagging, which, for a rottweiler, means rotating the entire lower half of the body. This effusive greeting done, it was time to amble into the examination room and get down to business: a check-up, followed by the booster shots, which Boo received as though they were presents. Somewhere during all this I asked Dr. Turoff how soon Boo, who was still squatting to pee, would graduate to the lifting of the leg thing. His answer: "When the hormones kick in. Any day now."

Sure enough, just as five months ago Turoff had predicted Boo's razor-sharp puppy teeth would fall out "Any day now" (the next morning those teeth came flying out of his head; for days it rained teeth on the rugs)—like clockwork, Boo's hind leg started to come up that very week. The second prediction Turoff offered this day, when we joked about how much Boo adored him brought a knowing smile to Turoff's face, when he said, "He may not love me the next time."

How right he was. The next time Dr. Turoff saw Boo some six months later, it was not a preadolescent puppy who ran down the hall to deliver his effusive greeting. The dog slowly walking down the hall this day was a sixteen-month-old, hundred-pound rottweiler who eyeballed Turoff with a touch-me-if-you-dare look. Turoff did not dare. He called for an assistant, who would need all his skills and all his strength to hold Boo down for the shot. And when the menacing growl through the snapping teeth still got too close for comfort, Turoff called for another assistant to bring him a muzzle. All traces of puppy love for Dr. Turoff were gone because the puppy himself was gone, blown away by adolescence, which, like a hurricane leveling the old, had ushered in this new Boo. Or was it the real Boo? Had adolescence only brought out the defiant, dominant dog lying dormant under the puppy fur all along?

This question would be answered soon enough.

For now, Dr. Turoff missed the sweet affections of the puppy who used to run to him. And no doubt about it, from this day forward, handling Boo would be a great challenge for him, for which I would offer many an apology. But the sad truth to be told is Boo would be the real loser, because this day, when Boo struggled to bite the hand—Turoff's—he once loved, was the day the curtain abruptly fell on Boo's carefree puppyhood. When the curtain came up again, the rest of the play, Boo's adult life, would read very differently.

As startling as Boo's display of aggression was this day, I rationalized it, chalked it up to his fright: he hadn't been here for a while, the assistant was too rough with him, the muzzle was too tight. Everything but the truth: *This dog has a dominance problem. Stop it now before the dominance evolves to dangerous*, and everybody suffers.

But I didn't stop it because I didn't see it as a problem. Not yet. I would need further proof, which Boo would provide in spades. For instance, much has been made of Boo's superior brainpower as exemplified by his exceptional trainability. Indeed, a few days after this vet visit, for fun and to see just how fast he could learn something, Lexie and I taught Boo to hop through her hoola hoop, in all of three repetitions.

Unquestionably, the issue was never *Did Boo understand what was requested of him?* The issue—as evidenced by the very audible growling that accompanied the hop through the hoop—was *Did he feel like doing it?* The answer was: He didn't.

Similarly, Boo continued to throw his paw out to shake hands, but he growled when I clasped it because even as he knew to offer it, it was clear he didn't want to. He came in short order when I called "Here, Boo!" in the house or at the store. But with increasing frequency, he arrived at my feet angry. In the park with its off-leash freedom, he started to not come immediately when called. The mere seconds that brought him running back as a puppy now lengthened to a minute, two minutes, and beyond. I could see he heard me, indeed, he was looking at me as I called him again, but he didn't interrupt his sniffing in the weeds around a tree. Not because he didn't understand the "Come!" command. I daresay he understood it better than any other dog being called back in the park this day. No, long after those far less gifted dogs were dutifully at their owners' sides, Boo was still wandering the rushes because he didn't want to comply. There were forces within him greater than his desire to do my bidding. They were the strength of his own will; his own wishes; his need to call the shots; his need to control the moment, in this case, to not come when called. This was the power dynamic playing itself out in the park. And, increasingly, it would find other ways to express itself.

At the same time Boo started that male-hormone driven rite of passage from puppy to dog—lifting his leg—his attitude toward other dogs underwent a startling transformation. He no longer ran tail wagging, mouth open, with bright eyes to engage fellow canines in the park. He walked stiff-legged up to them—large, small, male, female; it mattered not—the goal no longer *I'll chase you, then you chase me.* Or, *Isn't this a lovely day? Why don't we just loll around in the grass and enjoy it together?* The goal now was dominance: to overwhelm them and elicit their instant submission.

Did these dogs enjoy this contact, the threatening body language and its implicit *I am top dog here?* They did not. They did the submissive thing: tails tucked in, bodies hunched over, ears and eyes apologetic, little whines coming out of the ones who found him terrifying—and instantly gave up.

Did their owners appreciate this? Did they have any tolerance, any understanding whatsoever for this huge black apparition who came out of nowhere with the singular purpose of overpowering their dogs and making them cringe with fear? They sure as hell didn't. They were angry and resentful, frightened for their dogs, frightened for themselves. And I agreed with them. No one was more appalled than I that, in the blink of an eye, my "Little Man" Boo had turned into the playground bully. The writing, small but legible, that I had ignored on the vet's wall—*This dog has a dominance problem. Stop it now before it evolves to dangerous—* was now billboard-sized, its print huge, its message now irrefutable. Time to do what I should have done months ago: take back what you never, *ever* give to a rottweiler—control.

So I started to work with him. I didn't let him off leash in the park. I didn't subject other dogs to his problems until I got a handle on it, or—more accurately—he got a handle on it. With Boo now a year and a half old, I kept that leash on when we went to Prospect Park and fervently worked on training this dog-on-dog aggression out of him. I started with Boo heeling perfectly at my side, which he did as long as the sight of another dog didn't block the heeling section of his brain. It was only a matter of minutes before an off-leash dog ambled over. At the first sign of aggression on Boo's part—the mohawk that shot up his back, the tensing of his body, the low guttural growl—I was prepared to utter the loud "NO!" and give a sharp tug on his leash. The idea was to prevent the lunge at this dog before he had a chance to execute it. A split-second later, the lunge started. The loud "No!" and harsh tug got Boo's attention. It momentarily distracted him. But an instant later, he went for it, completing the lunge with double the voracity—this his solution to the fact that he not only had this dog to attack, but also the added burden of my trying to stop him.

And so it went: lunge after lunge at dog after dog, week after week in our training sessions in the park. Not very promising. In fact, very discouraging. I did have the strength in my arm to restrain a dog as powerful as Boo. But what, I rightfully worried, if I had a lapse in concentration? What if I looked right one day and failed to see a dog coming left? Furthermore, any strength I possessed was only a stopgap measure, and a flimsy one at that, like throwing paper over the tiger. And this tiger had split-second reflexes that made my reaction time look like slow motion. Bottom line: I was no physical match for Boo. Any human who thinks he can count on being able to outmuscle or outreact an angry rottweiler is in for a big surprise.

But I didn't want to fight with Boo every day. I didn't want to go to war every day. I didn't want to be on guard every second. I wanted to take my dog to the park so both of us could clear our heads and get some exercise before going to work. It was such a simple idea. But suddenly it seemed so unattainable, so impossible, like walking on the moon. To make matters worse, our sessions in the park, far from having the desired result—any reduction in his other-dog aggression—had had the opposite effect of making him more determined, more ferocious than ever.

Ten years ago, obedience training was the only tool available to the owner of a combative dog like Boo. Not so today. Although obedience training is still the cornerstone of gaining control over a dominant-aggressive dog, now there is hard scientific data suggesting that diet—what a dog eats—can play a significant role in affecting that dog's behavior. A diet too high in protein can up the ante, make an aggressive dog even more aggressive. So, too, can the artificial preservatives, like ethoxyquin, in that food. In addition, aggression problems are now being clinically linked with allergies to the chicken or beef content in the supermarket dog food that I and the rest of the world ran out to buy ten years ago.

Thus, dog behaviorists (who themselves were a rare breed a decade ago) and many veterinarians now tout the virtue of a low-protein, lamb-based diet—and one that is free of artificial preservatives—as corrective food for the combative. Big news to the dog world. Even bigger news, as veterinary medicine now wisely borrows a page from people medicine, is pharmacology for dogs; that is, the discovery that drugs like Prozac, which can temper aggression (and other negative traits) in Fido's master, lo and behold, can temper Fido's aggression, too. These drugs achieve their results by increasing the serotonin level in the brain, thereby reducing the aggression-reaction in any dog or human so afflicted. This is not to say one pill is going to change Jack the Ripper into Mother Teresa, or turn the Hound of the Baskervilles into Benji. What these mood-correcting drugs can do for Jack is enhance whatever progress he is making in talk therapy. What they can do for the Hound—for whom, alas, talk therapy is not possible—is enhance the effects of his corrective obedience training. And what they give to the Hound's owner is something he or she didn't have before: new hope.

But no such diet-to-drug arsenal existed ten years ago when I needed it. Suffice it to say, I would have leapt at any remedy as accessible as an adjustment in diet. Had there existed a mood-adjusting pill that held out the slightest promise for Boo, I would have bought a lifetime supply. But these clinical approaches didn't exist. Thus, I continued to work with what I did have: myself, and my past experience; the success with which I'd toned down Della's albeit much milder case of pushing other dogs around; the success with which I'd readjusted Timber's similar inclination to use her size to get her way in the other-dog arena.

But, unlike Della and Timber, what drove the power struggle in Boo's brain, that made him rage at other dogs, did not live on the outer rim of his personality. It was central; it was core. So core that the mere sight of any dog raised the hair on Boo's back and got him growling. And if that dog was a male, this was tantamount to waving a red flag in the face of a bull. It threw Boo into a frenzy of rage requiring all my strength to hold him back.

The vicious circle quickly tightened its stranglehold: The more Boo lunged at other dogs, the less he could interact with them. But only through exposure to other dogs could he learn how to behave normally with them. But I couldn't use other dogs as a training ground for Boo, knowing the threat he posed. Not until he was rendered safe. Which was not happening, despite all my efforts: the months of working with him in the park, each time trying to take a fresh approach, to not be discouraged by the previous day's fiascos, to just try harder, to be more creative. I was losing the battle that was bigger than my skills to stop it. Later, I would resort to last ditch measures to turn him around; for the moment, I acknowledged defeat.

The result was Boo's isolation from other dogs. No fellow canines to investigate interesting smells in the leaves with, or run in a happy pack across the fields with. No dog pals to chase after, then be chased by, then plop down on the grass with, tongues hanging out, and wonderfully exhausted. All this was replaced with solitary walks with me. I sought out areas not frequented by other dogs, and unleashed Boo there, and threw sticks for him to make sure he got a good work out. When I wasn't pitching sticks, we simply walked together and looked at things: the ducks in The Paddle Boat Lake; the kids playing ball on the newly constructed baseball diamonds at the far end of the Long Meadow; the flocks of seagulls who, when bad storms force them inland, alight on these same fields in the hundreds, until fair weather beckons them back to the harbor. Those rare instances when I could squeeze it in before going to work on a Saturday or Sunday, Boo and I would occasionally fast-walk the three-mile roadway (that is closed to cars on weekends) through the park, weaving around throngs of runners and bicyclists for the hour it takes to complete the circle. When we were done, he was nicely tired, which was the indicator I had done his exercising right.

But a great pleasure had been subtracted from my life. Beginning with Moppet, one of my great joys—like watching your child playing with other children—was watching my dogs interact with other dogs. I could throw sticks for Boo, I could play with him—indeed, there is a place for this in the dog-human bond. But it was no substitute for the simple, absolute pleasure of watching Boo play with his own kind. Neither was I a substitute for the other-dog joy Boo was incapable of. This is why I can barely remember Boo playing with other dogs. Because it was such a short time, the earliest sliver of his life, that was over even as it had just barely begun.

Was Boo's dominance-related aggression only directed at off-leash dogs in the park? I would have been grateful had the war zone stopped here. But it didn't. It started here, and quickly expanded to leashed dogs strolling down the street with their owners. To dogs tied outside stores. To dogs patiently sitting in parked cars while their owners ran into the bank. To dogs sitting, walking, waiting, anywhere.

Boo and I continued to walk down these streets; we had to, we lived and worked here. We walked to and from The Village Green each day. We did the treks down Seventh Avenue to Ace Market for a quart of milk or the Union Street newsstand for the *New York Times*. But the pleasure in these outings was fast being replaced by tension, as I had to be increasingly vigilant, constantly on the lookout for other dogs. When we encountered the many found in this increasingly dog-populated Park Slope, there was the inevitable confrontation as Boo jumped and snarled at them despite my loud "No!"s and sharp corrections with the leash. All I could offer was apology after apology to their owners.

Thus, there were instances, with another dog fast approaching, when I took the path of least resistance: I vacated the sidewalk to cross to the other side of the street. Did this evasive maneuver in any way help Boo deal with his aggression? It did not. In hindsight, it may have even reinforced it, as, smart boy that he was, Boo quickly learned there was always a four-legged reason why I suddenly stepped off that sidewalk. Despite being dragged away, he twisted his head around and issued his growled challenge. But when one is tired and exhausted from a long day at work and the other challenges real life has to offer, the energy was often not there to negotiate the obstacle course that a simple walk down the street with Boo had become. Even oncoming trucks looked easier than this one rottweiler hell-bent on attacking this dog and the next dog. On days like this, there was no surmounting the obstacle course, so I went around it. Thus, the short-term goal was met: I avoided the dog confrontation and got, even with the detour, a little closer to that quart of milk. But the other goal—Boo's training—also got detoured, put off to the next day when, hopefully, the obstacle course would look and be less daunting.

Along with other-dog aggression, another problematic trait was fast evidencing itself and gathering steam. Much was made earlier of the effective guard-dog Boo was even as a tiny puppy. As a strapping six-month-old, guard-dogging was more important to him than his toys, and he liked his toys plenty! At nine months of age, before adolescence hit, he possessed the ideal crime-deterring physical attributes: good size, rippling muscles, and a huge head equipped with intense brown eyes and Rocky Mountain teeth. He also had the mental equipment to go with that body: the ability to spot the one potential bird of prey in the flocks of decent, friendly, congenial, appreciative people otherwise known as our customers. Once he had this bird in his scopes, he stood up to keep a better eye on it. Then the bird saw him and flew away.

Far and above scaring away the bad birds, Boo had the acuity to make fine distinctions: like the subtle gradation to the left of low in the voice on the other side of the counter that inched that voice into ominous, something Boo didn't like, that made him tear over to the counter to announce this dislike, his blazing eyes instantly locking on its source, now his target. Needless to say, this individual with the not wholesome intentions beat a hasty retreat to the front door. Then, there was the silent treatment: the person who hovered not at the counter, but near it. This one said nothing, but his eyes said everything. He was casing the store, noting the location of the counter in relation to the front door, the proximity of customers, these dark calculations intermixed with furtive glances at the cash register and at us. Boo either picked up the discrepancy of the prolonged silence—no talk, no sound where there should have been—or he sensed something else very real, our mounting anxiety as this mute standoff continued. Either way, he was on it in a flash, leaping off the floor to hit the counter, front paws thunderously pounding it as he barked his ferocious *Back away now, or I fly over the counter*. Which I have no doubt he would have done. Had this individual done anything, had he produced so much as a toothpick, Boo would have scrambled over that counter and tackled the guy to the floor. But it never came even close to this, and we never wanted it to. The purpose of Boo, now official Village Green guard dog, was not defense, but deterrence, to discourage the criminal act, to stop it dead in its tracks before it occurred. Della did this. Timber learned to do it. Now, following the blueprint he was born with in his head, Boo did it with absolute precision.

He also did it with precision on the street. On a late night walk home, Boo zeroed in on the person walking behind us on the sparsely lit street who was following too closely. Ten paces back, this individual had stepped over that invisible line clearly understood by people—and sharp-minded dogs—in this culture that delineates our space from his space. Daytime "too close" is creepy enough, but "too close" on a dark street at night gets the heart thumping. But there was no need to start screaming. Boo was on to this guy the moment the tip of his shoe crossed over that line. Thus, even as we walked on, Boo turned his head around to make eye contact with this fellow and stared him back into the shadow from whence he came, there to wait for the person who did not have a rottweiler to walk her home.

He also did it with precision at home. He barked when the doorbell rang, only stopping when I told him too. He barked when he heard a strange sound coming from the street in the wee small hours. If that barking continued, David or I got up to take a look because when Boo barked there was a reason: something or someone was where it shouldn't be.

Indeed, Boo's guard-dogging knew no borders. In Prospect Park, I was the person who didn't have to worry she had stayed too late for safety after dusk. At Calendar House, when my mother informed me she had forgotten to lock the back door, I was the person who could reassure her with absolute certainty, "It doesn't matter. Boo's on the porch." In the deserted parking lot of a rest stop at midnight on the Massachusetts State Turnpike, I was the person in the passenger seat, with seven-year-old Lexie fast asleep in the back seat, who did not have to think twice about leaning back and closing her eyes for a quick cat nap while David went in for coffee. Why not? Boo was in the back seat. Awake and alert. Guarding us.

Then adolescence, that despoiler of reason and balance that a month earlier had ruined Boo's ability to run free with other dogs—hit full-force. Overnight, like a blowtorch igniting a keg of dynamite, Boo's *day-before* perfect level of protection skyrocketed into chaos. Suddenly, the mental machinations that could identify the one decibel between loud and too loud, that could distinguish dark clothing from dark intentions, a smile from a leer, were gone. From fine distinctions he went to no distinctions. Now anything on two legs was suspect: the teenager laughing at a joke his friend told him, the man calling out to his wife across the street, the little kid shouting so his elderly relative could hear him. Boo's overly sensitive alarm system was also triggered by any kind of sudden movement: someone tripping on a crack in the sidewalk, someone opening a car door to get out, someone plunking down a package of groceries before entering his house.

If such stimulus didn't present itself, Boo went looking for it, scrutinizing strangers, most especially men, on the street for the slightest provocation—any eye blink—that would green-light what his guard-dog circuits gone haywire directed him to do: seize control, overwhelm the enemy—now deemed anything that breathed—into instant submission. This achieved with his *get out of my way* glare, backed up by the ominous growling. Then, had I not prevented it, the lunge with its ultimate goal: to sink his teeth into the offending party until it gave up.

Boo put the fear of God in people. He terrified them. At high noon, pedestrians cut a wide birth around him. After dark, he cleared the sidewalks. I could have walked blindfolded into the darkest ally. I could have strolled the scariest docks of New York City at two A.M. with fifty-dollar bills pined to my back. But *what price this protection!* I had a natural-born guard-dog who had had the briefest fling with a normal level of protection, but was now out of control. The streets that only a month before bemoaned the other-dog obstacle course were now a minefield with a hidden explosive—Boo—that could ignite at any time. He was an accident waiting to happen. He was a loaded gun, his hair trigger poised and waiting for anyone to set it off.

We had started out, young Boo and I, with my protecting him from the world. Now, one short year later, it was I protecting the world from him.

Then, it became a matter of protecting us from him. That is, while Boo saved the high-voltage dominance-aggression for the world at large, he didn't leave it all at the front door when he came home. He brought just enough of it into our home life to make him unreliable, and sometimes dangerous, here, too. Thus, when I dared to suggest he vacate a chair so one of us could occupy it, this suggestion was met with his growling.

When I insisted he remove himself, he slowly got off, eyeballing me not with love as he skulked off to hunker someplace else. Fortunately, this was a sometimes event, as Boo didn't cotton to soft places unless they served as a proving ground for yet another I'm Top Dog routine.

What was not a sometimes event was the daily terror he engendered around his food bowl in the kitchen, the imagined threat here that I who filled that bowl would somehow want to take it away from him. Thus, be it filled to the brim or three crumbs full, Boo guarded his bowl with a vengeance, threatening David, me, Lexie, the cats, a *fly*—in no unmistakable terms—to stay clear of it. Not a pleasant scene in one's home. In fact, needless and pointless and nerve-wracking to all except Boo.

I put some strict rules into effect to lower the danger level around that bowl. First, at feeding time, I insisted that Boo sit, which he instantly did, as I got out the dog food bag and filled his bowl. Then, he had to stay seated, which he did with rapt attention, his eyes following me as I moved away from his bowl, until my "okay" released him to go ahead and have at it. While he was eating, Boo was as dangerous as a hungry lion thrown a zebra leg. Short of throwing a net around him, there was no getting around this. Thus, the number one rule in our household was especially directed at Lexie: to *never, ever* go near Boo when he was eating.

The moment he was finished, I told him to back up, and directed him to keep backing up until he reached the safe distance—ten feet away. Then I told him to stay there. Which he did. I then moved in, picked up the bowl, and put it away in the broom closet, there to stay, this object of such rabid contention, until the next meal. Thus, a small measure of peace was put back into our lives. And yes, it was an absurd price to pay for this peace.

But I couldn't put David away as easily. There were times, every other week or so, when Boo's dominance-aggression toward all men was directed at David, whose transgression could be as simple as coming home late and bumping into Boo in the hallway that was dark because a light bulb chose that moment to burn out. Which explained the late night growling coming from that hallway. Or, David might enter a room too suddenly for Boo's taste, which sent the mohawk up his back. Or the conflict could be David's telling Boo too aggressively to move out of the way because he was blocking the stairway. Or any other directive that pivoted on Boo's giving way—translation: *giving in*—to David. Half the time, Boo did give in, albeit angry in defeat. Other times, Boo stood his ground, not about to give a psychological or literal inch. Thus, the tense stand-offs: the family dog afflicted with the top dog syndrome challenging the other top dog for supremacy.

Not a pretty picture.

While David could have put on football gear and thick leather gloves to try to force Boo to do whatever was at issue, who wants to do literal battle with the family dog? And who is foolish enough to engage in a battle you cannot win? And who wants this insane violence with your daughter looking on? And the better question: who wants this violence *at all?* But there it was, and there we were, powerless at the moment to stop it. So we went around it (yes, déjà vu the other-dog obstacle course the streets had become). When Boo did one of his power plays with David, the simplest and only non-violent way to bring it to a swift end was to bring me in on it. David would call out, "Would you please call (expletive) Boo and get him out of here!" Or, "Tell Boo to get his (another expletive) ass off the sofa!"

Which I did. And Boo backed off, left the room, or whatever was necessary. Not happily, of course, but grumbling with resentment every inch of the way. Boo didn't like anyone telling him what to do, but he took it better from me than he took it from anyone.

Not good enough. And it was getting worse every month. A nervous diplomat with bare, minimum powers to diffuse the inevitable conflicts; that's all I was.

Boo is simply dangerous, David and I agreed during one late-night talk when both our workdays were done and we finally had a moment. *What if Lexie makes a wrong move? What if she trips on him? Is he going to challenge her?*

The next week, we did what we should have done a year and a half before: We sought help from a professional dog trainer. What happened here was no miracle. What it amounted to, this session with a well-known trainer and dog-book author, was Boo showing off how well he heeled, sat, stayed, did his 'downs,' and the rest of his repertoire. Yes, the trainer saw Boo didn't like him. He also saw Boo didn't like taking directives from me either. What he didn't see—because there were none in the room to elicit it—was Boo's violent behavior toward other dogs. He also didn't see the crux of what had brought us to him: that Boo had a dangerous streak, a *big swatch* of danger directed at people at large, that had now bled into his own family. All the trainer observed this day was what Boo demonstrated in this very controlled environment: a rottweiler—albeit a very belligerent one—who was trained to a very respectable level. The trainer had to take our word for the rest. Thus, his advice: "*Work* with him. He's very smart. Don't give him the upper hand; make him obey. And seriously consider neutering him. It may help."

The neutering idea had occurred to me before. Indeed, I had wrestled with it many times and rejected it just as many. I understood its health benefits: the avoidance of testicular and prostate cancer. I also understood—hence the trainer's advice—that neutering can tone down the aggressive dog. All this made perfect sense to me. But I couldn't get around the mutilation idea, the surgical removal thing. It seemed so drastic. Then the rationale: We never neutered Beau and he was fine, he lived to a ripe old age. And the other rationale: I had successfully bridged the gender gap from Timber, the most female creature of a dog, to Boo, the most masculine of dogs. And—I struggle to say this delicately—I had come to philosophically (or was it sentimentally?) equate the two items poised between his legs with the seat of this masculinity, a conceit much reinforced by Boo's dedication to them, the effort he regularly expended grooming them. On the other hand, the timing of his toilette on these objects did not serve to advance the cause of their retention. Boo would typically wait until David and Lexie and I were totally engrossed in some television show, then he would hoist up that back leg and set about polishing those precious orbs of his until they glistened. None of us worked all day or went to school to come home for an evening of looking and listening to *this*. Thus, my "Stop that, Boo!" Which he begrudgingly did. No sooner did we return to our show than he was at it again. But invariably, Boo saved the soup-to-nuts (no pun intended) *grand grooming* for when we had dinner guests at the table and the toasts had been made. All forks would be gaily poised to begin, when there would come the loud slurping from the living room. As our guests were not deaf, all heads turned to see the source of this enjoy-your-dinner sound effect. The big black rottweiler parked in the living room, who felt all these eyes on him, now answered this attention with a blasé *Is this a problem?* look on his face.

At moments like these, I felt like running to the kitchen, pulling out a cleaver, and doing the job myself—not in front of the dinner guests, of course, after they were gone—to be done with this maddening ball-licking once and for all. But then I calmed down and my old pre-judices sneaked back: the queasy feeling just the word "surgery" gave me. The what-if-something-went-wrong worry. The would-it-change-him issue. This, no doubt, the most ludicrous misgiving of all, as the point was precisely *to change him*, to knock down the dangerous male-hormone level that caused him and us so much trouble. But what, I obsessed, if it changed him in other ways, too? As stubborn and willful and obstinate as Boo could be, I had accepted these qualities, they were part of who he was. So we by no means discarded the neutering idea, we simply shelved it for the time being.

Three things now happened that improved all our lives. First, bol-stered by the dog trainer's advice to "Make him obey," I rededicated myself to Boo's obedience training. I got tougher with him, I upped the level of I-tell-you-and-you-*do*-it. It hardly achieved the transformation of Boo into "yes" dog, but it stabilized him. The small but meaningful victory was that his aggressive behavior did not increase.

Second—a big improvement—we moved. Not across the state or to a different neighborhood, but right up the stairs. We bought the brownstone house whose bottom floor had been our home. Thus we went from the very charming but very cramped "garden apartment" (as it's referred to in Park Slope) to much grander digs: the rambling three-story house above this apartment. And how wonderful it was! High ceilings. Huge windows. Rooms for this and that. It gave us literal and psychic space to spread out, to breathe, to not feel like we were constantly under each other's feet. It gave Boo these things, too, making him feel a little more relaxed, less likely to feel protective of his personal space, as there was so much more of it.

Third, something exquisitely sweet came into our lives. Her name was Daisy and she was an eight-week-old, chocolate-colored American cocker spaniel puppy. Why on earth bring a new puppy smack into the middle of ongoing travails with three-year-old Boo?

It's very simple. I wanted Lexie to have what I had as a little girl: a loving, outgoing, affectionate dog to share her childhood with. Boo was not this dog. He was a bramble bush with thorns, his heart much entan-gled and regularly obscured by those thorns. I could sort it out, I could see the goodness under the brambles. But Lexie was not always up to the task of deciphering the complexities of Boo. Bottom line: childhood only comes once and Lexie was well into hers. She needed her "Moppet" now. She got her, and so did I: a sweet little daisy of a dog whose most outstanding trait, without a doubt, was and is (Daisy is still with us) her capacity to love. She was the antithesis of Boo: small, soft, female, with a great need to be close to us. Further, she didn't give a whit about power playing. She was much too busy pursuing what she did care fervently about: her soft bed, a soft lap to hop up into, her thousand plush dog-toys. When Boo took one away from her, she shrugged it off good-naturedly and just picked up another one. Indeed, Daisy and Boo were polar opposites. Which may explain the first and only positive relationship—dare I say love?—that Boo would ever have with another dog.

It began the moment we brought Daisy home and he first laid eyes on her. His face lit up with *A present for me?* When she was in her crate, Boo would park himself right in front of it, staring in at her, curled up in a little brown ball, fast asleep. When I carried her to and from the store each day—in a big wool sock so she wouldn't get cold—he was so busy looking up at her little face peeking out of the sock that he often forgot about searching the streets for other dogs and people to attack.

At the store, she slept on his bed. Indeed, this was the first time he took the slightest interest in that bed—because she was on it. But one of the best things of all, when Daisy's puppy shots were complete, she came to the park with Boo and me. Now he had someone to run with, and what a sight they were: the little brown cocker spaniel running alongside the huge black rottweiler across the fields, the two of them tearing through the woods together. Daisy infused all our lives with a carefreeness I had forgotten could come with a dog. And she brought out a softer side of Boo. I let my guard down a little.

Then Boo almost killed Mama, our store cat.

I had come to The Village Green a half-hour earlier to give the plants in the garden a thorough watering before opening. The door was locked, and Boo and Daisy were walking around the store. I was out in the backyard, hose in hand and just about to start this very enjoyable task—when Mama streaked past me. Then Boo came thundering after her. Bad as this was, a second later he did something far worse: he caught her.

Screaming hysterically, I rushed over, throwing the hose at Boo. It may have hit him, or missed—it all happened so fast I wouldn't be able to reconstruct this five minutes later. But I do remember pounding on him with my fists, when suddenly he let go of her. Or it's possible Mama felt the instant when the right blow made him loosen his grip for a split-second, and she twisted herself free. Whatever it was, she dropped to the ground. In this instant, I caught a glimpse of the blood streaming down her back. Then she scrambled to her feet and raced for the back fence. She managed to claw her way up it, then jumped off or fell off into the yard on the other side. I heard her crashing through the bushes, then nothing. My heart pounding, I turned to Boo, screaming at him to "Go inside! Move! Now!" Which he did. No bullshit from him now. Boo slunk over to his bed, got on it, stayed there with Daisy, and didn't move for a long time.

For three days I didn't know if Mama was dead, or was out there suffering, or had recovered from her wounds but decided no home was better than this store home with its black hellion. All I knew was each day I went out into the garden to call her and she didn't come back. Then, the third day, I heard the scraping sound of claws on the fence, and she appeared at the top. She hopped down, and slowly walked over to greet me. I knelt down to stroke her and welcome her back. And then—it took some searching to find them—I saw a dozen little scabs that had formed over her puncture wounds, this, miraculously, the only evidence that one of her "nine lives" had been used up, now eight to go.

Drastic behavior required drastic corrective measures. It was time to have Boo neutered.

One week later, Lexie and I took Boo to The Heights Veterinary Hospital and turned him over to Dr. Turoff. Four hours later, we came back to take him home.

Ox that he was, Boo sailed through the surgery and walked out fit as a fiddle, albeit half an ounce lighter. If he remembered anything about this day, it was growling at Turoff when he arrived and growling at Turoff when he departed, the in-between a drug-induced blank.

The next weeks and months, I carefully observed Boo, looking for the slightest change in his personality, anything to indicate that his afternoon with Dr. Turoff had achieved even the most incremental reduction in his aggressive behavior. There was none to be found. He still tried to attack other dogs, still leapt at people, still growled at David, still grumbled at me. In short, the neutering of Boo was a classic case—my fault—of the right thing too late. The age to neuter a problematic male dog is not when he's three years old with the negative behavior dictated or exacerbated by high-dose male hormones firmly entrenched in his personality. The correct timing pivots on adolescence. That is, it must not occur before adolescence because a dog needs those hormones to achieve the full development of adult bone, muscle, stature, and secondary sex characteristics. The time to neuter is right after adolescence, before little hormone-driven aggression problems have a chance to become big aggression problems. Which explains why the neutering of Boo had no more effect on him than clipping his toenails.

But timed right, could it have made a difference? Could neutering have nipped the source of Boo's aggression in the bud before it had a chance to ripen and gain strength? Or, was the combative behavior dictated by those hormones and the dog producing them one and the same? Was the cause not so much hormones, but something far more basic, far more fundamental: Boo's genetic makeup, his genes, the DNA he was born with that, just as with humans, puts its immutable stamp on not just the physical package (size, strength, and so forth), but who we are, our gray matter, our talents, and yes, our temperament and personality? These are the right questions and they have no simple answers. It is not possible to know with absolute certainty what comes from where. But if I had it to do over again, there is not the slightest doubt in my mind that Boo should have been neutered the very day he went for Turoff's hand.

Further, Boo's genes should not have been passed on. He possessed the ideal physical characteristics of a rottweiler. He was virtual perfection. But his temperament was hardly the ideal, as he sorely lacked those other traits—balanced, tranquil—for which the modern day rottweiler was *also* bred, to balance and render safe all that physical power. Boo was either a throw back to the ferocity of the dog who hunted lions for the Romans, or a "throw forward" to the ills that have beset the rottweiler with its explosion of popularity in the last ten years. These ills include not just the physical instability of all the spindly over-bred rottweilers out there, but the mental instability of so many of these dogs who, sadly, now compete with the also horribly over-bred pit bull in the vicious-dog category. Indeed, the rottweiler and pit bull have been in a dead heat as to which one regularly makes more headlines in newspapers and on television for having attacked this person or that child or that other dog without provocation.

Further addressing the genes, the nature part of the "nature versus nurture" debate, the fact that Boo came out of the excellent stock of a very serious and dedicated breeder only underscores the unsettling truth that when all is said and done, what good genes will produce is still only a roll of the dice. In Boo's case, that roll resulted in a physically magnificent rottweiler with what the American Kennel Club—and anyone else— would classify a "defective" temperament of excessive protectiveness and aggression.

But maybe the nurturing, the home environment, socialization, and obedience training that Boo received was also defective. That is, in hands other than mine—in more experienced, more skilled, more confident hands that could have exerted more influence on him—Boo might have been a better-balanced dog. Putting some accountability square in my court, it is very possible that in my urgency to put a highly protective dog between me and the climate of fear that permeated the eighties, I may well have inadvertently encouraged these defective genes. Perhaps, ever the brilliant rottweiler with the guard-dog already in his head, Boo sensed my nervousness and rose to the occasion, upping the level of his ferocity accordingly. But once he unleashed this ferocity and it soared to dangerous levels, I lacked the necessary skills to curb it or ever get it appreciably back under control.

We humans, and our dogs, are shaped by, and are a product of, our times. Within this context is the subtle, or not so subtle, subtext of how we influence each other. Where nature stopped and nurture began for Boo has no clear-cut lines, no simple explanation. Indeed, a dog as complicated as Boo would raise more questions than he would ever answer.

What is for sure is that Boo went into surgery a tough guy and came out of surgery a tough guy.

But do not think that underneath all that toughness there were not nuggets of endearing sweetness in him, because they were there from the very beginning and golden they were. Boo just couldn't mine them every day, or every week, or every month.

There was the early-on nugget he gave Lexie when she was six. She reached down to pick a dandelion in the park and eagerly ran back to show me. Then, not about to overlook Boo's flower education, she reached over to show it to Boo. He gave it a sniff, then, to her utter amazement and delight, he ate it!

There was the time a few years later when a huge snowfall transformed Prospect Park into a winter wonderland replete with cross-country skiers tracking across the whiteness of the Long Meadow. Slews of kids and parents in brightly colored clothes were sledding down every hill, when Lexie and I, sled in tow, came across Alice and Brigitte. This day the thrill wouldn't be just the wonderful snow, but what Boo did in that snow. How he enthralled Lexie and Alice by doing something this rottweiler's genes also programmed him: to love pulling something. In this case, a sled carrying two girls (each weighing some forty pounds), who were laughing with glee as the great German rottweiler pulled them back and forth across great stretches of snow. Three hours later, it wasn't his joy or endurance that gave out, but rather the late-afternoon purple sky, that said it was time to go home.

Another wintertime story took place the night I had to walk Lexie to the birthday party of a classmate of hers who lived on the outskirts of Park Slope, ordinarily a ten-minute walk from our house. But not this frigid January night. The day before, a good foot of snow had fallen. The morning of the party, the sun came out. The temperature soared into the forties, melting some of that snow, only to plummet into the teens that night, turning the streets and sidewalks into skating rinks, with people slipping and sliding, and fender-benders on every corner.

It was clearly a night to stay at home unless you had to get someplace and had a four-wheel drive vehicle to get you there. We had the someplace to go, the party, and something, as it turned out, even better than a four-wheeler to get us there: a four-footer: Boo.

We set out to brave the icy streets with Lexie on one side, me on the other, and Boo sandwiched between us. As fun as the party turned out to be, the warm memory was not the party, but getting to and from it, something Boo made possible because this night he willingly let himself be the bulwark we glommed on to. It was as though he understood that we needed him to keep us upright, that our feet were no match for this treacherous terrain, but his were! Thus, he dug those huge black toenails of his into the ice-covered sidewalks and pulled us forward, foot by foot, block by block. And when we slipped and madly grabbed on to his neck to hold us up, he took this flopping all over him with total equanimity, waited for us to get our footing, and chugged on. In short order we were laughing hysterically every time we started to fall and glommed on to him, which amounted to bunches of laughter as we couldn't walk three feet without slipping on these city streets that were more Nome, Alaska, than quaint little Park Slope, Brooklyn.

It took us almost a half-hour to get to our destination. I deposited Lexie there, then Boo and I about-faced and retraced out steps for the arduous walk back home. Three hours later, we went back out to do it all over again, picking up Lexie and bringing her home.

This frigid January night, Boo was the guardian of our mission, the rottweiler with the tractor feet who got us through. This night, he had all my heart and all my gratitude. This night he was golden through and through.

Then, a summertime event, there was the hike up Mount Washington, the mountain with much dog and people history attached to it. Moppet and Beau, as already related, had hiked it with me when I was twelve. Timber had hiked it three times with David and me. Now, with nine-year-old Lexie alongside us, it was Boo's turn. And oh, the contrast between his climb and Timber's! She had been thirty pounds lighter, a veritable gazelle sailing over tree logs and small streams. Boo's boxy body was built for power and strength, not gazelle stuff. It was far easier for this dog to pull a log than jump over one. Nonetheless, he was thrilled with the big uphill walk that went on and on through the fragrant pine forest. By the three-hour mark, he was clearly getting very tired, his big feet starting to drag. By the time we reached timberline, the two-thirds mark, the poor boy was exhausted. But the hardest part, the final ascent over the craggy rock-covered terrain that required the most stamina and careful footing of all, was in front of us. So he trudged on.

With the top of the summit building in the distance, I observed something that got my adrenalin going. It was a long line of some twenty hikers—college kids—making their way, single-file, down from the summit and coming toward us on the foot-path that is so narrow even skinny people have to lean aside to let someone comfortably pass from the opposite direction. And, as the hike down from the summit is much faster than the hike up, these folks were fast approaching us.

My apprehension started to soar. What if they brushed Boo, or—God forbid—touched him? Was he going to bite one of them? But there was no time to pull him aside to tape his month shut because suddenly they were right in front of us, starting to file past us. Then, the leader of this friendly string of hikers did the something out of my Boo nightmares: he reached out to ruffle the fur on Boo's head the way grown-ups affectionately ruffle the hair of a three-year-old kid who's done something mighty cute. Then—it gets worse—one by one, all the hikers behind him did the same thing, ruffling Boo's head as they filed past him!

These twenty ruffles could have resulted in twenty dog bites one-half hour from the summit of Mount Washington in the White Mountains of

New Hampshire. But they didn't! Maybe it was the magic of this rugged mountain or the hard-earned thrill of walking among the clouds that got to Boo. Or maybe the truth is he was simply too exhausted to protest the twenty hands that reached out to him this day. In any event, after the adrenalin rush passed, what I saw in him this day was sweetness— yes, born of exhaustion, but sweetness nonetheless. When Boo dropped an unexpected nugget into your lap, nothing was achieved by overly analyzing it. Much better to do what I did. I took that nugget and quietly put it in my pocket where it has glowed right up to this day.

From a one-time nugget gathered high on a mountain top, I go to a very special everyday nugget: Boo's feet, which, for reasons only he knew, he would present to me each morning in the second floor hall by the banister as I headed down the staircase to get breakfast going. I would walk six steps down these steps. Then, with Boo still standing in the hallway, his chest now at my eye level, this dog who rarely let you hug him, this rottweiler who acted like his penis would fall off if he smiled, would wait for me to reach my hand through the banister spokes to play with his toes. He would shift his body weight to free one foot so I could touch and massage the offered paw's toes. Then, this paw done, he withdrew it and presented the next set of toes for their turn. The little miracle is that this golden ritual that started both our days was not just acceptable, it was at his instigation, and somehow needed by him.

Here's another everyday ritual. On our jaunts around Park Slope, it pleased Boo immensely, at some point or another, to ever so gently clasp my hand and take it into his mouth. Once in his clasp, with the expert but tender grasp of a mother cat carrying her kitten, he would gently roll my hand around in his mouth with his teeth and tongue, gently reveling in this contact. Not once in his six years of hand-holding did those huge teeth so much as graze one knuckle. What it did produce, this unusual union of big beast's mouth with little human appendage, was many a *My God, he's eating her hand!* reaction on the faces of passersby. So I'd led him indulge himself for a block or two, then I'd tell him, "Okay, Boo, this is very nice, but I need the hand back." I'd retrieve it, and on we would go, separate, but together.

It pleases me to relate that Boo occasionally gave my mother the "hand treatment." Morgan, as already set forth, was the love of my mother's life, the one she still mourns to this day. When he died, there would be no more dogs for her. Rather, she satisfied (and still does) her passion for dogs through my dogs. Thus, when big diffident Boo sometimes chose her hand to clasp, the compliment was not lost on her. Of course, the first time, as a strapping two year old, he reached over and took her hand, my mother nearly fainted, until I explained that this was Boo's little way of showing affection. Her hand was safe, I told her, and she could take it back at any time.

Then, there was the gem Boo gave to a perfect stranger which I include here because it was such a surprise, so out of character for him, and gave me such pleasure to see it. The recipient was an animal assistant at a boarding facility on Long Island where we brought Boo and Daisy because we were going to be out of the country for a week. The place came highly recommended and had everything one could possibly hope for: a very friendly staff; very clean, roomy indoor pens; and a large grassy outdoor run for the daily exercise they assured us Boo and Daisy would have. While they would occupy separate pens, I explained it would be a comfort to them if their pens were right next to each other so they could see each other—an accommodation they happily granted. I also explained that while Daisy, being the prima donna she is, would not like it here, she would be just fine. Then, the little talk about Boo. While he was extremely well trained, he could also, I told them, be extremely belligerent, as in "dangerous." Therefore, the staff had to exercise very careful judgment in handling him. Their response: "No problem."

The pats and "Be a good dog!"'s done, we turned Boo and Daisy over to the assistant, a dark-blond-haired woman in overalls with a friendly but very confident air, who led them away. Three hours later, we boarded our flight for Bermuda with confidence "the hounds" (as we affectionately called them) would be just fine.

A week later, we were back and drove straight from the airport to the kennel to pick up the dogs, our en route conversation punctuated with "I hope Daisy didn't get too upset" and "Christ, I hope Boo didn't bite anybody!"

Once there, we hurried in. A young man brought Daisy out first and she came charging over to us, her face screaming *Thank God you're back! It's been dreadful here. Absolutely horrible!* We gave her all the consoling she needed. Minutes later, the blond woman in overalls appeared with a Boo displaying not anger or resignation with the one holding his leash. This Boo was playfully cavorting with her, gleefully jumping around her, his eyes dancing with joy!

I stood there stunned. There was a part of me that didn't want to break it up, so amazing was this sight of my "bad boy" who far from biting his keeper, had fallen in love with her! This was not puppy love in action. Boo was six years old at this point. This was "big boy" love. Then he saw me and bounded over to deliver a greeting so hefty it almost knocked me off my feet. The woman was smiling as she walked up to me and said, "Great dog. Terrific dog."

Daisy couldn't get out the front door fast enough. Not Boo. While he was thrilled to be back with me, as we stepped outside and headed for the car in the parking lot, he turned back several times to look at the woman in the overalls who was waving goodbye to him at the door. And there you have it: the who-knows-what's-in-the-head, or the heart, of the dog you think you know so well. But there it was in plain sight at a boarding kennel on Long Island: absolute love for the once total stranger with the something in her or something about her that resonated in Boo that to this day remains a sweet mystery.

Then, of course, there was Boo's relationship with Daisy that would elicit many a display of genuine affection from him: his body wag when we came back from a (too strenuous for her) run in the park and found her at the front door to greet him. His joy when two leashes came out, which meant she was coming to the park with us. His absolute delight in her smallness. His fascination with her ruffled myriad brown curls, which he gave regular sniffing inspections to, as though he were counting them. But most especially, I think it was Daisy's absolute femaleness and her sweetness that got to Boo. Thus, the great rottweiler let the little brown spaniel with all the curls into his heart, as long as she obeyed his number one rule to stay clear of his food bowl when he was eating, because one step, one sniff in its direction would have made her dinner, too.

What are we to make of such a dog? What morals can be learned from the rottweiler who approached life in body and spirit like the great German tank he was? The morals are several. One, the most fundamental, would certainly have it that if life is war and the name of the game is search and destroy, a tank will do quite well, obliterating everything in its path. Absenting war, a tank is pointless, it lacks versatility, its very strength and rigidity seriously limiting where it can go, what it can do, not to mention the reception it engenders on the highways of life.

Boo taught me the foibles of self-defeating aggression and excessive rigidity that for dogs—and humans similarly afflicted—can seriously narrow the scope of life. In Boo's case, this rigidity negated, indeed it obliterated, a huge segment of his life: his ability to experience his own kind—with the sole exception of Daisy. It also profoundly limited his relationship with the humans he lived with, who had to curb their demonstrations of love and affection—which he missed out on—not because they didn't feel it, but because he couldn't handle it.

His other lessons? True to his breed, this rottweiler was extremely intelligent. But raw brains are not enough in this world. They must be tempered by reason—not to mention subtlety—that, for instance, can distill cause and effect: *If I keep up this attack-other-dog thing, I won't be able to play with those dogs. If I growl at the humans who love me, they will think twice about those displays of love.* As smart as he was, these were connections Boo's superior brain could not make.

As serious as these instructions are, Boo's most searing lessons were yet to come.

In July 1996, I decided to close The Village Green. It was a decision that evoked mixed emotions in me. After eighteen years, I yearned to have what the rest of the world had: free weekends. Lexie was growing up. There were her Saturday basketball and Sunday softball games to attend. There were writing projects that a six-day workweek could not possibly accommodate. Bottom line: I needed to start this new writing life with the flexibility I hoped would come with it, but was sad my Village Green days were over.

One doesn't walk away from something that has been so good without much rumination and many a glance back. This was the business I started from scratch, that let me raise my daughter within its fold, and that also enabled me to do something virtually unheard of in an urban setting: bring my dogs to work with me. But once freed from a six-day workweek, the prospect of setting a work schedule that would make possible long, vigorous (too vigorous for Daisy) runs in the park with Boo was a thought not encumbered with a wisp of wistfulness. Thus I could hardly wait for the days, coming soon, when I could lose myself in that simplest of pleasures: a walk in the park with Boo—unhurried—no time constraint—just he and I and the trees and the grass.

It was not to be.

In the early weeks, with my new work life barely begun, Boo started exhibiting some stiffness in his hind legs. At first I thought maybe in my enthusiasm, I'd overdone his exercising. Or maybe the culprit was that three-mile roadway around Prospect Park that we had begun to regularly fast-walk for our mutual health, whose asphalt surface was fine for my sneakered feet, but may have been too hard on his feet or the joints above them. But I wasn't particularly worried. I got a few aspirin in him (by slipping them into a chunk of ham that he scarffed down in one gobble) and restricted our walks, much shorter now, to the soft grass in the fields. I wanted for him to bounce back, but he didn't. The stiffness got worse.

Thinking this might be a total rest kind of injury, I cut out his exercising all together. Just the five-minute walks up and down the block to relieve himself at the curb, then back inside to rest. But there was no change. In fact, the stiffness grew even worse. While I couldn't believe his problem was serious—this was a dog who never suffered so much as a chipped toenail—dark thoughts of hip dysplasia began to erode my confidence. The next day, a Saturday, Lexie and I took Boo to The Heights Veterinary Hospital to have his hips x-rayed.

Ironically, it would not be Boo's once beloved Dr. Turoff who would see him this day. As fate would have it, Dr. Turoff was away for the whole week. Instead, we would deal with his colleagues, one of them Dr. Christine Norton, whose skill and compassion I would come to know well over the next seven days.

I stayed with Boo while they sedated him, then left with Lexie, prepared to spend the next hour investigating the shops on Montague Street. As we started to walk away, the door opened and one of the vets hurried after me, telling me he wanted me to "see something." Something in his tone—and the expression on his face—told me Lexie should wait outside.

I walked back inside with him to the examination room where Boo, unconscious, lay on his side on the table, with his mouth open. Then the vet showed me the "something" that made me gasp: a tumor, red and fiery, erupting through the teeth in a back section of Boo's gums. He told me that after x-raying Boo's hips, they would remove the tumor and have it biopsied.

Seven days later, Boo was dead.

Which brings me to the most searing lesson Boo taught me: that none of us, not the physically strongest of us or the mentally toughest of us, is excluded from that law that says *Anything can bring anything else down*. Like the mammoth dam destroyed by a raging flood that starts with one drop of water looking for someplace to go, Boo's great strength and iron will was no match for the one aberrant cell nucleus that started the raging cancer that would destroy him in the prime of his life. And it wouldn't take a year, or six months, or one month. This cancer would bring him to his knees in one terrible week.

From that Saturday, when we took him home from the vet, through the Sunday and Monday that followed, Boo could still walk. I would leash him and carefully walk him down the steep steps of the front stoop to the sidewalk. Then, we would slowly walk down the block so he could relieve himself at a tree or in the curb. I would watch him and wait, then offer encouraging words when his back legs began to wobble as we retraced our steps and slowly headed back to the house and up the stoop.

By mid-morning Tuesday, even this would prove too much for him. Our short walk done to the curb, we were halfway up the stoop when his hind legs gave way, his body collapsed backward, and I rushed to hold on to him. Between his will to get up those steps and my pulling him forward, we finally reached the front door, the tears streaming as I realized Boo would not be able to go outside again. So I slowly and carefully led him to where, days ago, he had taken up his new station: a large, circular, yellow cushion that I had taken from an old lounge chair and placed on the floor in the living room. From there he could see me and I could see him and talk to him as I walked around the kitchen or sat at the dining table working (or trying to work before I realized work, however urgent, was impossible). It was here that Boo spent his final days.

When I wasn't taking care of him, bringing him food or fresh water, I poured through my books on veterinary medicine, and spoke several times with Dr. Norton. Ever sensitive to my mounting fear, she assured me that my efforts to keep Boo comfortable were exactly correct, and that the results of the blood work and, more importantly, the biopsy report would "tell us what we need to know. We'll have it tomorrow."

Late in the afternoon of this same day, Boo began crying out from his bed. I called Dr. Norton again. He was in pain now, I told her, and needed something strong to block it. David picked up the painkillers from Dr. Norton on his way home from work. That night, I started slipping pills into Boo's food. They worked; he was able to relax.

Wednesday, the biopsy report came in. It was just as bad as I dreaded. Not just cancer in the mouth, but a bleak prognosis pointing to cancer in multiple sites, including his back and his hips, which explained his rapid deterioration. But I didn't need the report to tell me what I already knew. There was no hope for Boo.

But how could it be? my heart railed. This was a powerhouse of a dog who had never been sick a day in his life. This was the dog who I never saw shiver even in ten-degree cold. This was the Roman legion dog that herded the cattle to feed the marauding armies who came up through the centuries to haul my Lexie and Alice through a foot of snow all day. This was the dog who had hauled his own great bulk all the way to the top of Mount Washington. His powerful physique had scared away everything and anything with eyes to behold it. He was invincible. Nothing could touch him.

But then I would look to where he lay on that cushion with his small brown eyes looking intently back at me. The day before, he had fallen three times when he tried to walk around the living room, his legs simply giving out as he collapsed to the floor. This day, Wednesday, I realized with an ache, he had stopped trying to get to his feet. He just sat there, looking at me as I talked to him, choking on my cheerfulness as I told him "What a good boy" he was and asked him "Do you want some water?" which made his ears prick forward and his face brighten.

Then, the weight already melting off him—his hips looked gaunt, his rib cage was suddenly visible—he stopped eating. Desperate, I brought in other brands of dog food. I tried cat food. I offered him ham. I searched the refrigerator looking for anything he would eat, but he refused everything. I attacked the refrigerator again. There had to be something in there he would eat. Then I saw a package of hot dogs. I ripped the wrapping off and hurried over, hot dog in hand. He took it and ate it! I hurried back to the kitchen and grabbed the rest. One by one, he slowly ate every single one. I only left him long enough to bring in a good supply of hot dogs. But the next day, they lost their luster. I had to coax him and plead with him to eat. Then, later that day, came the final assault as this magnificent dog, so big on control, lost all control, barely able to move, and unable to control bodily functions, which distressed him terribly. I hurried to take care of whatever needed cleaning up, telling him "That's okay. It doesn't matter!"

But it mattered to him. His body was deteriorating by the hour, but not his brain. He was all there, his intelligence, his personality, the look in his eyes. And what I saw in them was not self-pity—dogs don't do pity, humans do pity—but something far more devastating that made his tragic plight all the more terrible: the bewildered *What's happening to me?* look on his great intelligent face.

Seven years earlier I had had to make for Timber the terrible decision that the end has come. There is no miracle cure. Prolonged life only holds prolonged suffering. This Thursday in the fall of 1996, I realized there was nothing more I could do for Boo but make preparations to ease his passage out of this world. I picked up the phone and called Dr. Norton to make the arrangements to have Boo put to sleep on Saturday morning.

But I couldn't take him to the vet and have people coming at him with tourniquets and a syringe. Yes, his body was ravaged, but his will was still intact. He would resist anyone who came near him; he would try to fight them like the dominant, controlling dog he still was in his head. I couldn't let him die fighting and struggling. To let this dog be conscious or in any way aware of his surroundings, with people touching him and he utterly helpless to stop it, was unthinkable.

For six years he had protected me (and then some, as detailed in these pages) with every fiber of his being. Now I had to protect him, save him from himself. I called Dr. Norton and made arrangements to have David pick up tranquilizing tablets on Friday night. I would administer them early Saturday morning before we left the house so that by the time we got Boo to the vet, he would experience no need to challenge, no need to dominate when the time came.

Then, the last call to the animal crematory to make arrangements for Boo's body to be picked up at The Heights Veterinary Hospital, cremated, and finalize details about his ashes.

The female voice on the phone was very kind, it not being a new experience for her to answer the phone and have the person at the other end already crying. So she understood when I had to put the phone down several times because I couldn't talk. When I came back, she picked up, explaining the details it was her job to impart. But when we got to the part about the fee, how it is based upon a dog's weight in categories of under twenty-five pounds, under fifty pounds, and so forth, she had to wait several long moments before I could pull myself together enough to get out the words that my once one hundred twenty pound rottweiler would qualify for the under one hundred-pound category.

Friday night, very little sleep came to me as the pills sat on the kitchen counter.

The next morning, I was up at six. The appointment at the vet was set for nine o'clock. At seven, I would have to administer the six pills that would need two hours to take full effect. But it wasn't seven yet. There was still time. I took my cup of coffee and sat down on the floor two feet away from where Boo lay on the yellow cushion, and talked to him—yes, only talked. I couldn't touch him. The cancer hadn't metamorphasized him into a dog you could do something so normal as touch. He was the same dog he had been all his life, who now, maybe especially now with him so vulnerable, would have interpreted the touching I yearned to give as a challenge to his supremacy. Even so, three times I ventured the lightest touch to his neck. Three times he met these touches with a growl to back off and keep my distance. So I gave him what he would allow, loving looks and soothing words, as I sat talking to him, hoping his great intelligence would not understand my red eyes or the tears streaming from them.

The last thing Lexie had said the night before as we sat talking in her room was to wake her up "in time," before I started the pills. I was about to go wake her when she walked into the living room, her face pale as she stood there, then sat down on the floor next to me. Now two voices sought to comfort Boo. A little while later, David came down and sat on the sofa a few feet away, a cup of coffee in his hand, but without the heart to drink it, as the room filled with a profound sadness.

It had started the very moment I walked into the living room an hour before: the aching realization that Boo's life had come down to lasts. The last time I would greet him in the morning, and he me, had already occurred. So, also, had the last time I could fill his water bowl and watch gratefully as he drank. I looked around. This was the last time he would be in this room, in this house, his home. I looked at Boo. These minutes were the last time he would recognize us, his family—or anyone else—with all his faculties intact. The pills that would ensure this could wait no longer. Time had run out. It was seven o'clock.

I walked into the kitchen, took out a package of hot dogs, opened it, and pulled two out. My hands shaking, I used a knife to make three slits in each one, then, wiping the tears from my eyes so I could see to do it, I pushed into the hot dogs the six pills that Dr. Norton had assured me were strong enough to bring down a horse.

I had carefully gone over everything with Lexie the night before, explaining what would happen to Boo once the tranquilizers took effect, the procedure at the vet, and that all of it would be very hard. The only way we could get through it, I told her, was to think of Boo. She said she understood. Now, as I walked back into the living room, I asked her if she was ready. She said she was.

I walked over to Boo, knelt down, and held out the first hot dog. He reached his head forward, took it, gave a few chews, then swallowed. My throat aching, I reached out and fed him the second one. It was done.

I sat back down on the floor near Boo. In a short while, Lexie began urging me to "Touch him, Mommy. He needs us."

"No, it's not safe," I told her. "We have to wait."

We waited, talking to him. Earlier, I had thought my heart would burst as I fed Boo the drugged hot dogs and sat there telling him not to be afraid of the strange calm soon to overtake him. Now I realized the real heartache had begun: the drugs were working. His body was beginning to relax. Inch by inch, he was slipping away. His eyes were open and looking at me, but little by little, the dog in those eyes had begun to recede. A half-hour before, I had urged him to not fight the drugs, to let it happen, to let go. Now, I wanted to cry out *Come back, don't leave. Come back!*

Instead, I reached out. Carefully watching his eyes following my hand, I ever so slightly touched his back, searching his face for even a flicker of objection. There was none. Only a peace, deepening by the minute, this the gift of the drugs now coursing through his veins that— *was it possible?*—gave him license, gave him the excuse he needed, to finally let down his defenses and feel the loving touches that—I looked into his eyes and thought I saw it—he wanted.

I turned to Lexie. "You can touch him now."

She drew closer to him, reached out her hand and, every so gently, started stroking his neck, telling him, "Good boy, Boo. I'm here, Boo."

We sat there, Lexie and I, gently stroking Boo with touches that were as gentle and respectful of him as our words. Those moments when we started to cry, we braced each other and pulled out of it with the truth that Boo needed us to be strong. We couldn't let him hear our grief or feel it in our touches. It would upset him, worry him. Later, when it was over, we could give in to our grief. Right here and now, we had to think about him and do the right thing: help him slip into this sedation overtaking him in total peace.

The next hour, as David joined us on the floor, was a blur of misery. But in this misery were also moments of awe and profound connection as, talking to Boo all the while, we touched his back, then gently stroked his still thickly muscled shoulders and neck. I'd seen these muscles in action, but what respect it inspired to actually feel them. Then, my hand sought the soft little flaps that were his ears. There had been a time, when he was a tiny puppy, when all his fur was this soft. Then he grew up and his fur grew up into the slightly coarse texture fur all rottweilers have. But his ears—my fingers sent the exquisite revelation to my heart— were still as soft and downy as the day I carried him home and into my life six years ago. The heartache picked up again as I began stroking his magnificent head, all the while looking at his immensely expressive face. Except for the emotion of joy, you can't read a rottweiler's feelings or thoughts in the actions of his tail—there isn't enough of it. But his face is an open book, as complex as its author. To read it, all you have to do is look at it. This day, this look brought me only pain. The dog Boo was, was still in his eyes, but flickering, like a candle starting to burn out.

All this week, he had laid upright on his cushion, his front feet out in front of him, his hind legs curled around his hindquarters, his head, when he wasn't sleeping, held high atop his shoulders so that he could look around to engage and be engaged by us. But now, suddenly, he began to struggle. In an instant, I realized what he wanted: he needed to lay down on his side. I moved quickly to help him, pulling his legs out of the way, as he rolled, groaning, over on his side. My heart lurched: *Animals do this when they are ready to die.* Even as I knew the drugs had brought Boo to this state, images from nature films streaked through my brain. The wild boar speared with the poison darts who finally collapses and rolls over on the jungle floor. The elephant with bullets lodged in his brain who can no longer outrun his fate, who sinks to his knees and rolls over on the savannah. *Animals do this*—a rush of tears fell out of me as I saw Boo's eyes glaze over, as his breaths suddenly came slow and labored—*when they are ready to die.*

It was eight-thirty. I called Dr. Norton and described his condition. "That's it," she told me. "He's ready."

David and I got a blanket and gently eased Boo onto it. With Lexie holding the doors open, David and I carefully carried Boo, comatose, out of the house and into the car.

Twenty minutes later, as Dr. Norton and another vet looked on, we gently lowered Boo onto the table at The Heights Veterinary Hospital. I stood next to Boo's head, with Lexie next to me, and David next to her, as

Boo lay there, barely conscious, his breathing very slow. His body was here, the moment was coming, but the dog inside his brain was where I wanted him to be: not here, someplace else. His eyes were open, but his brain was beyond processing the images they took in. So he did not see what our eyes saw: the moment the needle entered the vein in his front leg, and he did not feel it when the vet depressed the tip of the syringe that injected the solution that would stop his heart. If he could feel or hear anything these final moments, he felt my hand caressing his head and Lexie's and David's gentle touches as I told him, "Good boy, Boo. It's all right, Boo. Everything's all right."

He gasped a few times, then he was gone.

We had a few minutes to be alone with him, minutes of desperate sadness as he lay there, so still. Then, our time up, I braced myself for what came next: walking away from him. When all of us were ready, we said our final goodbyes and started to leave, when I stopped, went back, and kissed Boo on the head. A moment later, my heart already reeling, it reeled again when Lexie stepped over to him and kissed his head, too. David and I took her hands. Even as we walked out into the hall, I continued to turn around to look at him, my beautiful rottweiler there on the cold metal table, his life over.

There is great solace in knowing that, hard as it was, you did the right thing. It doesn't stop the heartache, you cry no less, but the tears aren't bitter, they have hope in them. Long before the heart stops hurting, this hope lets the brain start working again as you struggle to sort it out, to make some sense of tragedy. Along the way in this process that has no shortcuts, comes something that rarely occurs without pain. Indeed, it is the hard-earned gift of pain: new understanding.

This new understanding can take days, months, years, even a lifetime before it is fully grasped. Or, it can be immediate, it comes to you the next minute and changes you. From this moment forth, in large or small ways, you are a different person. If the pain that spurred this difference was really let in, you are a better person than you were a moment before: a little wiser, the heart a little larger, you and your perception of the world a little truer.

Even before we got back into the car, I already understood the irony of this anguished Saturday morning. The drugs, the gift I gave Boo to let him depart this world in utter peace, also gave me the gift of him. Because it was during those two terrible hours, from the first pills that melted away his resistance to the final injection he did not feel, that Lexie and David and I got to do what we had wanted to do from the first day Boo scrambled under that car seat as a tiny puppy: get close to him. To hold him, touch him, gently stroke his massive head, and tell him again and again how much we loved him. I hope, like the *toes* ritual, he did need this at the end. I know I did.

But it would take weeks to fully take in the most searing lesson that Boo taught me: There are no barriers strong enough to insulate or protect us from the bad things in life that can and will find us, no matter who we are. When Boo died, any illusion I had about any guarantees in life died with him, because when the strongest—dogs or humans—among us fails, the allusion that strength will protect us or somehow save us is gone.

Gone also was something as foolish as even an inkling of justice implied in any literal approach to that saying, "Every dog has his day," as Boo's day was much shorter than the day he deserved. Indeed, the most hideous disease had come out of the blue to sideswipe him and rob him of the longer day that should have been his. Where is the justice here? There is no justice, I say without bitterness. All there is, is life, the chance for life, lived to the fullest, this the only antidote to death, this the lessons of the dogs before him, and this Boo's lesson too.

But what an intense day this life of Boo's was. Yes, cut short; but filled with such energy, such extremes, the good and the bad. Think what you will of him, there was no doubt this dog was here, with a brain, even when its circuits misfired, of such extraordinary intelligence; and a personality, even though it often served him not well, of undeniable vitality. Thus, one simple sentence—usually reserved for humans— conveys what for me was the marvel of Boo: that, like Della, but in his own very different way, absolutely and irrevocably, "somebody was home" in that shinny, black, magnificent head.

This somebody never offered unconditional love, which we humans attribute to anything with four legs that barks and walks on a leash— because it suits us, we like it, indeed we love our dogs for it. Who else could give us such longed for affirmation but a dog? I had basked in this glorious affirmation for fourteen years with Della, who thought the sun rose and set very close to anywhere I stood. But Boo thought the sun rose and set very close to anywhere he stood. His love—when he gave it—had dozens of conditions attached to it: Don't stand too close, don't look the wrong way, don't breathe the wrong way, don't confuse me with some other dog because I *will* bite the hand that loves me.

We humans can reshape, modify, alter the outer rims of our personality. We can attempt this same remodeling on our dogs. But that's all it is, outer rim remodeling. At our core—humans and dogs—*we are who we are*. In this core is how we love. Some of us love unconditionally, and some of us do not because we cannot. Boo and I shared six years. Somewhere along the line, I finally came to understand he needed to be himself, just as I need to be myself. It was a lesson I needed to learn.

Mismatch that we were, my unruly Boo and I, this was no loveless marriage. He loved me as much as he could love me, and I loved him as much as he would let me. But love it was.

I end with an image of Boo that I love. It didn't happen at home or at The Village Green or some familiar haunt like Prospect Park. Rather, it happened six months earlier at a kennel near Calendar House where we had to board him one weekend.

We'd dropped him off Friday night. Now it was Sunday afternoon and we were back to pick him up. We had just arrived and were standing in the office with the owner and his wife, when Lexie happened to glance out the window and see Boo standing at the end of an outdoor dog run next to the office. A moment later, we would call out to him and he would whip his head around looking for us, the total body-wag instantly set in motion. Sweet as this was, it was not this that moved me, but what happened right before we called out his name, before he knew we were there, when he calmly stood there this lovely summer day, not fighting anybody, not challenging anybody, just standing in the warm sun, looking out on the world.

5

The Inimitable Miss Daisy

I t was a listing of breeders that I got from The American Kennel Club that led me to the inimitable Miss Daisy, my sweet little chocolate American cocker spaniel with the big expressive eyes in her little brown head. But, like all good things in life, it took some work to find her.

The information I received from the AKC—whose language, appropriately, makes clear, as it does with all inquiries, that this is a listing, not necessarily an endorsement—included some thirty breeders of American cocker spaniels. But I felt confident I could sort out the right breeder from the wrong breeder. I went down the list. There were so many of them—across the country, and nearby—that I narrowed the choices down to kennels in reasonable proximity to New York. I made the phone calls, and over the course of a few days, I talked to a range of breeders.

Some of them had buff (cream to red colored) puppies, but not the more rare chocolates. Two breeders had chocolates and passed everything but the gut feeling I got that they still weren't right. What happens between breeder and buyer is an ongoing relationship. Apart from the essential determination to be made that this is a source for a sound and healthy puppy, a breeder has to be someone you feel comfortable with, who you can call with questions and who will take the time and want to answer those questions. If it doesn't ring true in the first five minutes, it isn't right. You need to thank the person for his or her time, and keep calling until it is right. My sixth call, to the breeder in upstate New York who bred blacks and buffs, but specialized in chocolates, felt right. I passed her suitability test. She passed mine. I told her we were looking for a chocolate female. She informed me she was expecting a litter of chocolates in two weeks and then did the something that makes that right even better: She invited us to drive up and take a look.

Two weeks later, we pulled into her driveway and parked in front of a most pleasant house and small kennel set in the woods. As we approached her front door, what awaited me was yet another example of how breeders "do" their breed, but seem to go for polar opposites in their "personal" dogs. Della's breeder bred great big Danes, but her personal menagerie of pets included those little dogs who ran around underfoot. Boo's breeder bred burly rottweilers, but had elongated dachshunds scurrying about. Daisy's breeder's personal dogs were a pair of two-hundred pound Mastiffs who lumbered around the place.

As majestic as this duo was, we hadn't come to admire them; it was that litter of chocolates we'd come to see.

As it turned out, this time choosing which puppy would be ours was not done by the breeder or me. Daisy's mother had made the choice. Her litter—born two days earlier—had produced four males and one female. That female was Daisy. After explaining this, which sounded fine with us, the breeder left the three of us sitting in her living room. Minutes later she returned with something wondrous cupped in her hands: the generic little puppy the length of a hot dog, with four little feet (we had to look close to make out the tiny little toes), eyes closed of course, and tiny little flaps for ears. She was very sleepy, having been just plucked from a puppy nap with her littermates. We couldn't touch her, of course. Our hands had germs. But we could look. And look we did, standing in close to marvel at tiny little Daisy, so sweet, so new, on this, her second day of life. When the breeder left to return her to her mother, David and I turned to Lexie. But we didn't have to ask her opinion, she was already crying, "Yes! Yes!" and she already had the perfect name for this wondrous little creature.

When we returned eight weeks later, that generic little hot dog of a puppy had rearranged all the nondescript parts and there she sat: a little miniature cocker spaniel in a big crate in the middle of the breeder's kitchen, her floppy ears already beginning to sport tiny little brown curls. Daisy looked up at us with the sweetest expression as we peered down at her with big smiles on our faces. But she didn't have to look up very long. As David took care of the paperwork, Lexie and I got right down on the floor with her, talking to her, our fingers venturing through the crate to touch her. This was hardly good enough, so we opened the crate door and let Daisy out. Now our hands were gently all over her, and she liked their touching. This idyllic little scene was interrupted a moment later when the family cat wandered in to see what all the fuss in the kitchen was about. Daisy, who had never seen a cat, ambled over to it, and the cat gave her a swat in the head that sent Daisy, yelping with astonishment and fear, back to the safety of our hands and voices that leapt to consoling her. Fortunately, she wouldn't hold this cat event against other cats. Which was good, because there were two of them waiting to meet her at home. Before we left, I tended to one other, not small detail: a crate. Recalling all too well the travails of housebreaking Moppet, I bought a crate right then and there from the breeder.

From the first minute, Daisy was everything I hoped for: a loving little dog for Lexie. A loving little dog for all of us who we could lavish with love without fear of loosing a finger. Indeed, unlike Boo, who felt so confined and was so unhappy there, Daisy rode home snuggled in Lexie's lap. When I saw her look up trustingly at Lexie's face, I thought here was a match made in heaven. As I continued watching, my eyes could hardly decide where to look: at this adorable puppy in Lexie's hands? Or at Lexie's adorable hands holding Daisy? But there was no confusion in the gratifying realization that a part of my life had come full circle. I had given Lexie exactly what I had had as a child: a sweet little cocker spaniel. Not when she was six, but nine. Still plenty of childhood left.

From where I stand and what life has taught me, apart from a parent's love, there is no greater gift, nothing more meaningful or of greater or lasting value that we can give a child than a loving little dog to share a childhood with. Lexie didn't need Daisy the way I needed Moppet. I had made sure of this. She *wanted* Daisy. Fulfilling this want made for one of the happiest days of my life.

Now this may beg the question: Is Daisy Lexie's dog? Or my dog? If the answer pivots on who cleans up after her, there is no question she's my dog, as I have mopped up a hundred pees to Lexie's one. If it pivots on who takes her to the park to run virtually every day, she's my dog. If it pivots on whom she loves, the answer is Daisy is both our dogs. Indeed, she is a little dog for all of us to love and be loved by. The dog waiting

for us at home that day, three-year-old Boo, was not that dog for Lexie.
He would never be that dog.

As already related, Boo was delighted with this new little puppy in
our midst. She posed no threat to him. He saw in her the opposite of a
threat. She was the very small, very sweet, very female little creature
with the big brown eyes in the little head, whom he found fascinating.
He opened his carefully guarded heart and took Daisy in.

With her shots still incomplete, I carried Daisy to The Village Green,
where she sat on Boo's bed and played with the toys he had long abandoned. Practically every hour, I would take her out into the yard for
bathroom duty. And, of course, feed her and make sure her water bowl
was filled. But when Lexie came back from school, it was her time with
Daisy. She'd scoop Daisy up in her arms and carry her down the little
hall to her room to play—or Daisy would trot down the hall on her own
steam after Lexie—and I'd hear Lexie laughing and little excited barks
from Daisy. Later, when I would realize there were no sounds coming
from Lexie's room, I'd quietly walk down the hall and find Lexie asleep,
with Daisy asleep too, in her lap or curled up against her neck.

In short order, Daisy's shots were completed and she could walk on
the streets of Park Slope with Boo. They were the quintessential Mut and
Jeff: the sweet-faced little brown cocker spaniel trotting alongside the
growly black rottweiler, the top of her head barely reaching his knees,
her taking five steps to his one.

When I gave up my plant business two years later to write full-
time, Daisy switched gears too, becoming my cheerful work-at-home
companion. She and Boo still went to the park every morning, but instead
of trotting down Union Street to start their day at the store, it was home we
came, where the leashes came off and up I went to my office. Boo stayed
where he wanted to be: downstairs in the hallway, guarding the front
door. Not Daisy! Up she hopped, two staircases worth, to follow me into
my office, where she sits right now as I write this.

Is she a cocker true to her breed? Daisy's genes have produced her
own version of the lively, affectionate little cocker of my childhood, with
the indelible stamp of her very unique personality. For instance, her little
obsessions, like the one with the ping-pong balls that would invariably
escape from the playroom. She would rout them out from the rest of the
house, madly hopping on and off furniture, creating all manner of havoc
until her hot pursuit would lead her to the one lone dusty little ball that

had found its way under the living room sofa six months earlier. The ping-pong ball obsession only ended when the ping-pong table came down. She spent weeks rounding up the last of them, then, with no balls left anywhere to sustain her interest, she forgot about ping-pong balls and stopped looking for them.

For several months there was stillness. Little pieces of furniture that she had pushed around stayed put, as did the stacks of books on the coffee table and throw cushions on the sofa. But no sooner did we get used to this normalcy than Daisy's proclivity for obsessions resurfaced and found a new outlet, this one with a much broader base of operation that has lasted to this very day. Indeed, it is so entrenched in her personality that it has earned her the title "Inspector Daisy."

While its explanation yet eludes us, its modus operandi is very simple: Daisy walks around looking for things. Be it Lexie's bedroom or ours, the dining room, the living room, she walks around the perimeter of rooms, dipping into corners, snuffling around in closets. She uses her nose to lift the lids of file boxes. She stands on her hind legs so she can see what's on a dresser. She peers into shopping bags. When we open the cabinet doors under the kitchen sink, we have to be careful how we close the doors lest we close them on Daisy's neck, because her head *will* be in there. This behavior has prompted the question that has been ongoing in this family for years: *What is she looking for?* We haven't a clue. I'm not even sure she knows. But it's so funny, so amusing, that to take a break from homework, Lexie will call me into her room, we'll sit on the bed together, and then call Daisy. A few seconds later, in she trots. She gives us both a nice little greeting, then—she can't help herself—she starts inspecting. One after the other, she checks the lowest shelf of a bookcase. She sticks her nose into a wastepaper basket. Takes a look-see into Lexie's backpack. Stands on her hind legs to inspect the rack of CDs. The more she looks around, the more we laugh until finally, the tears coming down, Lexie cries out, "Take her out! I can't take it anymore!" And out she goes. Or, rather, out I take her.

"Inspector Daisy" knows no borders. She inspects wherever she is. At Calendar House, because of deer ticks and Lyme disease, the dogs are no longer allowed into the house; they're restricted to the closed-in porch. Not a problem. This long triangular place is a catchall for bins of old tennis rackets, ancient badminton sets, and boxes of whatnot collected over twenty years. Here, Daisy is the wind-up doll you don't have to wind up. Just put her down anywhere and off she goes, snuffling, sniffing, looking.

Then there's her obsession with Teddy, a fake sheepskin, beige dog toy in the shape of a bear that I picked up at a pet shop when Daisy was three. I barely got him in the house when out came David's reaction: "Another toy?"

"That's right," I told him.

In David's defense, Daisy must have had thirty toys to her name at this point. In my defense, I loved buying her toys. Boo found them frivolous. His idea of recreation was chewing on somebody's arm or leg. But Daisy liked toys! And I liked getting them for her. Every month or so, I'd stop off here or there and bring her home a little something. She would dance around at my feet as I pulled the cellophane off whatever it was, and could barely wait for me to hand it down to her. But as happy as she was to have this new toy—and the many others she played with— none of them delivered the goods: the lasting thrill. For a while there was the big rubbery caterpillar toy that squeaked. (Boo's pleasure was to take it away from her, but she'd wait till he lost interest and lumbered off, then she'd scamper back to reclaim it.) But soon the squeaking caterpillar lost its luster and joined the ranks of the thirty other ho-hum toys laying around, which Daisy would pick up, play with, drop, then go find another because one was as good as the other. Then—you never know what's going to score a home run in a little dog's heart—came Teddy. I didn't have to pull any cellophane off him. All he was wearing was a price tag. I barely got it off him when Daisy, who couldn't wait a second longer, jumped up, grabbed him right out of my hands, and dropped down on the floor, thrilled to pieces, her little tail beating a mile a minute, her mouth glommed on to him, and she has never let go.

A good quarter of Daisy's waking hours involves Teddy one way or the other. She plays with him, then leaves him to check out what Snowball's doing, comes back to chew on him for a while, leaves him to go do something else, comes back to carry him around for a while, then drops him. A little nutty to be sure, but it works for her. When she forgets where she left him, it's finding Teddy that occupies her. But downtime is when Teddy really works his magic as Daisy relaxes on the floor. Her front feet extended with Teddy in their clutch, she mouths him and chews on him with such sublime satisfaction that she falls asleep with him in her mouth. At night, God forbid we should forget to toss him into bed with her because Daisy without Teddy will not go to sleep! She will whine and cry and make everybody miserable until we get him and give him to her.

Teddy started out fat, but there have been several episodes when Daisy's chewing has made holes at his seams, then she has yanked out major portions of his stuffing. Each time I collected up as much of his stuffing as I could find, shoved it back in him, and sewed his seams closed. But over the years, this reduction in stuffing has caused Teddy to loose much of his girth. He used to be round, now he's flat. One of these days Daisy's going to pull off an arm or a leg, and then my challenge will be to reattach it. But stuffing and arms and legs don't matter to her. The more ragamuffin he looks, the more she loves him.

Needless to say, this little flop of a toy collects dust and dirt like a magnet. In his dirty state, it's hard to distinguish him from Daisy. Which means from time to time (when he turns the exact color of Daisy) it's time to pop him in the washing machine. The challenge is how to sneak Teddy out of the room without her knowing. I trick her with cat food. I put a few dollops of Snowball's food in the dog bowl, wait for her to start eating, then fast! I snatch Teddy off the floor and run through the house madly gathering up Daisy's three beds and their fake washable sheepskin bedding (and dirty sneakers and anything else funky enough to join this barnyard group of collectibles) as I race for the washing machine. But in a second, she's on to me! She quickly gobbles up huge mouthfuls of Snowball's food, then runs after me, barking *Give him back!* I try to comfort her as best I can, but into the washing machine he and the rest of my cargo go, along with some heavy-duty detergent and a major dose of bleach.

Daisy's been through the laundering of Teddy a hundred times. She knows she'll get him back in about half an hour. Sometimes she sits down in front of the washer and waits it out. Most of the time, she comes where she also wants to be: with me, as I work in my office or take care of household chores. In a half-hour—to delay one minute longer would be cruel—I stop whatever I'm doing and head for the laundry room where, to Daisy's infinite relief, up pops Teddy, still raggle-taggle, but miraculously beige again. I consider a roll in the dryer that fluffs out his flatness a bit. But Daisy is so anxious to have him back (one time she jumped into the dryer after him) that I usually pass him down wet. She grabs him, sinks down to the floor on the spot to chew on him, the stress of enduring his absence only matched by the joy of having him back.

One time I lost Teddy (he somehow fell behind a shelf in the laundry room) and Daisy was so upset that I ran out and got her a new one. Not exactly like Teddy, but close enough—fake sheepskin, beige, and a bear—hoping she wouldn't know the difference. Foolish me. She took one look at him with a *What's this?* No doubt I should have dragged this one through the streets for a week to lend him some authenticity and make him acceptable to her. But Teddy turned up. As for that new bear, he's as beige and round and clean as the day he arrived because he's barely been touched.

So what is it about Teddy? Despite his hundreds of washings, is he so steeped in the smells of home that no other toy could possibly compete with him? Is the attraction here his curly wool looks and feels like her fur?

I don't have the answers to these questions. What's important, what matters, is that Daisy knows. We love who and what we love in this would, and Daisy loves Teddy.

With or without Teddy in her mouth, there's what the tip of her Daisy's tongue does soon after she falls asleep, which is to stick out, eventually drying to the consistency of a pink potato chip, a condition mercifully remedied when, upon wakening, she pulls it back in.

This tongue-protruding vision notwithstanding, how is Daisy's intelligence? It's right up there. To recall, in his *The Intelligence of Dogs*, Coren ranks the American cocker spaniel in the very respectable number twenty slot, suggesting a wide range of training possibilities. But somebody forgot to tell Daisy about this wide-range idea. This little cocker's brain power was accurately summarized when Lexie said lovingly of Daisy that hers is a "selfish intelligence," that she restricts herself, without a whit of guilt, of course, to learning what suits her, what's important to her.

For example, how to use her paw to bang her metal water bowl when it's empty so someone will make the banging stop by filling up that bowl, pronto. Boo taught her this one and it stuck. What he didn't teach her— because she was not interested in learning it—is the following: As a twelve-week-old puppy it was not important to Daisy, and nine years later, it is still not important to Daisy, to housebreak herself. Why wait for someone to take you out in the morning to pee at a cold curb when you can simply hop out of your bed at some point in the night as the spirit moves you, take three steps, pee on the soft oriental rug in the living room, then hop back in the comfy bed and pick up that dream where you left off?

The fundamental mistake here? I threw out the crate Daisy used her first year because she tricked me into believing she didn't need it. For four whole weeks—with the crate door deliberately left open, even at night—she had saved the puddles and other things for outside. I took this to mean we were done with the crate thing and triumphantly carried it out to the curb for any passerby that might want it. No sooner was it carried off, then the indoor peeing and so forth started again. Loathe to buy another crate, I did the next best thing: I put Daisy on a strict schedule that, because I'm here to do it, has her going out at eight o'clock in the morning, then noon, then three, then six, then out for the last time at nine or ten at night. But should there be the slightest delay—a minute, a second—because the phone rings and I run to answer it, or we're headed for the park and I dash into the kitchen to make sure I turned the coffee maker off—the dash back to Daisy finds a puddle or some brown offering on the floor. And she's not sorry! If she wore a watch she'd be pointing to the second hand with a "Don't blame me. You're late!"

It's déjà vu Moppet, minus Moppet's sincere regret every time she piddled in the house. If stock in a mop company was what I should have had in the fifties, stock in a paper towel company and a foaming rug cleaner company would have lined our coffers in the nineties and the new millennium.

Bottom line: If housebreaking means—and it does—that a dog learns to exert her own control over elimination, Daisy is not house-broken. It's I who exert—or do my best to exert—the control over her. And I do it like an army sergeant, by cutting off her water supply at five in the evening; by getting her out first thing—it used to be eight, now it's seven—in the morning; by never, ever feeding her anything but her dog food, because while she loves table scraps and cat food, changes in her diet can prove disastrous. Her digestive system can't handle them; it gets upset and unmentionable things pour out of Daisy for days.

A small footnote to the above: Last week David removed and threw out the antique red oriental rug in our living room that Boo used to sit on, we walked on, and generations of people before us walked on. It couldn't survive Daisy. We now walk on the hardwood floor. The question now is: Do we get another rug that will only amount to a huge pee pad for Daisy? Or is it hardwood floors for us? This dilemma remains.

So Daisy gets a big F in housebreaking. But she did learn—she must have deemed it useful—to heel nicely. She learned to sit, as, no guessing the usefulness here, this got treats handed down to her. And—this one Lexie taught her—she learned the down in all of five minutes as it too proved useful: It elicited the Cheerios Lexie popped into her mouth every time she plunked her little brown body on the floor. And the interesting thing here is we rarely ask her to do this. Indeed, I had forgotten Daisy even knew it, when, a few months ago, Lexie was playing with Daisy when—with no treats, no incentives of any kind—for fun, she told Daisy, "Down!" Daisy hit the floor like someone yanked her feet out from under her. It was that fast, that crisp! As for the stay, Daisy hasn't added this one to her repertoire because she doesn't like to stay anywhere and have people walk away from her.

Where do Daisy's genes depart markedly from her breed? Cocker spaniels are supposed to be outgoing and affectionate with people in general. Not this cocker. Daisy restricts her affection—and lavish it is—to the people she knows and likes, and a small circle it is. It includes my sister, Paula, who delights in Daisy and loves her quirkiness, but not my brother, as she senses he doesn't like dogs (they're too messy, too earthy for him). It includes my mother, as Daisy loves her and her kitchen, where my mother is known to slip her little treats. And she loves Shawn. After Shawn moved away, Daisy hadn't seen her for a year or so. When Shawn came to visit, Daisy tore down the stairs and practically leapt into her arms, absolutely thrilled.

The rest of the world, those "people in general," Daisy does not like, most especially strangers. She abhors them, shuns them as though they had the plague. Despite their efforts to befriend her, Daisy also gives the plague treatment to the neighbors. Children (except my brother's little boy, RJ) she finds absolutely horrible. They run up to her on the street expecting the sweet-looking little brown spaniel with big ears and chocolate curls to be happy to see them. She isn't. Her dislike, while great, would never escalate to a growl, no less a bite. The point is she can hardly wait to get away from them.

Although most spaniels exhibit laudable displays of courage, "display" is all it is for this cocker. But herein lays one of Daisy's most endearing traits. When confronted with something alarming—the ring

of the doorbell, the late night barking of a dog several backyards away—
she tries to be brave, meeting these challenges with a flurry of her own
barking, no doubt praying there's nobody at the front door, and please
God, let there be fifteen fences between her and what's making that dog
bark. But hers is the true definition of courage: the show of force in the
face of fear. This show was easier to put on when Boo was alive because
he took care of the heavy-duty guard-dogging. After Boo died, there
were several months—hard, scary months—when Daisy had to go it
alone.

But not for long. Four years ago, when Daisy was four, Tyler, my
Bernese mountain dog arrived. The day we brought him home, she eyeballed the chunky puppy already half her size with a disdainful look that
said *Do we really need this?* It was a question her rolled eyes would ask
again and again, particularly as he continued to grow larger and larger,
like he'd fill up the house if somebody didn't put a lid on him. But soon
enough, he won her over, her aversion melting in the face of his infinite
charm and easy-going ways. More to the point, she rediscovered the
advantages to the two-dog thing: somebody else to run barking to the
fearful front door with. Somebody else to answer the strange sounds in
the night with. But make no mistake about it: it's Daisy who takes the
first turn at the food bowl. It's the little brown cocker spaniel who rules
the roost.

The sporting dog in this cocker spaniel? Dog sporting events happen
outside. Herein lies a knotty problem for Daisy as hers is a huge disdain
for the natural elements she encounters on a walk down a city street. It's
the rain: her head might get wet. A puddle: her feet might get wet. The
wind: it ruffles her curls. (If the wind comes from behind to blow on her
little rear end, so disagreeable is this sensation to her that she sits down
and refuses to budge.) Then there are the awful leaves and twigs that
fall down from the street trees to plague her. Daisy's fur attracts them
like a magnet. They stick on to her legs and underbelly and won't let
go. So she has to stop every two feet to madly yank them off. However,
take her to a woodsy section of the park or Calendar House and all this
nonsense is forgotten as she jumps to life, leaping around trees, tearing
through the underbrush with total zest for all this naturalness. But this
nature stuff can only occur in the spring, summer, or fall. It cannot, in
other words, occur in the winter. With winter comes the awful cold.
Despite enough fur on her to suffocate any other cocker, plus her red

dog coat, Daisy shivers and shakes. Walking her is like trying to walk a log with a leash attached to it. She does what I call her "slug thing," where she drags her feet and no amount of tugging is going to speed her up. As for snow, she likes hopping around in it for about five minutes. Then the trouble starts, the hard little balls of snow that form in the curly fur between the pads on her feet and turn into hard little balls of ice, which she has to stop and remove every two feet. And she won't let me help (which might speed things up). She's got to do it herself, punctuated with the reproachful looks she directs my way: *Why do you subject me to this?*

Cocker spaniels are supposed to love the water and be good swimmers. Not Daisy. She hates water. Like puddles, it's too wet. Hardly a good swimmer, the one time she mustered the courage to venture into the Paddle Boat Lake in Prospect Park, where Moppet had dog-paddled after all those generations of ducks and Timber had displayed such prowess, Daisy almost drowned in two feet of water!

Boo was with us. It was before 9 A.M., and the two of them were off leash, when he decided a little stroll in the water might be nice. A few weeks earlier, we'd been at Calendar House and had taken Daisy and Boo to a small stream where—for the first time—Daisy had overcome her aversion to water and actually done a little paddling around with Boo. Hers hadn't been blue ribbon swimming (neither was Boo's for that matter). It had simply demonstrated she could swim.

So here we were in Prospect Park, with Boo gently swimming around as Daisy stood on the shore watching him, the steam coming off her head as she was trying to decide whether to follow him in, when she took the big psychological plunge and pushed off. My mother had joined me for this little walk, so it was the two of us standing there watching them swim, and it was so much fun. Boo was doing okay, lazily swimming around. Daisy was doing well, too. She was in the horizontal position with her head and the top of her back above water, her feet paddling away below the water. She actually seemed to be enjoying herself, when, four feet away from the store and in all of two feet of water, she forgot how to swim! Her body instantly lost its horizontal position. She turned vertical in the water, her front feet splashing like crazy, her head still above the water, but the rest of her was sinking like a rock and she was in a complete panic! And the more she panicked, the more she sank!

I turned aghast to my mother. "My God, she's drowning!" I was going to have to go in and pull her out! Of course, on this, the water-rescue day, I wasn't wearing my usual casual dog-walking attire which wouldn't have suffered the dunk in the drink. I had on a very tailored, very nice, long black coat and unusually nice shoes. I made the split-second decision: The hell with the shoes, but damn it, I'm not sacrificing the coat! So I tore the coat off, shoved it into my mother's hands, and was a second away from tearing into the water, when Daisy scrambled to shore and hauled herself out, one dripping, horrified mass of sputtering dog. So much for the good swimmer in this spaniel.

If Daisy sometimes forgets she's a cocker spaniel, half the time she forgets she's a dog altogether, finding the company of other dogs—with the exception of Tyler—highly disturbing. They're too noisy: dogs are known to bark. Too unpredictable: they might accidentally brush up against her. Too messy: they might accidentally breathe on her. Indeed, the running joke in this family is that Daisy's not a dog at all. If her fur came with a zipper and we could unzip it, out would pop a rabbit! Rabbit jokes aside, this—my fault—is the socialization she didn't receive as a puppy, as she was raised with Boo whose other-dog belligerence pre-cluded any interaction with them. Where Boo went, Daisy went. Thus her knowledge of other dogs started and stopped with him. This big gap in her education is much improved since the arrival of the affable and outgoing Tyler, whose example of total pleasure in fellow canines has raised Daisy's abhorrence to a tolerable level, her occasional little tail wag suggesting one day she just might be able to pump herself up to liking other dogs.

But before Tyler, other dogs made her so nervous she'd drool with anxiety and emit not exactly a growl, it was more like a nervous hum. For weeks after Boo died, I carried her around in the park so she could reacquaint herself with her own kind from the security of my arms. At one point we were making such good progress—she still drooled but had stopped the humming—that I thought I'd try putting her down on the ground near some friendly little dogs that were gently playing. Then—wouldn't you know it!—some Dalmatian tearing around with his dog pals who wasn't looking where he was going ran right into her, knocking her off her feet. When I hurried over to make sure she was okay, her eyes were livid: *You see how awful they are? Get me out of here!*

She overcame this setback, but Tyler would prove the real catalyst in bringing her out of her shell. These days, Daisy is almost to the point where she knows for certain she is a dog. While she still shuns large dogs, she will occasionally stand and sniff noses with little dogs like herself. Interestingly, she's warmed up to being around other cocker spaniels, most especially other chocolates. There's a wonderful one near us; his name is Buddy. He's a sweet, gentle creature, just like his owner, Nancy. At first, Daisy wouldn't even make eye contact with Buddy, her theory, no doubt, that if she ignored him long enough, he might do what she fervently hoped: disappear. But little by little she let her guard down. Now, some three years later—Daisy doesn't like to rush things—they're pals, and the two chocolate cockers walk side by side through the Long Meadow as Nancy and I joke about the "cute little couple" they make and I marvel how Daisy finally found the gumption to make herself a friend.

Then, just the other week, Daisy did something that was an absolute first: she chased a dog! It was a fluffy little white thing who came trotting over to say hello. Instead of giving him the big chill—the stiff back and glaring eyeballs—Daisy ran forward and gave chase! For fun! It wasn't thirty feet of fun chase. It was more like ten feet. But ten big feet for the cocker spaniel who used to shake in her shoes at the sight of another dog. Other distinguishing physical or emotional traits that set her apart from other spaniels?

Daisy is a very small cocker spaniel. Recalling that female cockers stand approximately fourteen inches at the shoulder and weigh between twenty-four to twenty-eight pounds, Daisy measures twelve inches and weighs all of eighteen pounds. Many are the people who see her on the street and come over to warmly exclaim, "She's so cute! Is she a puppy?" I thank them for the "cute" remark before providing the information: "She's nine years old."

What anyone admiring her couldn't possibly imagine is that this "cute" little eighteen-pound cocker spaniel snores like a five-hundred pound rhinoceros. It's so loud that, years ago, Lexie expelled her from her bedroom, as did David and I. She sleeps in a basket in the downstairs hall. Even so, her snoring rumbles through the house. During the day, she takes naps in my office as I work, but I have to poke her when the racket starts. Watching television at night, we keep the magazines handy to throw not on her, but close enough to wake her up when she slips into rhino mode.

Speaking of TV, she watches it. Not the news or music videos, but nature programs, especially when the bear, wolf, or whatever it is makes barking or whining sounds. Many a dog's ears prick up at these sounds and the heads zip around to their source. But without the smells and other real-life effects, few dogs continue to watch the screen. Daisy does! There's something about the way her eyesight or her brain interprets the images on the screen that finds it real enough to sustain interest. Not your usual dog, cocker spaniel or otherwise.

Then there's her coat. Remember the maddening curling fur on Moppet's ears that caused so much trouble? This fur grows all over Daisy. Unclipped, she turns into a poodle; she looks like a brown Grover from Sesame Street. Lexie grooms Daisy with the regularity I groomed Moppet: not often. Then again, Daisy is impossible to groom. The fur on her ears, her body, her legs, even her tail, sprouts out like a brown Chia Pet. It even grows on her face, obscuring her eyes to the point that someone viewing her in this state might well wonder *Is anybody in there?*

The first time her fur got hopelessly out of control, I took her to a professional groomer and had her clipped all the way down. When I went back to pick her up, much to my distress I found that underneath the ball of fur, she was too thin! Her little ribs were showing. I immediately set to feeding her more. The next time, some six months later, it turned out that extra food worked a little too well. When the fur ball came off, I discovered she'd turned into a fat little barrel. Now, like the Goldilocks story, she's just right. Not too fat, not too thin. I've also reached—with the help of the groomer—a nice balance with Daisy's infamous fur: not too long, not too short, but just right, with a little extra left on the ears.

As for her nails, I've never read in a breed description that the cocker spaniel "grows eagle talons for nails." Most cockers wear their nails down as they run around. This is particularly the case for urban cockers who walk, as Daisy does, on concrete and slate sidewalks. But because of the natural angle at which Daisy's nails emerge from her toes, they don't make contact with these sidewalk nail files. So she grows eagle talons, thick hard curls of steel that merrily grow on and on. And they do it at an astounding rate. We clip them down. Three weeks later, the talons are back and she's clicking around the house on the hardwood floors, like little metal pellets pinging on a tin roof. Of course, she doesn't sit still for the nail trim. It's a wrestling match we engage in to immobilize her so we can isolate each toe. Now comes the high stakes part: to clip off just the right amount of nail. Not easy with black eagle talons. Cut too much and we cut into the "quick" where the vein (and nerve) is, which causes the vein to bleed and the jangled nerve to instantly send its message to the brain: *pain*. But cut too little and we don't cure the maddening clicking.

The clicking aside—no less the fact that it can't be fun for the dog— too long nails can pose health issues. They cause the toes to splay or spread out, which can misalign the bones in the foot, which can throw off the leg, ultimately affecting how it rides in the shoulder socket. So there are real reasons to keep a dog's nails trimmed. Forget about scissors. The only tool that does the job safely is that little guillotine dog nail clipper (which works for cats, too). The portion of the nail to be cut goes in the little circle, and down comes the guillotine blade to slice the appropriate section off neatly and cleanly.

"Cut them until you hear *nothing*," David used to tell me. But the procedure is so nerve-racking that I now tell David, "*You* cut them until you hear nothing." Then I take myself as far away as possible so I won't hear what brings me to Daisy's next distinguishing trait: that hysterical screaming she does when she's really upset. Nothing gets that screaming going faster and louder than a nail cutting session. It's a wonder the neighbors have never called the police; these are bloodcurdling screams that sound as though strips of her flesh were being peeled off.

Other events can trigger it, too: the moment at the vet's when the syringe comes at her. It's what happens when a stranger on the street accidentally steps on her (the trauma here two-fold: she got stepped on and it was a horrid stranger who did it). It's also—fortunately not an everyday occurrence—"separation anxiety" that, done Daisy's way, is separation hysteria. No one captured this hysteria better than Boo's breeder, a woman not known for her sense of humor, but this time, she found some.

Daisy was three then; Boo was six. We'd taken the dogs to Laura's to board them for a week. We dropped them off at seven in the evening. Three hours later, Daisy reached the horrible conclusion we weren't coming back, and she wasn't going to take this horror silently. To whit, as Laura put it, "At ten o'clock the siren (that would be Daisy) went off. We thought the rottweilers had caught one of the dachshunds and were killing it!"

As fixed as Daisy's little idiosyncrasies are in her personality, they pale in comparison to her most outstanding trait, that trait that more than any other defines the cocker spaniel: her capacity to love. The pleasure she takes in pleasing us, providing, of course, it doesn't go against her wishes. It's her need to be close to us. The affection she showers on us. These emotions are rendered with the fullest heart as, more than anything else, this is who Daisy is.

When I head up the two flights of stairs to go to work in my office, she runs up the stairs so fast to be with me she trips on them. When she has to choose between following me around the house as I do chores on a hot summer day, or luxuriating in the wonderful chill of an air conditioned bedroom, she chooses me. She may be little, but her heart is big. What it also has—indeed, no small contradiction in a dog so into herself—is an amazing ability to feel and demonstrate compassion for others.

This wasn't something she grew into, or that came with maturity. Daisy was barely a year old when the events of a particularly bad day spiraled me down into a state of dejection such as I hadn't felt in years. That night, I couldn't sleep and went down to the living room to sit on the sofa and cry my unhappiness out in the darkness. Then I felt the brush of soft fur against my legs, and a little hop. Daisy was up on the sofa next to me, then on me, licking my arms over and over, my heart rescued by this show of compassion from the little dog whose only feeling was for me.

Her capacity for compassion continues. Many is the time I find myself overwhelmed by the frustration of something as simple, but not easily solved, as too much to do and not enough time to do it. Or I loose heart because something very important has gone very wrong and I don't have the wherewithal to fix it. Or I feel dejected because justice looked the other way when someone I care about needed it to look his way. These are no more or less than the troubled waters that rock anyone's life. But no one picks up on my troubled waters faster than Daisy. She rises to undo my unhappiness, to reverse it, with her solicitousness, the concern in her big eyes fixed on my face, the hopeful little wags of her tail, as she stays close to me and helps me weather the storm until I see the light again.

Lexie and I have this thing we've laughed about for years, that if she went to some foreign land where the camels, and incense, and too many cobras rising out of too many baskets began to do her in and make her long for places and faces familiar, I would arrange to have a box arrive and out would pop Daisy and Lexie would instantly be home. As Daisy is synonymous with home, with things sweet, and hopeful, and good.

Daisy's lessons? She woke me up to something long overlooked in my life: the importance of "creature comforts," those basic fundamental forms of comfort that are so attainable, so within anyone's reach. It isn't the once-a-year, big vacation that restores (in fact, it often exhausts), but the little pleasures we put into everyday life. So expert, so discerning, so versed is Daisy in this arena that she earned herself yet another title: the "Master Instructor of the Merits of Creature Comforts."

Far beyond the warm bed and good food that would satisfy any reasonable dog, this stubbornly-pursues-her-comforts little dog insists upon warm places to be when it's cold; cool places to be when it's hot; a very nice bed to sleep in; her used-to-be-fat but still fuzzy Teddy to sleep on; premium dog food, preferably topped with cat food to please her palette; and lots of nap time to prep and refresh her for the next round of pleasures. Conversely, she stubbornly avoids what is not comfort: having the water bowl empty, which, as we already know, makes her bang on it. She isn't going to go thirsty silent. It's being alone, which means nobody to do her bidding. And at all cost, it is the avoidance of any sensation even remotely resembling pain.

This attention to and absorption in self was stunning to someone who, except in August, worked six days a week for years. Who didn't let the cold or the heat stop her, or various aches and pains. Who skipped lunch half the time. Who worked weekends when the rest of the world rested, worked holidays when the rest of the world partied. Who went to work sick because where I came from you didn't fail to go to work unless you were dead.

This stoic work-life thing, however, did not for a second apply to Lexie. As already related, I saw what Della did for her puppies, and I carried her example right up through the years to emulate when my time came to be a mother. So Lexie's comfort, from infancy up, was of paramount importance to me. If she woke up in the middle of the night and cried out, I raced to her aid. Before she could talk, if there was one wrinkle in her blouse that looked like it might feel uncomfortable, I smoothed it out for her. When the old air-conditioners weren't doing the job, she was the first to get a new one. But I couldn't apply anything near this comfort level to myself.

My workmate and friend Shawn would see how tired I sometimes got, and plied me with that classic women's remedy to combat fatigue and other ills: her cheery "How about a day of beauty?" (Translation: Go out and get a massage, a facial, anything relaxing. Or, do the beauty on your own turf. Lock the bathroom door and take a long hot soak in the tub and don't come out until you're good and ready.) She'd see the incredulous look on my face at the suggestion of "A *day* of beauty" and knock it down to "An afternoon of beauty?" When the look still hadn't changed, it was "An hour? *Ten minutes* of beauty?"

Shawn's wise counsel fell on deaf ears. When you're a mother with a child to look after and a husband to try to keep happy and writing deadlines to meet and the rest of it—your own needs get lost in the shuffle. You forget you even have needs. And not even a friend as close as Shawn could jar me out of this misconception.

And then came Daisy with that masters degree in the pursuit and enjoyment of everyday comforts that was so extreme—and provided so many examples—that it finally opened my eyes to the fact that there's nothing wrong with these things. There's much right with them. To put a little pleasure or relaxation into my day wasn't selfish, it was essential. And I needed to do it the way Daisy does: without a shred of guilt.

It wasn't Daisy's over the top comfort I was after. It would take a household staff of fifty and three secretaries to reach Daisy's comfort level. Rather, as with so many things in life, I needed to strike a balance. I needed to find the little everyday things that would deliver the big result for me. I found them. A cup of tea: not just any tea, but lovely teas simmering to perfection in a lovely cup to enhance the experience. A new comforter to deliver just that: comfort. A moment—or two—in the morning to step out on the deck and smell the roses. Not prune them. Not fertilize them. Not take cuttings to make more of them. Just smell and enjoy them.

I began to do these things. I continue to do them. It takes practice. I'm working on it.

This comfort idea brings me to the puppies Daisy never had. As already related, dogs can surprise you: You never know who has it in her to be a whole-hearted mother. As related, Moppet couldn't get out the door of motherhood fast enough. Della was the mother extraordinaire.

Timber I suspect would have been a lovely mother. But Daisy? With that masters degree in creature comforts, motherhood was out of the question! For starters, she would have never even made it through the mating; she would have become hysterical. And forget about the main event: giving birth. One real contraction and she would have fainted. Then nursing? Keeping track of puppies? Cleaning them? Dedication, in other words, to *other* lives? Daisy is dedicated to herself. I say this as lovingly as Lexie said Daisy's is a selfish intelligence. There wasn't a bunch of thinking to be done about puppies for Daisy. She was spayed.

Life with Daisy is also illuminating the amazing inconsistencies that can exist within the same dog's—or human's—personality. The fearful little creature who also has in her to summon (albeit, a show of) great courage. The sporting dog who can't stand the natural elements on a street, but take her to the woods and she jumps to life. The smart little cocker who can't remember to pee outside, but out of the blue remembers and does a trick she was taught a year ago. But nowhere is the lesson of inconsistencies driven home with greater heart than the example of this "selfish" little dog who is so capable of feeling and displaying such great compassion for others.

The lesson of inconsistencies goes further, into *seeming* inconsistencies. When Daisy was six, I thought I had her pretty well down pat, knew what was in her heart and in her head. But sometimes I wondered what else was she thinking? What was the depth of her thoughts? Did she ever think about Boo? Did she miss him?

I couldn't imagine she missed his threats and growling at feeding time. Nor did I think she missed the hundreds of times he practically knocked her over to lunge at all those dogs on the streets. Had these things hastened to erase him from her mind?

I cite an example that shows you never know for sure what goes on in the head of any dog, or any other cognitive entity, for that matter. Be ready for surprises. Be ready to be humbled by the wrongness of your thought.

As already stated, about the time Boo died, rottweilers burst on the scene. Suddenly they were all over the park, on the streets, in the news— they were coming out of the woodwork. But they didn't look like Boo. These spindly-footed, undersized, misshapen, ill-begotten rottweilers were (and continue to be) the watered-down versions that happen with an explosion in a breed's popularity.

But one time, some three years after Boo died, Daisy and I were approaching the entrance to Prospect Park at Grand Army Plaza, when she suddenly stopped walking and stood there frozen. I gave a gentle tug on the leash. She didn't budge. I gave another tug. She ignored it. "What is it?" I asked her. She didn't even look at me. Her eyes were sharply trained on something. I looked where she was looking, and then I saw it: a large and very beautiful male rottweiler walking with its owner across the broad expanse of Grand Army Plaza. Daisy continued to stare, her head slowly turning as her eyes followed this dog. *She thinks it's Boo.* Or maybe he simply reminded her of Boo. Something moved in my heart. A respect for her, for her feelings, and her memories. We stood there together as she watched this rottweiler until he was a tiny figure in the distance.

Life goes on, and so had we. There was Tyler at home. There was the walk in the park waiting for us. But there are moments when you stop, as Daisy did at Grand Army Plaza, to remember who came before.

6

Tyler: The Joy-of-Living Dog

A love affair with life. We humans are born with it, but, alas, soon outgrow it. Or life tramples it out of us (but never without our permission). Or we forget it. Or if we remember, we put it off to that great usurper of life—"some other time"—as though we had not one, but three lifetimes to play around with. But if we're lucky, something or someone comes along to turn us around, to remind us, even better, to show us by the very fiber of his being and actions, the joy of living. In my case, it is a beautiful Bernese mountain dog who came along at this special juncture in my life—with one half essentially lived, and the other half waiting to see what I will do with it—to show me the gift that *any day* we get to live is. And how essential to really live it as it is offered, one precious moment at a time.

I had never seen or even heard of a Bernese mountain dog until three or four months after Boo died. I was standing with Daisy at the bottom of our block one morning, when I happened to look across Seventh Avenue. There, standing at the corner, was a strikingly beautiful, big, tricolored dog, with glossy jet black fur, a white blaze on his chest, symmetrical white and brown markings on his feet, and a beautiful face with a white streak between his eyes that ran up his forehead. What was equally stunning was the look in his eyes—the look his entire body radiated—of serene confidence and friendliness. When the couple accompanying this lovely creature crossed over to my side of the street, I approached them to ask the question people now stop me on the street everyday to ask, "What breed *is* that dog?"

I'll answer that question right now.

The Bernese mountain dog (known in his Switzerland as the Berner Sennenhunde) derives his name and origin from the Swiss canton of Bern, and is one of the four breeds of "sennenhunde" (Alpine Herdsman's Dog) that are the oldest living breeds in Switzerland. (The other three are the Appenzeller Sennenhunde; the Entlebucher Sennenhunde; and the Greater Swiss Sunnenhunde, or Great Swiss Mountain Dog.) While all four breeds share similar markings, only the Bernese sports a long coat.

The Bernese mountain dog has worked in conjunction with people for thousands of years. Indeed, evidence of his ancestors dates back to the dogs used by Stone Age farmers in Neolithic Switzerland. In recent millennia, Alpine herdsmen used the Bernese as a herding dog to drive and protect their flocks, pull carts to market, and guard the farm and family. Pulling a cart required traits of physical size and strength and endurance. Guarding and protecting the flock required a dog with a "low-prey" drive where the flock was concerned, but a high level of protective instincts regarding predatory animals. Because he is so amenable to training, in modern times the Bernese mountain dog (classified in the Working Group) has also been used as a police dog. While he still enthusiastically herds and willingly pulls carts, nowadays the Bernese is an esteemed companion dog.

In appearance, the Bernese is an arrestingly beautiful dog of jet black color, with rich mahogany markings on his legs, cheeks, over each eye, and on either side of the showy white chest marking that forms a Swiss cross. A white blaze adorns his face, muzzle, and forehead, with further white on his feet and tail tip. His bushy tail must not curl or curve over the back, but fall straight down. His outercoat is thick, moderately long, glossy, and straight or slightly wavy. A profuse, soft, undercoat enables him to endure harsh winters. His eyes are dark brown (the occasional blue eyes he sports is a disqualifying fault in the show ring).

Male Bernese measure twenty-five to twenty-eight inches at the shoulder and weigh eighty to one hundred twenty pounds, whereas females measure twenty-three to twenty-six inches at the shoulder and weight sixty-five to ninety pounds. This is a breed, like the Great Dane and rottweiler, in which males appear distinctly masculine, while females are distinctly feminine.

The temperament of the Bernese mountain dog is, in a word, lovely. He's confident, sensitive, and serene, but also delightfully alert and outgoing. He's energetic outdoors, but calm indoors. As mentioned, he is highly trainable. (Coren ranks this breed in the very respectable number twenty-two slot.) He is most agreeable toward other dogs, very friendly (particularly males) with people he knows, gentle with other animals, and very affectionate with his owner. He exhibits endearing traits like the "Berner smile" that forms on his face when he's pleased with something (which is most of the time), and the "Berner hug," something he does with his front paws to hold on to the object of his affection: his owner. Like the herding dog he is, the Bernese trails his owner around the house until the owner stops moving, perchance sits down, whereupon the typical Berner will step over and sit on his owner's feet (an effective way to keep track of him), until, of course, the owner gets up and the trailing starts anew.

The Berner's attitude toward strangers varies from friendly to aloof, but sometimes—this is not considered ideal—this aloofness, particularly in the case of female Bernese, can be excessive shyness that needs to be remedied early in puppyhood with deliberate and regular socialization to strangers.

While this large, beautiful breed is readily found in Canada (and, of course Switzerland), it is still somewhat uncommon in the United States. As I waited for breeder information from The American Kennel Club, I set about researching the Bernese mountain dog. I went to bookstores where the shelves were overflowing with general breed books, and many breed specific books, six on rottweilers, seven on golden retrievers, five on West Highland white terriers. But there was only one Bernese mountain dog book to be seen. When I finally found it, I grabbed it, bought it, and hurried home to read it: *The New Bernese Mountain Dog*. Its author, Sharon Chestnutt Smith, is not only a highly respected, AKC approved judge of Bernese mountain dogs in the United States, she is the delegate to The American Kennel Club from the Bernese Mountain Dog Club of America. She also—my heart leapt when I saw it—maintains a small, select kennel, where she and her husband breed some of the finest Bernese mountain dogs anywhere. And her kennel is only in Catskill, New York!

It sounded too good to be true! When I called her up, it would only get better. The breeder-prospective buyer relationship instantly clicked. And then, as we further questioned each other, it turned out that earlier she had lived in Park Slope for fifteen years! We even had a few longtime acquaintances in common. But no, she didn't have any puppies available by any means. Her current litter, born five weeks earlier, had been spoken for many months before. She only bred a few females each year, and like any highly respected Bernese breeder, she had a long waiting list for her puppies. She said she would enter my name on her list for a future litter, but the wait might easily be a year. In the meanwhile, she would send me her questionnaire to fill out. I was so completely impressed with her in every possible way that I was prepared to wait that year. Several days later, she called. Due to personal circumstances in their prospective buyers' lives, two puppies in the current litter had suddenly become available: two beautiful males. She invited us to drive up and have a look.

That Sunday, David, Lexie, and I took the two-hour trip that had us eventually driving down an asphalt road that turned into a gravel road and ended in a quiet cul-de-sac. Her charming home—and the kennel on the hill above it—was situated in the trees on a bank very close to the shore of the Hudson River. Sharon, even more gracious in person, came out to greet us. We went into her home filled with myriad blue ribbons and awards. We then entered the kitchen to meet the parents of the litter we were here to see, who—coming upon them so suddenly—gave the initial impression of two black Saint Bernards! Indeed, David exclaimed, "They're *so* big!" (As in *too* big!) I gave him a "relax" look. Put two adult Bernese mountain dogs in a kitchen, even a large one, that kitchen shrinks and the dogs look even bigger. "It's an optical illusion," I told him.

Sharon gave us a tour that included going up the small grassy hill to the kennel and outdoor pens where a dozen gorgeous Bernese greeted us with barking and much tail waving. These adults now viewed, and much admired by me, it was time to see the Bernese babies.

Sharon took us into the comfortable, very clean building that housed the pen, where David, Lexie, and I peered down with excitement and sheer delight at ten beautiful little five-week-old Bernese puppies in various states of puppy behavior. Some were jumping around on the papers. Others were playfully gnawing on each other. Two were doing the tug of war thing with a cloth toy. One or two, standing amid the jumble, watched us watch them. And then—there's always one—there was the one puppy fast asleep on his side, his feet out straight, his plump little belly rising and falling as he breathed. "That one!" Lexie cried out.

"Which one?" I asked her. "*That* one," she said, pointing to the one who was fast asleep. I checked with Sharon, who said he was one of the two "show-quality pet" males available. His markings were perfection, he was absolutely beautiful. But ever the dog person, not sure if his sleeping indicated lethargy, I directed Lexie's attention to the other lovely available male puppy. "But look at this one," I said, pointing to the little creature who was right next to us, jumping up against the pen wall. "Look how lively he is!"

"No," Lexie said. "The sleeping one."

Sharon reached in, picked him up, and let us touch him. He instantly woke up and was completely alert, and so adorable. His markings, as stated, were perfection. In the Bernese world, the right markings make for much excitement. But far beyond this, there was a sweetness about him beyond description. We fell in love with him right then and there.

So it was not I who chose Tyler, it was Lexie. It was her unfailing eye, that sensibility of hers, even at thirteen, to spot the someone with something special. It is Lexie who I have to thank for Tyler. And Lexie who I also have to thank for giving him the perfect name.

Three weeks later, we went back to get our baby Tyler. He was a much bigger baby now! And not asleep! He was wide wake and hopping around when Sharon picked him up. We did the paperwork in her living room, met her equally gracious husband, and she gave me a fat blue folder with some fifty xeroxed sheets detailing Bernese diet, health, exercise, training—the works!

Tyler rode home in my lap and Lexie's lap. When we stopped on the highway for a snack, David finally had his turn holding him; then I got him back. Tyler took all this passing around with total equanimity.

Do Tyler's genes conform to his breed? They do, right down to the white tip of his otherwise black fluffy tail, as he is everything the ideal Bernese mountain dog is supposed to be, taken to the third power.

As a puppy who I carried around until his shots were complete, Tyler was so unbelievably adorable, people would stop me on the street to ask, "Is he *real?*" All Bernese mountain dog puppies are adorable, as are all puppies, period. But the Bernese puppy takes adorable to the category of unbelievable.

The unbelievably adorable puppy Tyler was then grew up into the spectacularly beautiful Bernese mountain dog he is now some four years later. He stands twenty-seven inches at the shoulder, with a broad chest, and weighs one hundred pounds. His markings are stunning. His coat is glossy and slightly wavy. Underneath that beautiful coat, he's heavily muscled. His head, the crowning glory of the Bernese, is glorious. In it, on either side of the blaze that runs up his forehead, are two lovely, dark brown eyes whose gaze says much about him. Because if Tyler's outside is something to behold, his inside is golden through and through. Not just for me. His golden quality, like the sun, shines everywhere he goes, eliciting smiles from strangers on the street, who are certainly struck by how beautiful he is. But it's also what radiates from Tyler, the friendliness, the sweetness, the fresh-new-puppy optimism on his face that produces those smiles and draws people to him. Indeed, I haven't seen anything like it since Timber.

Tyler's take on the other Bernese traits explains the rest of him. It includes the "gentle with other animals" characteristic that is core in the Bernese. This is the farm dog in him, the dog bred through the millennia to guard the flock, not eat them, to keep track of the chickens, not chase them. Tyler doesn't live with chickens, sheep, or cows, but he does live with cats, not to mention the inimitable Miss Daisy.

When we first brought Tyler home, Daisy's initial reaction, as related, was a stunned, dismayed, disapproving, *What's that?* Worse, this *that* grew at an alarming rate. He started out half her size. In a matter of three weeks, he reached her size. Then he doubled it, tripled it, quadrupled it. When he stopped growing, in height, anyway, at the age of a year and a half or so, Daisy was the length of Tyler's head plus his neck. To be sure, Daisy might have had a lot of dog to be upset about, had Tyler not completely won her over in a matter of days with his sweet and gentle ways. To win over Daisy in any capacity—no less total conversion—is a feat only a little short of miraculous.

He did the same thing with the cats.

Twinkie and Snowball have always been engaged in a happy life. But for Boo's six years, their indoor happy life had them wisely keeping to the safety of kitchen counters and snug spaces under the furniture. After Boo died, they were just getting used to being able to walk across the living room floor without nervously looking over their shoulder, when in came Tyler. The fact that he was little was no reassurance to them. Boo started out little, too. So it was *Oh, God, here we go again* on both their faces.

Tyler would prove them so wrong. His genes didn't have built into them any "high-prey" drive to chase, harm, or even intimidate other animal species. His genes were "low-prey," designed to cohabit peaceably with them. But Tyler took it many steps further to develop a very loving relationship with the cats that includes the category at which even the most gentle dog will draw the line in the sand: his food.

The cats are fed their cat food, but often the dog food in Tyler's bowl looks more inviting to them, so they take themselves over to have a serious munch in it. As a little puppy, and as the hundred-pound Bernese he is today, Tyler willingly lets the cats eat from his bowl. If he's really hungry and there's a cat head where he would like his head to be, his peaceable solution is to slowly move in, start eating at the far side of the bowl, then ever so gently he inches center, effectively nudging the reluctant Snowball or Twinkie out. A very different scene from the terror around the food bowl that Boo engendered.

As to affectionate behavior, Snowball often seeks Tyler out, rubbing herself back and forth against his tall front legs, gazing appreciatively up at him, as Tyler stands and waits, enjoying this contact. Many is the time I come down late at night to find the two of them sleeping together in the front hallway, Snowball using Tyler as a giant pillow.

Tyler is even nice to tiny animals! When we first got Tyler, Lexie had a hamster. Tyler would stand next to the bed in her room, watching the hamster run around on the covers. She also had a parakeet. He would sit below its cage and amiably watch it fly around. He would even park himself in front of her fish tank to observe what was going on in there. With all of them, it was look, not touch, not frighten, not disturb in any way.

When I first started taking Tyler to the park, our jaunts then, as now, often took us to the Paddle Boat Lake where we paused and looked at the ducks. Which is exactly what Tyler does: look.

Is he a saint of a Bernese? If you waved a squirrel under his nose and then let it go, would he chase it? He might, but never seriously. He might chase it for several yards, but all in play, before, a moment later, he remembered himself and stopped.

His intelligence? His trainability? Tyler isn't just the very intelligent dog all Bernese are, he's exceptionally intelligent, his brain-power exhibiting amazing versatility heightened by another Bernese trait: a great sensitivity that takes in subtlety and nuance. And all of it is instantly switched on for any given task at any given moment by another Berner characteristic Tyler possesses in spades: his great desire to please. To do virtually whatever is asked of him, and then be praised, as he loves that praise.

I pause here to make clear how sensitive—a sensitive not to be confused with timid—the typical Bernese mountain dog is. You don't have to shout at him, you must not shout at him (or any other dog, for that matter) in the training process. It upsets the Bernese, it bewilders him. He doesn't need or want any kind of strong-arm tactics. Just quietly tell him, or gently show him, what he needs to know. And get ready to praise him, as there will be cause. He will willingly and quickly learn the lesson at hand.

As a puppy, there was very little of teaching Tyler the basics; he picked them up on his own. All the more to his credit, as he didn't have a fellow canine—that would be Miss Daisy—providing a positive example. In fact, her example, as already indicated, was often the opposite of what we wanted him to observe. But it worked, taught him anyhow. For instance, that all-important housebreaking that Daisy never learned. Baby Tyler arrived peeing and eliminating on the floor like any puppy. But he caught the look on my face when I saw his puddles on the floor and he changed his ways almost overnight so he would never see that look again. Yes, a far cry from the free-to-pee Miss Daisy who makes no apologies for her ways. Indeed, it's *Tyler* who is embarrassed; it's the distressed look on his face that tells us Daisy has left a wet circle or a little brown present in the hall.

Then there's the more sophisticated training his terrific brains coupled with his sure-I'll-do-it attitude sponsors: he heels perfectly on and off leash. He drops things when asked, even stuff he really enjoys, like his toys. He calmly walks past any dog on the street even if it's acting like a real maniac. He's learning hand signals. I'm grateful he doesn't need to, as Timber did. I'm just throwing them in because they're so easy to do and he's so quick to pick them up. The wave of my hand beckoning him to come, along with the verbal, "Come, Tyler!" The back up signal at the same time I tell him, "Back up, Tyler." The "move left" command, coupled with a wave of my hand to the left. The "move right," the hand gesture so indicating. All of these directives and their results are achieved in a harmonious manner with this finely tuned, exceptional Bernese.

The description of the Bernese as "friendly with other people" does not come *close* to describing this Berner with the fan club in Prospect Park: the fellow dog owners in the dozens who have fallen under his spell. Their faces light up when he runs over with the "Berner smile" on his face to say hello. They delight in how he invites them to pet him, leans on their legs (another Berner trait he's adept in plying) to press his point, and how this big beautiful dog is just as sweet as he can be. Some people give him an affectionate round of thumps to his side. Others squeeze him. Some just plain out hug him. There's one woman in the park who is so enamored of him, she gives him massages. Whatever they do, they don't want him to leave. He's so *nice*. He's so friendly. He's so much fun to be around. But he can't stay too long. There's somebody else he likes coming across the field who he now has to run over to greet, tag wagging, the smile up. If Tyler doesn't see this person right away—because he's so busy enjoying the person he's already with—he gets called over. Because they want to see him, be near him, touch him, and have their moment with the Bernese mountain dog, who, as one fellow dog owner who's known him since the first day he showed up in Prospect Park calls him, "The great affable Tyler."

As for children, Tyler loves them, and the feeling is mutual. He stands there, tail gently fanning back and forth, and lets them pet him, play with his ears, run their hands through his fur, touch his whiskers, count the brown freckles (he has three of them) in his white muzzle, as he gazes sweetly into their eyes. With children, Tyler is Timber redux.

Indeed, this Bernese is the dog for people with dog-phobia. Spend an afternoon—or fifteen minutes—with Tyler and you're cured.

What is Tyler's take on the typical Bernese's attitude toward strangers that "varies from friendly to aloof?" Stop right at friendly, and make it very friendly. Tyler has lots of opportunities to be friendly because Park Slope is a very popular place these days. For three decades, Manhattanites have been immigrating across the Brooklyn Bridge in droves to stake their claim in the "urban neighborhood with the small town feeling." The tour buses now come down its landmark-designated streets to view the Victorian brownstones and see the stunning examples of every architectural style popular in the late nineteenth century. Seventh Avenue, particularly on weekends, is brimming with people. While many people know each other, there are many strangers irresistibly drawn to Tyler who stands, as nice as he could be, letting them touch him, as I field the question Tyler raises every day he leaves the house: "What breed *is* he?"

So nice is Tyler to all people that, truth to tell, I had begun to wonder, *Did I have a special place in his heart?* The answer was revealed when, after a three-year absence from the horticultural world (which I missed, because I love it), I began working two days a week—two intense, very demanding days—at a leading and very large garden center in New York City. I leave the house at 9 A.M. in the morning, and return at 7 P.M. Prior to this, Tyler had only experienced my work-at-home writing life.

When I returned home the first day, Tyler was extremely glad to see me, and he seemed fine. But when I went into the kitchen to set about dinner preparations, I saw he wasn't fine. His food bowl was completely untouched. When I returned home the second day, it was the same thing. Not so much as a crumb had been touched. As friendly as he was to people he knew and strangers he didn't know, he did care about me in a special way. His take on that "very affectionate with his owner" trait was so deep, so profound, that he stopped eating for two days. It was only over time, and with practice seeing me leave in the morning and always coming back at night, that Tyler began eating again on Thursdays and Fridays.

Does Tyler's amazing "gets along with people" include, as it certainly does with the typical Bernese, "gets along with their dogs?" It does, and how. I went from Boo who couldn't be let near other dogs, to its absolute, polar opposite. Tyler doesn't just get along with other dogs, he delights in them: big dogs, small dogs, male, female, neutered, unneutered, spayed, not spayed, old, young, it matters not.

For many a Bernese mountain dog, this social trait is there in the genes, but it's not dominant. This is the Berner who must be deliberately socialized with other dogs (and their owners) to bring it out so he—more often she—can relax and enjoy himself in their midst. While Tyler had much exposure to other dogs from the moment his shots were complete—his daily runs in the park, our jaunts through Park Slope, and every place else we went—Tyler was born socialized. He popped out of the egg ready to partake of his own kind with a joy and pleasure I have never seen in any other dog, ever.

This sociability has also sponsored some funny moments. Prospect Park, particularly on weekend mornings in the off-leash hours before 9 A.M., is the dog show described earlier. Hundreds of dogs—in good weather, easily a thousand dogs—of all breeds run and play on the open expanse of the Long Meadow. There are the dozens and dozens of retrievers, the "Westies" (West Highland white terriers), the field spaniels, Vislas, Weimaraners, Basenjis, dachshunds, several greyhounds, salukis, Airedales, terriers, pointers, beagles, bulldogs, collies, Dalmatians, cocker spaniels—the full pedigree spectrum, with a good mingling of mixed-breeds thrown in.

While he's nice to all dogs, Tyler has favorites among them. Some are small like Fiona, the West Highland white terrier who he runs to greet, and she, him. He likes Buddy, the chocolate cocker spaniel who is also Daisy's (one) dog friend. There's Bear, the golden retriever. Leo, the black Labrador retriever, and Square Bear, the big wonderful Tibetan mastiff. He makes a bee line for Tyler, who is mighty glad to see him, too, as these two have been good friends from day one.

If one of Tyler's friends—or another dog he would like to befriend—is busily playing or running around in a cluster of dogs, out comes another Bernese trait. The herding dog in Tyler, in this application, knows how to separate out this dog from the herd and drive him away from it so he can have this dog all to himself. Tyler is nice enough about it; he's very gentle, but also very effective. With the dog in his sights, Tyler runs over and puts himself between this dog and the rest of the pack. Then, with gentle little clomps of his muzzle to this dog's behind—or with total body pushes—he drives this dog away from the pack so he can play with him alone.

If the object of his attention is running with other dogs in great big circles around the meadow, as is often the case in an open expanse like the Long Meadow, out comes the strategy and economy of motion in the herding dog. Tyler stands there—letting the other dogs do the running—as he waits, his forehead wrinkled with concentration, for the exact moment, as they circle closer, when the dog in question is the shortest possible distance from him. Then Tyler leaps into action, running forward into the pack, using the body blocks and muzzle clomps to separate this dog from the rest of the pack, driving him several yards away to keep him isolated, as they start to play.

The first time I saw Tyler exhibit these behaviors, I stood there laughing. It was so amazing, and he was so good at it! Then came the warm appreciation that made me smile as I realized what I was looking at: the herding dog *herding*.

Other things have made me laugh too. They speak not so much to Tyler's breed as they do to Tyler himself.

While there are a good number of dogs in Prospect Park, like the Tibetan mastiff, Square Bear, who are as large as Tyler, not too many dogs are significantly bigger than Tyler. But there are some. There's a Saint Bernard (who's still growing), several Old English mastiffs, several Great Danes, some Borzoi, even a Kuvasz or two, that Tyler regularly encounters. Big as they are in height or weight, these dogs don't dwarf Tyler. However, one day a black Newfoundland, this one some three feet tall at the shoulder, approached Tyler from behind. Tyler didn't see him coming, but sensing something, turned his head around, looked at him with utter disbelief, looked away for a split-second, then looked back—did a double-take—at this wall of dog suddenly right next to him. Another time, an exceptionally tall Great Dane also caught Tyler unsuspecting. He was walking with some dogs when the Great Dane stepped over. Tyler stopped walking, and—I caught the surprise on his face—looked *up* at this Great Dane's face.

Tyler's beauty, his high level of training, his congenial temperament, his friendliness toward strangers, and his ability to amiably roll with the punches have also put him in front of the camera.

Through the years, Timber's agent would occasionally call. She had been so impressed with Timber and her training, and also very saddened by her death. But knowing I loved dogs and that my life would always include dogs, she would call from time to time asking, "Anybody new to tell me about?" One of these calls came when Boo was three, when rottweilers were still relatively rare. "A *rottweiler?*" she said. "Is he trained? *Like Timber?* Could he—?" "Not a chance," I got right down to it. "Not unless you want everyone in the room bitten." She got the message.

She called a year later. I explained that we now had a chocolate cocker spaniel. "A *chocolate* cocker spaniel?" she said. "Is she trained?" "It's not her training," I explained. "It's her. She's not wired for commercial work. She'd hate it; couldn't do it. Not possible." We hung up the same professional friends we'd always been.

This lady was persistent, and she knew I tended to have two dogs at the same time. Two years later she called again. "Anybody new to tell me about?" "There is," I said. "His name is Tyler. He's a Bernese mountain dog. He's two, he's beautiful, he's trained, he's perfect." She requested I send her pictures of Tyler. I sent them.

Three months later, she called with work. It was a thirty-second TV commercial for Lysol. The segments included teenagers lounging around with their shoes on a bed, and a living room with grown-ups in another "dirt" situation. Tyler's segment would be with a six-month-old baby in a high chair, with Tyler very tight and up close to the baby—the point being that Lysol can even handle the germs on a highchair that a dog generates.

I had Tyler professionally bathed and groomed the day before. The morning of the shoot, equipped with water, brushes, and whatnot, we took a car service to the huge Silvercup Studios right across the East River from Manhattan. There Tyler wowed everyone—the director, producer, production assistants, lighting people, and sound people—first, with his looks, then, with his training, his behavior, his attitude. He was calm, but also wonderfully alert. All of this came across beautifully on film. And yes, he was extremely gentle and winning with the babies—three of them.

There was baby number one, and two "backup" babies. What Tyler had to do—and what he did—was sit right next to each baby in the highchair and look up alertly but sweetly at the baby. At the same time the baby had to look down adoringly at Tyler. The camera shot started out "wide" (filming the baby, the highchair, and Tyler), then slowly moved in for a tight shot of just the baby, and Tyler reacting to him, to end up on the baby's face reacting to Tyler. Thirty times, as the camera came to end on the baby's face, it literally brushed against Tyler's face. Thirty times, he took this brushing with absolute calmness.

But the babies weren't always calm. When the first baby began to fuss, they brought in the second baby and filmed Tyler with him. When this baby eventually got upset, too, they brought in the third baby and filmed Tyler with him. They ultimately used the footage with the baby whose performance best meshed with Tyler's. But Tyler had no backup. There is no backup for "dog talent." The dog is expected to do it, himself, over and over. Which Tyler did.

When Tyler's segment was over, five hours later, everyone broke for a late lunch and headed for quite an impressive spread, where the producer and crew people, utterly taken with Tyler, petted him and hugged him (a few slipped him little pieces of ham). Tyler had enjoyed getting to know these people, and he went right down the lunch line to socialize with all his new friends, affectionately leaning against a few, thoroughly enjoying himself as he had all morning long. And yes, he enjoyed the ham.

Next, Tyler did a photograph for a print advertisement—this one arranged by Tyler's other agent, a woman just as professional and nice as the first—that was shot in a very large loft in Soho in Manhattan. The ad was for a flea and tick product with, as its copy says, no pesticide residue, so that, as the happy family in this black-and-white photograph shows, there is no need to be afraid to get very physically close to the loved family dog.

When we arrived, the producer, the photographer, their crew, representatives from the flea and tick company, and so forth, were setting up. The models—an older but extremely attractive "father" and "mother," plus their two grown "children;" a good-looking man and woman in their thirties—were being made up. Also present was Tyler's agent, whose suggestions and help would prove most helpful throughout.

The shoot was set up with the parents sitting together on a sofa, their children leaning in close to them from behind the sofa, and the family dog—that would be Tyler—positioned by the parents' feet, looking alertly and sweetly into the camera.

To have Tyler at exactly the right height required that he sit on a wooden box and position himself so that the parents could put their arms around him. But, as the shoot began, the box proved to have insufficient traction. Despite Tyler's efforts to stay in position, his feet kept slipping out from under him. They put sticky tape on the box, which solved the sliding feet problem. I took up my position again, right behind the photographer, making sounds and hand gestures to keep Tyler angled in exactly the right position and have him look alertly right into the camera, as the shoot picked up again.

Whenever they broke to change cameras, adjust the lighting, change the position of the models, or adjust their clothing, I took these opportunities to brush Tyler's coat, making sure he was visually perfect. I also walked him around the loft to let him refresh himself. At one point, when everyone broke for lunch—a catered affair in another part of the loft—I took Tyler took down in the elevator to the sidewalk and curb so he could relieve himself.

Near the end of the shoot, with what they needed "in the can" and a little extra time still left, as an afterthought, the photographer suggested, "Why don't we try something different? Maybe Tyler on the sofa with them?"

I didn't have to tell Tyler twice. This was the command he'd been waiting for. He jumped up on the sofa, pushed himself around the father, to squeeze in tightly between the father and mother with real joy, even leaning against the mother. He'd come to like all these people whose hands in one combination or another had been all over him all afternoon!

And they liked him right back! In fact, the official shoot now over, the models who had been professionally smiling for hours now smiled for real, and so many hands genuinely came down and around to touch Tyler that the photographer, looking through his camera lens, loudly declared, "They're too many hands on Tyler! We can't see enough of him. Only the mother's hands on him!"

As the camera started to click away, with everyone genuinely animated—and Tyler leaning all over the mother with her arm around him—the photographer shot this last roll of film. That roll would produce the ad that demonstrates with heartwarming clarity, *this* is how close you can get to the family dog—and he to you—with this product.

Moving back closer to home, much has been said about beautiful Prospect Park, its Long Meadow, and, especially on a Saturday or Sunday morning, the thousand dogs who come here to exercise. It is therefore a fair assumption that half of them—some five hundred dogs—also eliminate here. After the morning dog people come the picnic people, and the Frisbee and volleyball people, and the just lounge around on the grass people. They do not do these things amid five hundred dog droppings, because the sanitation laws here are obeyed. Dog owners pick up after their dogs, almost to the person. They are also extremely civil and congenial in other ways. The dog scene here is the strong subculture described earlier, where people avidly discuss training, dog food brands, collars, and leashes, pass along breeder information, and trade vet information, all the way to the merits (or uncertainties therein) of holistic dog medicine.

What we also talk about is how very lucky we are to have this place. Prospect Park and its Long Meadow, the longest unbroken swatch of green space in New York City, with its off-leash hours, enables us to have all these dogs and exercise them. It also allows us to get to know each other, but rarely by our names. It's the dogs' names people know. When referring to the woman who walks Fiona, nobody knows her name to say it. She is "the woman who owns Fiona." Somebody else is "the woman who owns Sunny." I am "the woman who owns Tyler."

But not all is continually rosy on the Long Meadow of Prospect Park.

Put a thousand people in any space, and not every single one of them is going to be congenial or respectful of fellow dog people and the rules. To whit, there is the one person in the hundred people who does not pick up after his dog, who leaves the dropping behind, and calmly (or furtively) walks away. Obviously, the dog is not to be blamed. It's his callous owner. Then there is the woman who seems otherwise sane, but who walks from one end of the meadow—and back—bellowing out the names of her dogs, who are running close by in the little hills alongside the meadow. She can see them, they can see her, yet the bellowing, whose purpose remains a mystery, continues. Its effect, however, is not. It blasts into other people's right to the peace, calm, and quiet fun they and their dogs come here for. Clueless to this imposition, she bellows on.

There are also the twenty-foot long "training leashes" that, yes, are a wonderful boon to training a young dog to come when he's called. If he doesn't come of his own accord, he can be reeled in to show him what is intended by the "come" command. However, when these long-leash training sessions occur in the middle of several groups of unobserving dogs playing and running around every which way, their legs get caught up in the long leashes and many a dog takes a tumble. Similar, but far worse because they are effectively invisible, are the retractable fifteen-foot wire leashes also used on untrained dogs. Other dogs, who are playing freely, run headlong into these "invisible" wires and are harmed.

Then, there are also the problem dogs, and yes, what invariably comes with them, the problem owners, whose dogs—I tread as carefully as I can here—more often than not, are the "problem breeds." Somewhere there is a basset hound biting somebody as surely as there is a rottweiler safely playing with a baby. But the fact is, statistically, it isn't the basset hounds who are doing the biting. It is the rottweilers, the pit bulls, the Akitas, the Dobermans, and so forth. But having only said what statistics bear out—plus my own, and many other people's experience in the park and on the streets—a problem dog is any dog of any size, sex, breed, or mixture of breeds who poses a threat to other people or their dogs due to dominance aggression, fear aggression, sexual aggression, learned aggression, protective aggression, territorial aggression, or any kind of potentially dangerous behavior.

What saddens me, of course, is that—as has happened in the last decade—the moment one says *the* pit bull or *the* rottweiler, *all* pit bulls and *all* rottweilers are automatically viewed as dangerous, which of course, they are not. I may have had a dangerous rottweiler, and I see a lot of dangerous rottweilers, but the woman who owns Lady does not have a dangerous rottweiler. Lady is one of the sweetest, most well-mannered dogs in the park. Then again, there's Rocky, owned by a fellow I've known for years. Rocky has it in him to be ferocious toward other people and dogs. This fellow responsibly walks him on a leash, takes him deep into the woods to run, then the leash comes back on when Rocky crosses the Long Meadow where other dogs and people are.

But not all people are always this careful.

Tyler was about six months old when a male boxer dog mugged him. The boxer was accompanied by a well-known dog walker who takes a number of peoples' dogs to the park every day, and usually handles them with judgment. But this day he made the wrong decision when he let the boxer—known to sometimes engage in other-dog aggression—off the leash. The boxer spied Tyler and rushed over. The next second, he was all over Tyler, snarling and snapping his teeth, as Tyler tumbled to the ground. The fellow instantly jumped into action, pulled the dog off Tyler, was extremely sorry, and took full responsibility for what just happened. I checked Tyler. While the boxer's saliva was all over him, beyond this, it appeared that no harm had been done. But harm had been done. As it turned out, Tyler had been bitten on his ears, and also on his head. The head puncture caused a very nasty bacterial infection (pyrotraumatic dermatitis) known familiarly as a "hot spot," that oozed, itched, hurt, and spread rapidly. I took Tyler to the vet where he got an intravenous shot of antibiotics and cortisone. All the fur on his head had to be shaved off, and he was on oral antibiotics for two weeks. All of it to the tune of one hundred fifty dollars—and much worse—a lot of pain and discomfort for Tyler.

When I ran into the dog walker three weeks later, I told him that the boxer had bitten Tyler, and about the infection that followed. He was terribly sorry about it all. I appreciated his regret, and told him so. Afterwards, I invited him to reimburse me for the veterinary bills I had paid. A responsible fellow, he accepted that invitation.

Then there is the opposite of this scene: total irresponsibility, followed by maddening unaccountability.

A year ago, Tyler and I were walking on a path in a hill that over-looks the Long Meadow, when we encountered a large black Doberman coming toward us. Fifteen feet behind him were his owners, a couple in their forties. Having encountered enough aggressive Dobermans to now be leery of them—and this one had a ridge of hairs rising up on his back as he stiffly walked toward Tyler—I called out to the woman the question I and all dog people use: "Is he okay?" (Meaning, is he safe?) This is a yes or no question. The woman hesitated. Bad sign. If you have to think about what to say, the answer is, "He isn't." Which the Doberman proved a second later when he ferociously attacked Tyler, growling and trying to bite him as I screamed, "Get him off! Get him off!" The husband, or the wife—I can't remember which, it all happened so fast—finally managed to pull the dog off Tyler. Then, after quickly making sure Tyler was okay, I began to shout at them, "What is the matter with you?! What is that dog doing off the leash!"

There was no apology, no "My God, I'm terribly sorry!" No less, "Is your dog all right?" Instead they stood there glaring belligerently at me, as though I were the one at fault because I happened to come along when they were walking their obviously dangerous dog off the leash. There was also no surprise on their faces. Clearly, this Doberman had done this before. Knowing the level of responsibility of his owners, he would do it again.

Seeing I would get nowhere with these people, all I wanted now was the something that would protect Tyler if their dog had bitten him. "I would like the name of your dog's vet," I told them. "I need to know if he's had his shots, to know my dog is in no danger." Their response? They turned and walked away. "Just your vet's name!" I yelled after them. At this point, I came across my friend, Robin, walking her dog Sunny. Her daughter and Lexie are good friends. Robin and I had been very nice acquaintances. This day we became friends as she joined me in my outrage—and commiserated with how upset I was. And yes, she joined me in yelling at these people so irresponsible as to let their dog attack another dog, then walk away and out of the park doing and saying nothing except, "You are harassing us."

In all fairness, I must follow this attacking-Doberman story with one about the woman who walks her five Dobermans all at once, off leash, on the Long Meadow—quite an amazing sight under any circumstances. But these five dogs are exceptionally well trained by a highly responsible and astute owner. Her five sleek Dobermans are obedient to a degree one rarely sees in any dog of any breed. They do not pose a threat to anyone or anything but the blades of grass on the Long Meadow their twenty feet cannot help but tread upon.

But what was Tyler's response to the boxer who assaulted him? And the Doberman who attacked him? In the case of the boxer, Tyler, six months old, was knocked off his feet so fast and then bitten so fast, he never had a chance to do anything. In the case of the Doberman attack, he tried to get out of this dog's way, but the Doberman wouldn't let him. The Doberman needed to fight. Tyler didn't.

Which brings me to one of the lessons Tyler is teaching me: How pointless and stupid it is, and what an energy-waster and life-waster to needlessly engage in the negatives that dogs and we humans encounter, or—much worse—create. Beyond the boxer and the Doberman, Tyler is often approached in the park by other male dogs with a need to prove dominance—and there are plenty of them. Hardly ruffled, he simply walks away, invitation after invitation to duel calmly refused. Why? Because in these moments and all his moments, Tyler has better things on his mind: harmony, joy, pleasure, affection, love, and the rest of the good things a dog's—and human's—life has to offer.

So he didn't hold a grudge against the boxer, as I did for a time. He didn't shout at the people with the Doberman—and continue to shout at them—as I did, even though the momentary crisis had come and gone. He let it go. He walked away, unruffled, ready to enjoy life again, as I should have, but couldn't. I'm learning.

Can there possibly be protectiveness in all this affability? Is the Alpine guard-dog who defended the flock and hearth and home in Tyler, too? I had wondered about this. Dividing protectiveness into the two categories it is, the "watchdog" protects by sounding the alarm to danger. The next step up in protectiveness is the "guard-dog" who does something about that danger. He physically intervenes by attacking the intruder, or by holding the attacker at bay.

Taking them in order, the watchdog alerts to danger by barking. The first several months of Tyler's life, as Daisy ran barking to the front door at the slightest disturbance—and Tyler ran tearing to the door with her— we never heard a single bark, not so much as a peep out of him. Indeed, I had begun to wonder if he would bark? Then, at about six months of age, out it came. When Daisy ran screaming and barking to the front door, Tyler suddenly ran barking, too. And it was a deep, rich bark at that! He's been barking ever since. But, unlike Daisy, who gets a little carried away with herself, Tyler never barks frivolously. Little kids on the street don't set him off. A radio suddenly turned on, he ignores. But at the sound of the front gate squeaking as it opens, or footsteps coming up the stoop—or any other sound that he deems needs announcing—Tyler sets to barking immediately. His judgment is so accurate, so dependable that no matter what hour of the day or night, be it broad daylight or 2 A.M., when Tyler barks, we pay attention. There's always a reason; something or someone is amiss. Further, he stops barking just as fast if the hand on the gate turns out to be David's, or the turning of a key in the front door lock is Lexie coming home, or the noise was just the friendly kids next door.

This is the watchdog in Tyler. I've seen him in action a thousand times. He is very, very good. But what about the guard-dog in him? Would this calm, peaceable creature who in four years has never so much as growled or shown his teeth at anyone, four-legged, two-legged, or otherwise, actually leap to defend me if the need arose? A fellow Bernese owner who I occasionally come across in Prospect Park—who has had these dogs for fifteen years—said it best when she told me, "You'll never see it (the guard-dogging in a Bernese), until you need it."

She then proceeded to tell me the story of how she had been walking with one of her female Bernese in a woodsy area of the park one time, when fifteen feet ahead of her, an unsavory fellow stepped out of the bushes and advanced threateningly toward her. The next moment, her five-year-old Bernese, who had never shown an inkling of defensive behavior, because she never had to, "went absolutely nuts!" leaping after the guy, snarling, snapping her teeth, knocking him to the ground, before he managed to escape with his life—"and his torn clothing"— back into the woods. "*That's* what you can expect from a Bernese," she said. "And you can trust it."

As Tyler, to date, has never had reason to display this trait, I take this woman's word for it, and other Bernese owners' very similar stories with the same reassuring message.

The Bernese mountain dog has that aforementioned trait of "high activity outdoors, low activity indoors," which for me—and I think all Bernese owners agree—is a winning combination. But make no mistake about it, a walk around the block does not cut the mustard with this large athletic breed. The Bernese is a Working Dog; he needs to exercise, to work himself for, ideally, an hour or so every day in order to happily and healthfully be that "low activity" (and nicely tired, good dog) when he gets home.

Just like any large-breed puppy, this exercising must never be over-done until his bones are fully grown, which, for a female Bernese, re-quires a year or so. For a male, it's a year and a half or so. Over-exercising the Bernese puppy or adolescent courts the same bone and joint stress injuries for exactly the same reasons outlined earlier for the Great Dane, and all large-breed puppies. The idea with a juvenile Berner is just the right amount of exercising, no less, never more, that will enable him to develop full musculature and strength, without risking injury.

To whit, the immature Bernese must not be allowed to roughhouse with larger or more agile dogs, or even more agile puppies. Seek out gentle dogs and puppies with whom he can exercise and socialize. At this stage, just like the Dane, he also must not run or exercise on hard surfaces like asphalt. Grass or soft ground is the right surface. If he is destined, only after he's fully grown, to accompany his runner-owner, the Bernese must very gradually move up into this kind of endurance. But never forget he is not a greyhound! He is hardly designed for speed or hours of trotting alongside the long distance runner. The Bernese is a short distance runner. The moment he appears to be tiring—when in doubt, make the decision for him—it's time for the Bernese mountain dog to call it off and walk home.

Well acquainted with these precautions, I applied them to Tyler's puppyhood and adolescence. Even so, between the ages of six months to two years, Tyler would occasionally "run out" too fast—because I misgauged his speed and let him—or jump over some rocks—when I should have stopped him—and came up a little stiff in the joints. A call to Sharon (which she always took, or graciously called me back with dispatch) would confirm what I already suspected: He'd overdone it. Time to back off the exercising and let him rest for a couple of days. Then, gradually, if the stiffness disappeared, which it did, I slowly eased him back into those walks and runs in the park. It worked. Tyler bounced back each time.

I purposefully digress to mention that the Bernese mountain dog is a happy stoic when it comes to pain, or enduring discomfort of any kind. Tyler is so typical here. Where Daisy screams if Snowball should accidentally brush by one of her toes, a steamroller could run over Tyler and you'd never hear a peep out of him. He'd get up and still happily walk all day. Which means I must assess any potentially bruising experience and determine what, if any, restraints to impose on him.

Unlike short-haired dogs of any breed, the Bernese mountain dog of any age must never run or exercise in the heat. This is a dog whose thick outer coat and dense undercoat are designed to insulate him from the harshest Swiss Alpine winters. These same insulating properties (enhanced by the color of his coat, *black*, which absorbs heat) that serve the Bernese so well in the most extreme cold, work proportionately against him in the heat. So he doesn't just dislike the heat, he hates it because he suffers in it. In extreme heat, even the most well-conditioned, athletic Bernese can succumb to heatstroke, or worse.

New York City—no less regions farther south—is famous for its hot steamy summers, which, Park Slope, a skip and a hop from Manhattan, shares. To exercise the "strong, athletic dog" in Tyler, but not endanger his health and happiness, on a hot August day, I get him up to the park for his daily run and out of the park by 9 A.M., before the real midday heat hits. So he gets his exercise, and he's happily tired. Once home, to keep him happy, he goes right into the air-conditioned bedroom. (If I forget to get him there myself, he takes himself there, pushing on the door until it opens.) Late afternoon or early evening, when the heat's toned down, he gets a stroll up and down the block, or to the newsstand with me. In between, it's just runs to the curb, strictly to take care of business, then in he comes and back up the stairs he bounds to return to the wonderful chill of the bedroom.

With the same passion the Bernese mountain dog hates the heat, he loves the cold! Ice. Hail. Sleet. And he is beside himself with joy in snow, the more the better. Tyler is no exception. He bounds into it, tears around in it, chugs into snowdrifts. This joy isn't like Timber's, but suffice it to say Tyler is very, very happy when it snows. I make sure—and New York winters oblige—that he has every opportunity to be this happy.

What the Bernese mountain dog of any age also needs is never to be allowed to become fat. Hip and elbow dysplasia are issues with the Bernese. Then again, they are an issue with any dog, particularly dogs over thirty-five pounds, which includes many breeds.

Hip dysplasia, in a nutshell, is an orthopedic disorder in which the ball of the hip, to one degree or another, doesn't fit properly into its socket, resulting in correlative degrees of rear leg lameness that can also pave the way for arthritis. Elbow dysplasia, encapsulated, is a catchall term that encompasses several degenerative disorders of the elbow joint, resulting in front leg lameness. Heredity is clearly involved in both diseases. Thus, it's important that both parents of a prospective Bernese puppy be OAF (Orthopedic Foundation for Animals) certified. In the case of hip dysplasia, the rating is broken down into seven categories, from "excellent" hip joint confirmation, to "good," to "fair," on down. In elbow dysplasia, a similar rating system exists, though not as specific, that indicates the degenerative condition (or absence thereof) of the elbow joints. But it's important to point out that a Bernese breeder can only guarantee "clear" hips and "normal" elbows in the parents (as designated by the OAF rating), not in their offspring. This is because inheritance for hip and elbow joint dysplasia can be "multiple," that is, not directly inherited from parents, but from a grandparent.

How is this related to being fat? Excessive weight puts more stress on joints—all of them in a dog—thereby exacerbating even a minor case of hip or elbow dysplasia, or even causing one or both when neither existed. (So, too, can an injury caused by rough playhousing, tackling stairs, or jumping hurdles in puppyhood or adolescense before the bones are fully grown.)

Is all this talk of bones and joints suggesting the Bernese mountain dog isn't as strong as he looks? Hardly. He's a Working Dog athlete. When grown up and properly conditioned, he's a gifted athlete. But when he's a young athlete, he won't put on the brakes himself. He's too enthusiastic about having fun and pushing the limits. This is where his caring and informed Bernese owner steps in.

The grooming of the Bernese mountain dog is relatively easy. That is, no fancy stuff, no poodle or cocker spaniel clipping and snipping, is required. But—it's a big one—the Bernese sheds year round, most especially in the spring as he "blows" (as it's called) some of his outer coat and most of that famous undercoat of his. This isn't a fur ball or two quietly collecting in the corners. This is a blizzard of black fur balls that rolls across the floor, sticks to the carpet, and snares on the edges of furniture. But there's no reason for furry mayhem. An every-other-day brushing in the spring removes the fur before it flies into the air and lands on home and furnishings. The rest of the year, a weekly brushing suffices. Nonetheless, the Bernese owner does well to keep the vacuum cleaner handy year round.

Tyler, like the typical Bernese, likes being brushed. For him, it's contact affection, and much praise for standing perfectly still. What he can't stand is the vacuum cleaner and the racket it makes. At the sight of it—and he sees it a lot—he hightails it upstairs. Interestingly, not Daisy. Ever the paradoxical little dog, she loves the vacuum cleaner. As Tyler runs away from it, she runs for it, standing right in front of it to get a closer look, and I constantly have to nudge her away so I can proceed.

The Bernese mountain dog only needs to be bathed when he gets dirty. We bathe Tyler when his whites start to look dingy. He doesn't like being bathed, but he puts up with it in the typical, patience of a Bernese. Unlike a certain Miss Daisy who puts up a huge struggle because water doesn't feel good to her, Tyler simply stands there and lets us do what we need to do. His whites now bright, and the rest of his fur returned to its former glossy state, his reward for being so good is the run in the park that always follows the bathing of Tyler.

Much was made earlier of the eagle talons that sprout from Daisy's toes, and the hellish experience of trying to keep them under control. Blessedly, Tyler spares us this agony. While breed books include the clipping of the Bernese's nails as part of his regular grooming, we have never had to clip Tyler's nails. His feet, as they should be, are round and compact, with well-arched toes whose nails make contact with the side-walks he walks on, thereby filing them down. But the nails of the Bernese who doesn't regularly walk on abrasive surfaces need to be clipped. As mentioned earlier, long nails, apart from looking unsightly, cause the toes to splay out, affecting the position of the foot bones, and ultimately the position of the leg joints above the foot.

Before Tyler, there was only one Bernese mountain dog in the Slope; his name is Luke. He is the dog I saw standing on the street corner that day with Daisy four years ago. Tyler and I would occasionally run into Luke in the park, but then he and his owners moved to Vermont. Then we met Hope, a female Bernese, whose owners drive over from neighboring Borum Hill to exercise her in Prospect Park. With these two dogs, Tyler first showed a most endearing trait: his excitement at seeing other Bernese mountain dogs. He might be busily engaged in play with his regular dog friends, or actively making new ones, when he chances to look up and see another Bernese coming across the meadow. Tyler drops whatever he's doing or whomever he's with, and runs over, the "Berner" smile on his face, to greet this other Bernese mountain dog, bounding around it with total joy!

These days, Tyler has more opportunities to feel joyous, as he has started something of a Bernese mountain dog movement in Park Slope.

Our neighbors two houses down, a lovely family with two very nice children, had it originally in mind to get a golden retriever (whose temperament, of course, is much like the Bernese). They had purposely chosen this breed because they had children. Also, Jennifer, the wife, had never had a dog before and it was important to her husband that her first dog be a very positive experience. So it was a "golden" in their heads, until they saw the unbelievably adorable puppy Tyler in my arms, which enthusiastically prompted that question: "What breed is he?"

I explained the breed question and put them in touch with Sharon, calling her later to alert her to a wonderful home for one of her future puppies. Almost a year later, they got Ike, a fabulously beautiful Bernese, who is Tyler's half brother! (They share their father in common.) The entire family fell in love with Ike. Then, friends of theirs saw puppy Ike. They contacted Sharon. A year later, Mary Jane arrived, who is a cousin to both Tyler and Ike. Then—it continues—an athletic instructor at the Berkeley Carroll School saw Lexie walking Tyler. Lexie put her in touch with me. I put her in touch with Sharon. Now, suffice it to say, there's Bella, a very sweet six-month-old female, also related to Tyler, who he and I regularly run into in Prospect Park. So now there are four of Sharon Chesnutt Hill's October Bernese mountain dogs in Park Slope, all loved by their families—and vice versa—and all beautifully representative of the breed in every way. This also means three more Bernese—and counting—for Tyler to get so joyous over.

There is a Swiss saying, "Three years a young dog, three years a good dog, and three years an old dog. All else is a gift from God."

I think about those first three years that we've already passed. Then, the next three years that Tyler, at four, is in. Then, with unavoidable apprehension, about the following three years that make a Bernese mountain dog "old." But Tyler wouldn't see it this way. All he would see is the word "gift" which he has applied to every single day of his life that has so graced mine.

Which points me to the most important lesson Tyler is teaching me: how essential it is to really live this gift that life is. His instruction is how he greets each day with enthusiasm; the way he expects good things—and therefore elicits good things—because he's so receptive to them, and he knows how to enjoy them when he finds them. Tyler's is a love affair with life. He is "the joy-of-living dog" who is teaching me, like no other dog before him, how to really live life as I see how he delights in most everything he experiences, his optimism at age four that of a newly minted puppy. He is the dog who is showing me how to live for today in the precious increments in which it is offered: moment by moment. As what matters is not yesterday or tomorrow, but right now. This moment. Here.